ASPECTS OF THE VEDĀNTA

ASPECTS
OF
THE VEDĀNTA

M.C. Alasinga Perumal

Edited by
Dr. N.C. Panda
VVBIS & IS, Panjab University
Hoshiarpur, Punjab

BHARATIYA KALA PRAKASHAN
Delhi : : (India)

Revised Edition : 2009

Published by **C.P. Gautam**
BHARATIYA KALA PRAKASHAN
3421-A, IInd Floor, Narang Colony Tri Nagar,
Delhi-110035. Telefax : 27393083 Phone : 32967505
E-mail : bkp3421@yahoo.com
Website : www.bkpbooks.com

ISBN : 978-81-8090-226-0

Laser Type Setting :
Creative Graphics

Printed by :
G.S. Offset Printers
Delhi

DEDICATION

Dedicated with Profound regards

To

Professor Dr Godabarisha Mishra

A Prolific Writer, a true Thinker and
an Eminent Scholar of Indian Philosophy

Hon'ble Member Secretary
Indian Council of Philosophical Research (ICPR)
Darshan Bhawan, New Delhi

Contents

Preface

The word 'Vedānta' literally means 'the end of the Vedas'. The Vedas were devided into two great divisions, 'the work portion (*karmakāṇḍa*)' which teaches man how, by the performance of duty, the observance of morality and other acts, he might be go to heaven, a better of enjoyment, and the 'knowledge portion (*jñānakāṇḍa*)' which teaches him that not even the enjoyments of heaven should be his aim inasmuch as they too are fleeting and transitory, but to go beyond all relativity and find in himself the Divine, the centre of all knowledge and power. Of course, it took ages for the Hindu mind to evolve this system of Philosophy.

The Upaniṣads may be ragarded as the end of the Vedas also in the sense that they mark the culmination of the Vedic speculation. In the Upaniṣads themselves we are told that even after the study of the Vedas with other branches of learning a man's education is not complete till he receives instructions in the Upaniṣads. Besides, the Upaniṣads were regarded as the inner or secret meanings of the Vedas, hence their teachings were sometimes called Vedopaniṣad or the mystery of the Vedas.

The sages of the Upaniṣads claimed that they had discovered the gist or purport of all Vedic teachings in the knowledge of the absolute, of whom the gods worshipped by the authors of the *mantras*, as well as all objects in creation, were, they taught, names, forms or relative manifestations. The final end of all Vedic discipline were, they thought, union with Brahman, the Absolute Being. In this latter sense, therefore, in the sense of the gist or purport of the Vedas, it was the Upniṣads, again, which were called the 'Vedānta' or

'Vedāntas'. But the term came gradually to mean something quite different from, through closely related to the Upaniṣads.

The Vedānta, as scripture, consists of the Upaniṣads. Their traditional number is one hundred and eight; but modern scholars have found out that there are no fewer than one hundred and fifty bearing the name. All of them, however, are not genuine parts of the Vedas nor do all truly represent the spirit of the original Vedāntic teaching. Practically, twelve Upaniṣads are recognised as forming the Vedāntic canon and the basis of the Vedāntic Philosophy. They are the Īśa, Kena, Kaṭha, Praśna, Muṇḍaka, Māṇḍūkya, Taittirīya, Aitāreya, Chāndogya, Bṛhadāraṇyaka, Kauṣitakī and Śvetāsvatara Upaniṣads. The most honoured exposition of the Philisophy of the Vedānta is the body of aphorisms ascribed to Vyāsa or Bādarāyaṇa. Bādarāyaṇa himself is named in these aphorisms as one of several teachers of the Vedāntic Philosophy; so that Vedāntism, as a philosophical system, must have existed and been widely taught long before the composition of these aphorisms, however ancient they may be, and possibly there may have been previous compendiums of the Philosophy on which they were based. But, as a fact we possess none more ancient than they. Some of the names by which these aphorisms are called deserve to be mentioned and remembered by the student of the Vedānta Philosophy. They often go by the name of the Vedānta Darśana, though all exposition of the Philosophy of the Upaniṣads may claim the name. They are called Uttara Mīmāṃsā; because they are a Mīmāṃsā or reasoned exposition of the *Uttara* or latter part of the Vedas; i.e. of the Upaniṣads. They are so called in distinction from the Pūrva Mīmāṃsā ascribed to sage jaimini, which expounds the *Pūrva* or earlier parts of the Vedas. They are called the *Brahma Sūtras,* aphorisms expounding the nature of Brahman, in distinction from the Dharma Sūtras or aphorisms expounding the nature of Dharma or duty, the subject matter of Jaimini work. They are named as the Śārīraka Sūtras, because they treat of the true nature of the Śārīraka, the embodied soul. Other names are the *Brahma Sūtras*, the *Vedānta Sūtras*, the *Bādarāyaṇa Sūtras* and *Vedānta Mīmāṃsā*. This great work is divided into four chapters and sixteen sections, consists of five hundred and fifty eight pithy utterances, many of which contain the concentrated gist of a great deal of maditation and reasoning.

Besides the Upaniṣads and the Vedānta Sūtras, another work, the Bhagavadgītā, is held by all Vedāntic schools as embodying Vedāntic teaching of an uncertain nature, and this inspite of the apparently sectarian character of the book inspite of the fact that Lord Kṛṣṇa is theirin represent as the Supreme Being. So it has happened that ever since the time of Śaṅkarācārya, and perhaps, since a time anterior to him, the Upaniṣads, the Vedānta Sūtras and the Bhagavadgītā have been held to compose the complete Vedāntic canon. These are called the three *prasthānas* or *prasthānatraya* or the three basic works of Vedānta on which almost every great Ācāryas have commented. Various commentaries thus came to be written to elaborate the doctrines of the Vedānta in their own light. Each tried to justify its position as the only one consistent with the revealed texts Vedas and the *Sūtras*. The author of each of these chief commentaries became the founder of particular school of Vedānta. Thus, we have the schools of Śaṅkara, Rāmānuja, Madhva, Vallabha, Nimbarka and many others. Each school of Vedānta consists not simply of the philosophers who theoretically accept its views but also of a large number of moks and common followers who try to mould their lives accordingly. It is in this way that the Vedānta in its different forms still persists in the lives of millions. After the main commentaries (*bhāṣyas*), the literature of the Vedānta developed through the innumerable sub-commentaries, glosses and other indipendent works written by the leading exponents of each school to support its views and refute those of the other schools. However, Ācārya Śaṅkara's exposition of these Vedāntic texts is monumental.

Besides, the commentaries on the *prasthānatrayas* written by the great founder of Vedānta schools, a good number of hand books expounding the philosophy have been composed by the founders themselves and their followers. Unfortunately it is only works belonging to the schools of Ācārya Śaṅkara that are well-known throughout the country. Mādhva's Tattvamuktāvali is read in Bengal, But Ācārya Rāmānuja's Vedānta Saṅgraha and other minor works, and even his commentary on the Upaniṣads are only heard of. Of works of Śaṅkara's school, the Upadeśasāhasrī and the Vivekacūḍāmaṇi ascribed to him are well-known and so are several smaller texts said to be written by him. The Pañcadaśi by Mādhavācārya and the Vedāntasāra by Sadānanda are among the best known of minor works on the Vedānta, and have been translated into English. One of the most ancient books of this class, but not strictly philosophical in method, is the celebrated Yogavāsiṣṭha.

The Ultimate Reality, according to Ācārya Śaṅkara, is Ātman to Brahman which is pure conciousness (*jñāna-svarūpa*) or consciousness of the pure self (*svarūpa jñāna*), which is devoid of all attributes and all categories of the intellect, Brahman associated with its potency *māya*, appears as the qualified Brahman (Saguṇa Brahman) or the Lord (*Īśvara*) who is the creator, preserver and destroyer of this world which is His appearance. Ācārya Śaṅkara emphasizes that from the phenomenal point of view the world is quite real. It is not an illusion. It is a practial reality. He distinguishes the dream state from the waking state. Things seen in a dream are quite true as long as the dream lasts; they are sublated only when we are awake. Similarly, the world is quite real so long as true knowledge does not drawn. *Jiva* is ignorant of the essential unity and takes only diversity as true and wrongly regards himself as agent and enjoyer. *Avidyā* conceals the unity (*āvaraṇa*) and projects names and forms (*vikṣepa*). Īśvara never misses the unity. Māyā has only its *vikṣepa* aspect over him. When *jīva* realizes through knowledge and knowledge alone, *karma* being subsidiary, this essential unity, liberation is attained here and now (*jīvanmukti*) and final ṛelease (*videhamukti*) is obtained after the death of the body.

The religion of Vedānta is inseparable from true science and from true philosophy. Why? Because, all sciences and all philosophies are nothing but so many attempts of human minds to grasp some particular phase of the eternal truth, the Infinite Reality. As truth is the goal of all science and philosophy, the same truth is the goal of the Vedānta; and as Vedānta attempts to lead all human minds to the realization of that Absolute Truth of the oneness, so it embraces all the philosophies of the world.

In fine, the Vedāntic Religion, accordingly, believes in one and only one God, i.e. Brahman, in His omnipenetrativeness, as it has been aptly termed, and in the spiritual oneness throughout of human nature and human destiny. It enforces self-discipline and self-culture, and teaches man to realise the life of righteousness as the best means of worshipping God and of obtaining deliverance and Bliss.

The teachings of Vedānta drive away the fear of death, because they say that death can not attack our souls; we are immortal; by our birth right we are children of that Universal Spirit, and therefore we are immortal. Fear of death will never trouble the mind of a student of Vedānta Philosophy. So, the teachings of Vedānta take away all fear of death and make us happy and contented in our earthly life. Another great help in practical life which we get from Vedānta is the knowledge of Divine Being. The Divine Being is not far from us. He is the soul of our souls. He is dwelling within us. He is both personal and impersonal, and beyond both. Moreover, He can be worshipped under any name, in any form, by anyone, under any sect, creed or denomination. He is one and eternal and when we understand this, all religious animosities, quarrels, fights, cease for ever. Then we consider all sectarians as our brothers and sisters and we embrace them as the children of Allmighty (God). This is the real teaching of Vedānta, which is more practical today.

The work entitled 'Aspects of Vedānta' is a collection of twelve articles written by various eminent scholars of Religion and Philosophy. The first edition of this work was came out in 1921, which was edited by M.C.A. Perumal. I have tried my best to modify these articles and given the correct references of the textual quotations. Besides, the diacritical marks are also furnished for proper reading and understanding of the Sanskrit terms. In addition to these, Glossary is also appended at the end of the book. Hope, this New Revised edition may be benefitted for the Researchers for furthering their Research work in the field of Religion and Philsophy.

Acknowledgements

It is a great pleasure to acknowledge my obligations to the eminent scholars, whose articles are being published in this book. Infact, these scholarly articles have been a real source of inspiration for me re-edit the work after a long period. I am indeed very thankful to these illustrious authors for their scholarly contributions. I record my profound obligations to Prof. D.B. Sen Sharma, Kolkata, Prof. Radhavallabh Tripathi,. New Delhi, Prof. Dharmanand Sharma, Chandigarh, Prof. Surendra Mohan Mishra, Kurukshetra for their enlightening inspiration and scholarly suggestions.

I feel highly delighted in dedicating this book to Professor Dr Godabarisha Mishra, Member Secretary, I.C.P.R., New Delhi, for his constent inspiration and scholarly guidance.

I am extending my sincere thanks to Prof. B.B. Chaubey, Prof. Indra Dutt Uniyal, Prof. Shuk Dev Sharma, Prof. Vikram Kumar, Prof. Raghbir Singh, Prof. Rajinder Sharma, Prof.

Prem Lal Sharma and Prof. Gopabandhu Mishra, for their valuable suggestions to complete this work in time.

I am also thankful to Shri C.P. Gautam, Publisher of Bharatiya Kala Prakashan, Delhi, for kindly undertaking the publication of this book.

15th August 2009
Sadhu Ashram
Hoshiarpur

N.C. Panda
V.V.B.I.S. & I.S.
Panjab University

List of Transliterations

अ	:	a	क्	:	k	ध्	:	dh
आ	:	ā	ख्	:	kh	न्	:	n
इ	:	i	ग्	:	g	प्	:	p
ई	:	ī	घ्	:	gh	फ्	:	ph
उ	:	u	ङ्	:	ṅ	ब्	:	b
ऊ	:	ū	च्	:	c	भ्	:	bh
ऋ	:	ṛ	छ्	:	ch	म्	:	m
ॠ	:	ṝ	ज्	:	j	य्	:	y
लृ	:	lṛ	झ्	:	jh	र्	:	r
लॄ	:	lṝ	ञ्	:	ñ	ल्	:	l
ए	:	e	ट्	:	ṭ	व्	:	v
ऐ	:	ai	ठ्	:	ṭh	श्	:	ś
ओ	:	o	ड्	:	ḍ	ष्	:	ṣ
औ	:	au	ढ्	:	ḍh	स्	:	s
•	:	ṃ/ṁ	ण्	:	ṇ	ह्	:	h
:	:	ḥ	त्	:	t	ळ्	:	ḷ
			थ्	:	th			
			द्	:	d			

The Vedānta : Some Reasons for its Study[1]

Mr. N. Vythinatha Aiyar, M.A.

The Vedānta has been described as being both a philosophy and a religion. And it has been thought that this combination of the two into one marks a low stage of civilization. But any sharp separation of the one from the other is logically impossible; and if these stand united in the Vedānta, it is because the two are so intimately connected, that we cannot possibly, investigate the one without being inevitably drawn into the other. Philosophy is the science of sciences; its subject-matter is the whole range of scientific phenomena; and its aim is to combine all these into a consistent whole, to dive deep into the verities, underlying them and to decide upon the First Principles which form the bases of scientific certainty. Thus, Philosophy is necessarily drawn into the problems of ultimate realities, their nature, origin and mutual relations. It is the handmaid of science, for science depends for the justification of its methods and of its premises upon philosophy. It is also the twin-sister of religion, for in giving a verdict on the foundations of science, it decides the nature and scope of religion as well. The question of the origin of the world and of its phenomena is only another form of the question regarding the existence and nature of its Creator, be it a blind force in independent control of the force-manifestations in the perpetual stream

1. A lecture delivered to the Presidency College Literary Society by the late Mr. N. Vythinatha Aiyar, M.A.

of causation, into which science has resolved and is resolving the march of cosmic events; or be that Creator of the world an intelligent, omnipotent, and benevolent Being, who is immanent in the world, or who watches and controls its process from the outside. The philosophy of the phenomenal cosmos, of its nature and origin, leads us unavoidably to the regions of religion, and the inherent connection between cosmic facts and events on the one hand and their metaphysical explanation and divine origin on the other accounts for the dual character of Vedantism.

It may be thought that we of the nineteenth century, enriched as we are with the intellectual harvest of so many ages can do better than go back to the thoughts of the primitive minds of India. Our intellectual inheritance is the ever-growing accumulation of the mental activity of many centuries and of more than one continent. We are masters of the distilled knowledge of thousands of generations, of which each has sat in judgment over its inheritance from the past and has passed that inheritance through the searching crucible of intellectual criticism. Physical science was literally unknown to the thinker of the Vedānta; and a reasoned concatenation of the facts and doings of nature was not theirs. They had not therefore that discipline of the intellect which comes of our logical search into the ways of nature; and it may be asked whether we are to sit at the feet of the antiquated Ṛṣis of the Vedic times, while our intellect has received such training and while we are in possession of such stores of reasoned knowledge.

But a deeper investigation into the nature of the human mind on the one hand and of the problems here taken up for solution on the other cannot but give us a pause in this fancied pride of intellectual growth. The province of Reason is not unlimited and illimitable; and even within its legitimate sphere; its sway is not absolute. The whole body of classified and well-arranged facts, in their particular or in their generalised form, and the whole body of inferences from those facts, or briefly, what we call science is confined to human experience; that is, to the interpretation by the subjective mind of the perennial currents of sensations and ideas. Our reasoned knowledge is limited to the contents of our minds, and to the sphere of our consciousness. It is true that of these contents of our minds we project more than one-half into the imagined void which we conceive to lie outside our consciousness. We erect the material world upon the basis, one may say, of our mental states. But in any view we may take of the scope of reason, it must be granted that the mind is ever making irrational leaps into the unknown, which lies beyond the province of reason and of science. There are also phenomena, mental and volitional, which are ultra-rational or irrational if you please, which, as phenomena must be amenable to scientific enquiry, but as irrational, break loose from the legitimate moorings of science. At the one extreme stands the well-ordered science of objective nature, and at the other, the apparently chaotic, phenomena with which the name of metaphysics is connected. The external world of nature is observed and examined; its several aspects are abstracted; and there arises the hierarchy of the sciences. And these same experiences rightly when looked at from their subjective side melt away into sensations and ideas, and reason is irresistibly led to furnish them with a substantial basis in the eternal realities of metaphysics. In building up the elaborate system of the objective sciences, the material world is assumed as a reality; and this reality glares us in the face in the machinery of modern civilisation, and its social and political movements. But these same phenomena, so vast in their multiplicity, are all contained in some mysterious fashion within the four corners of the human mind. Reason is the name given to but a change in the form of the presentation of the contests of the mind. The sciences are all of them but emanations from the contact of the mystery known as the human mind with the metaphysical , entity which has been supposed to stand outside the mind and contra-distinguished from it. Thus, for our reasoned knowledge a metaphysical basis at each one of its limits is required. It is connected on the one hand with an unknown but assumed matter and on the other with an equally unknown and unknowable mind. Its vision abuts on every side on metaphysical pre-suppositions which go under the names of matter, mind, causation, space, etc.

These metaphysical realities or assumptions are thus required to round off the dominion proper of reason and science. And we should also remember that all our boasted intellectual advance is as nothing in regard to them. They now stand and have always stood, outside the pale of what we ordinarily understand by the term knowledge. The blaze of intellectual light that has grown in intensity and depth with the progress of civilization has been strictly confined to this side of the impenetrable veil drawn over metaphysical entities. All that reason has done in regard to what lies or may lie outside the range of sense-perception is only this—the declaration that it is unreachable by sense and that it is hence unknowable. Of what lies thus beyond the reach of reason, even existence, it may be thought, cannot be predicated. But Spencer and Huxley, while confessing to the impotency of reason to penetrate into the recesses of the eternal realities of the universe, will not yet push their agnosticism so far as to deny even their reality. "Though as knowledge approaches its culmination" says Spencer, "every unaccountable and seemingly supernatural fact is brought into the category of facts that are accountable and natural; yet, at the same time; all accountable and natural facts are proved in their ultimate genesis unaccountable and supernatural."

Now philosophy ventures to pry into what is thus screened off from our empirical vision. The empiricist resolves all knowledge into sensations, and this leads him logically to agnosticism. If we accept that our knowledge is limited to what is revealed to our mind in its commerce with the external world; if we confine our vision, as the empiricists do, to the knowable revealed to the perceiving mind through the agency of the senses, then indeed should we declare that the ultra-sensual region claimed as its peculiar sphere by metaphysics is impassably shut off from us; agnosticism proclaims this and this alone; its dogma is that the sphere by of knowledge is limited to the world of sense-perception; and that non-knowledge or ignorance is the right frame of mind in regard to what lies or may lie beyond that world of sense-perception. But there is one important fact that empiricism seems to ignore. Science under its guidance has brought or tries to bring within its sphere, the whole range of phenomena, physical and psychical. And its grasp of the physical half of the phenomenal cosmos is thorough-going and secure; but its work in regard to the other half of its subject-matter—the psychical,—is not equally exhaustive. It does not seem to have even a comprehension of the whole range of psychical phenomena. And it is exactly that portion of these phenomena which it ignores, or of which its view is half-hearted and halting, that is of the utmost importance to man. Among the phenomena most characteristic of man are his religious convictions and beliefs. These with his ideas regarding his moral responsibility fill no small space of his life. In no country and in respect of no nation can it be said that these phenomena relating to religion and morality are insignificant or that they are unimportant. They occupy not only much of the time and attention of all nations, including those who are the most civilised, but exercise also a considerable amount of influence over their conduct through life, as sons, fathers, citizens, etc. It should not be supposed that in modern times the influence of religion has waned. It may be that the fire of the Inquisition and the slaughter of the Crusades have disappeared; and in India the cruel pike may have forgotten its function. Our age has learnt to be tolerant in matters of religion, but not thereby to lose sight of the existence, of a craving for something other than empiricism and its teachings. These moral and religious phenomena have changed their form of external manifestation, but their springs in our innermost nature yet run fresh and full. And these inherent tendencies that draw us towards the supersensual now act mainly upon the ethical side of our nature. Their force is now strong as ever, but it is felt mostly in the shaping of our social deportment. The extended vision of modern times has served to extend the sphere as well of our ethical sympathies.

Now it is this side of our nature, these religio-ethical phenomena so strikingly present in us and so potent over our feelings and actions, that modern empiricism has failed adequately to grapple with. If science is to take under its wings the whole range of phenomena falling within our observation, the neglect by it of these is by no means justifiable. It is not a scientific explanation of the ethical side of man simply to state its psychological origin and development. Our conscience may have come into exisence in the particular manner described, by the empirical moralists; our religious instincts and beliefs may have been developed out of some of the primitive elements in our nature as the sociologists assert. But the question of their growth is not the question of their authority. And there is the further question of the nature and origin of these primitive instincts themselves from which our notions on religion and ethics are said to have sprung up. It is here that modern science has failed in its mission; and it is exactly here that the metaphysician comes in with his ultra-physical data to emancipate the Scientific Reason which stands entangled in the meshes of First Principles and primitive instincts.

It should not be supposed that in going back to the Vedic times of India for a solution of these metaphysical problems, we are seeking refuge in darkness from light. The thoughts of our ancients have lost none of their wisdom and weight because of their antiquity. It is not simply because, as has been pointed out above, these thoughts refer to a department of our nature on which modern science has not and cannot shed any light that was not within the reach of the ancient sages. This is true no doubt. But there is a stronger reason for this search into the past than this mere lack of advance is metaphysics since the days of our Upaniṣads. It is that the sages of ancient India have brought to bear upon these questions an acuteness and strength of intellect which is surprising in itself and is almost unequalled, even by the foremost of modern minds. You should not suppose that I am asserting a mythical impossibility in claiming for the ancient India as a vigour of intellectual perception matchless in its degree. There has been immense progress, indeed, since their time. But this progress has not been in the perspicuity of intellectual comprehension. "The secrets of the universe have indeed been plumbed, and with the knowledge so obtained, man has turned the world into a vast workshop where all the powers of nature work submissively in bondage to supply his wants." The almost universal tendency has been to regard the intellectual factor as the ruling and dominant one in the advance made by modern nations. But quite recently attention has been directed to a comparison of the average intellectual development in the old civilizations, with the average mental development under modern civilization; and the result of this comparison is found to be against the latter. Although Western civilization of recent centuries has "developed a strength, a magnificence and an undoubted promise which over-shadows the fame and the achievement" of the civilizations of ancient Greece and Rome, " the fuller knowledge and the more accurate methods of research and examination of our own time," says Mr. Benjamin Kidd, "have only tended to confirm the view, that in average mental development, the moderns are not the superiors, but the inferiors of those ancient people who have so completely dropped out of the human struggle for existence. Judged by the standard of intellectual development alone, we of the modern European races who seem to have been so unmistakably marked out by the operation of the law of natural selection to play a commanding part in the history of the world, have, in fact, no claim whatever to consider ourselves as in advance of ancient Greeks, all the extraordinary progress and powers of the modern world notwithstanding. The marvellous accomplishments of modern civilization are not the colossal products of individual minds amongst us : they are all the results of small accumulations of knowledge slowly and painfully made and added to by many minds through an indefinite number of generations in the past, every addition to this store of knowledge affording still greater facilities for further additions. It must not be assumed, even of the minds that have from time to time made considerable additions to this common stock of accumulated knowledge, that they have been separated from the general average or from the minds of other races of men of lower social development, by the immense intellectual interval which each, achievement standing by itself would seem to imply." The great strides of modern civilization have been the products of the time rather than of individuals. Even those nation which are generally styled the lower races do not appear to be lower than the so-called higher races in point of mere intellectual power. This applies to the Maories of New Zealand as to the natives of this country. Of our countrymen, Mr. Benjamin Kidd, from whose remarkable book and Social Evolution I have already quoted, says : "These natives have proved themselves the rivals of Europeans in European branches of learning. Indian and Burmese students who have come to England to be trained for the legal and other professions have proved themselves not the inferiors of their European colleagues; and they have, from time to time, equalled and even surpassed the best English students against whom they have been matched."

If this be the verdict of modern science even in regard

to the degenerate race now inhabiting India, degenerate through centuries of Moslem invasions and anarchy, what necessity is there to press the argument in favour of the intellectual greatness of the ancient, authors of Indian metaphysics ? And as in the region of ultra-sensuous perception, modern researches have proved inefficient and ineffectual, and as in consequence the perception of truth depends necessarily upon our innate powers, it stands to reason that the philosophical thoughts of the ancients, endowed as they were with an extraordinary acuteness of mental vision, may be studied to advantage even after the lapse of so many centuries.

What is this philosophy and this metaphysics to which so much importance is here attached? This high estimate of its value should not be imagined to be due, in any the least extent, to the unconscious predilection in us for what belongs to our country. Oriental scholars enjoying a wide reputation and accepted as undoubted authorities on the subject are unanimous in their praise of the Vedānta as a philosophy. Professor Max Müller's views on the subject are too well-known to need repetition here. In his lectures on the Vedānta, he says, for instance : "Such speculations are apt to make us feel giddy; but whatever we may think about them they show at all events to what a height Indian philosophy had risen in its patient climb from peak to peak, and how strong its lungs must have been to be able to breathe in such an atmosphere." "The system of the Vedānta," says Professor Deussen, "as founded upon the Upaniṣads and Vedānta Sūtras and accompanied by Śaṅkara's Commentaries upon them,—equal in rank to Plato and Kant—is one of the most valuable products of the genius of mankind in its search for the eternal truth." And it is not too much to claim the right at least to a respectful hearing for that which has evoked such, feelings from European *savants*.

As a philosophy, the Vedānta inquires into the ultimate bases of phenomena. We interpret the material world and the world of mind, so mysteriously joined to our bodies, through our sense impressions. Matter is to us coloured; its sounds are caught by our ears; we perceive its surface as hot or cold, rough or smooth, plane or spherical; and we enjoy its smell and tastes. The forces that sway matter, both molar and molecular, we ponder and study. In these and other ways we grapple with the material world with the senses as our instruments, and it is through these alone that we can reach the world. Now the question arises as to the existence of a something behind these attributes, as the substratum, of which colours, sounds, smells, tastes, etc., are but appendages and belongings. This substratum, if it exists, cannot be known through sense-impressions. For then it will become a colour, a sound, a taste, etc., and thus will be brought down to the category of attributes. The Vedānta declares therefore that the eternal cannot be known through the transient. This eternal substratum of the world, not thus accessible to our senses, we yet believe to exist. We may go the whole way with the, philosopher who would resolve all our knowledge into sensations; it may be a matter of rational conviction to us that what is inaccessible to the senses must necessarily be beyond the sphere of knowledge. And it is but reasonable to say that we are not entitled to speak of what is unknown and unknowable. Yet the conviction of the existence of a material is too strong to be got rid of by such arguments, cogent though they appear to be when looked at from the analytical point of view. It is insufficient to say that the mind has built up a world of its own from the materials supplied to it by the senses. The repeated experience of sensations by us in particular groups and in particular successions, it has been said; explains the growth in us of material objects and their orderly arrangement. But whence this possibility of experiencing them repeatedly? Why should the same group of sensations recur to us and to others in any particular order or arrangement? Why this perdurability among the groups of number of sensations? A material object is not simply the summation of a number of sensations. These sensations are permanently bound up together into inseparable bundles. What is the explanation of this permanent bond among these attributes of matter? Is there a nucleus corresponding to our idea of matter around which these experienced attributes cohere? Or, is it the mere play of fancy to ascribe to them a permanency which does not belong to them?

Here is a question before which science along with reason stands discomfited and spell-bound; and in despair, it would destroy and deny what it cannot comprehend. The perceiving mind is no less mysterious than the perceived matter; and Nihilism has solved the mystery by destroying the former as well as the latter. The existence of these mysteries both in the sphere of sensations and in the external world does not in the least affect the practical concerns of life. The objects continue to be what they are and continue to serve the usual purposes of life even though we may be unable to comprehend their innermost texture. They may be but airy combinations of sensations, tangible to the muscular sense, coloured to the vision and so on. Or they may be substantial realities of which these attributes are only the outside varnish. So also is regard to our minds. There may be nothing in the background of our consciousness corresponding to our notion of mind and self. The *I* of our conviction may be an illusion built on no logical basis. The fleeting experiences of the mind have, it is true; a bond of union, which bond is a mystery unsolved by sense-experience and rationalism. Here also what is insoluble has been destroyed and the Gordian Knot has been cut by an easy process. But these ghosts of a material world and a mental world cannot be so readily allayed. Nor can we rest satisfied even with a simple negation with the possibility of knowing them. The Vedāntic philosophy fully recognizes this element of permanency in our psychological structure of a material world and of a mental world. To the knowledge of these two departments of experience resolvable into sensations we have to add the notion of permanency. The attributes of matter are permanently bundled up together in various ways; and so also the attributes of mind. And whatever explanation may be attempted of this notion of permanency as due to variations in our experiences, such an explanation cannot do away with the fact. A residuum there is, all must admit, which sensations do not and cannot account for; and of this residuum, Western philosophy does not seem to have attained to a clear vision. It has either to rest contented with the assumption of gross material world as present to our ordinary vision or it has destroyed it completely. It has not śifted its contents with care and laid firm hold of their ultimate meaning. Even Mill, whose analysis of matter is so striking and acute, did not see that the permanency or perdurability which he asserted as the residual factor both in his analysis of matter and of mind, required a fuller recognition as an ultimate element in the philosophy of preception than he was willing to accord to it. This element of permanency in the material world of perception and in the mental world of self-consciousness is set up as an ultimate fact of philosophical analysis by the Vedāntins; and they call it *Mūla prakṛti* or *Māyā*. The term *Māyā* has no doubt come to mean *illusion;* but this was not its meaning in the text of the Vedānta as originally expounded. The word *Māyā* occurs but very rarely in the Vedas; and it means in them not illusion, but Divine power. The same is true of the significance of the term in the few pages of the Upaniṣads where it is used. When the Lord is said in the Brihadaranyaka-Upaniṣad to appear as multiform through the *Māyās,* the reference is clearly to His creative *Śakti.* The Lord is represented as careering rapidly through the appearances of the world with "the horses yoked." The mind has the horses or the senses under its control; and with these yoked or controlled-horses, it proceeds to its work of creative knowledge. But in the ultimate analysis, the horses, the world and all resolve themselves into the Brahman. "This

Ātman is the horses, this is the ten, and the thousands, many and endless". In the Śvetāśvetara-Upaniṣad, it is said that "the sages, devoted to meditation and concentration, have seen, the power belonging to God Himself." The sages "meditate on the river whose water consists of the five streams, which is wild and winding with its five springs whose names are the five vital breaths, whose fountain-head is the mind, the course of the five kinds of perception". The five streams here referred to are the five percipient senses which wind about the material structure of the world; and the river of the phenomenal runs along the course of mental perceptions. It will be seen that here again the idea of illusion is entirely absent. And when the student is called upon to identify *Prakṛti* or nature with *Māyā* in the same Upaniṣad and the Lord is spoken of as the *Māyin*, the reference is, as Professor Max Müller observes, only to the creative power of the Lord.

The Vedānta corrects the popular notion of the material world and contends that it has no essence independent of mental perception—a contention which is amply sustained by modern science. That material existence is to us known only as perception is a doctrine of the Vedānta, as it is a doctrine of the modern theory of knowledge. The former is perhaps more emphatic in maintaining the unreliable character of sensations and appearances—unreliable as implying anything more than what they are; as contrasted with noumenal realities—a doctrine that has the full support of modern psychology. To revert to the Vedāntic doctrine of *Māyā*. Now this *Māyā* is the *Śakti* or power of God and is *Anādi*—beginningless. It is divine in its origin but is not eternal, for it may come to an end. Reserving this latter aspect of the question for the present, the significance of the statements that *Māyā* or *Śakti* is Divine and that it has endured from the beginning should be attended to. We found that beyond and behind the phenomena of perception, underlying the attributes or bundles of possibilities of sensations, constituting the objects of the material world, there is the important fact of their permanancy. Sensations viewed as elements in our experience are fleeting; one sensation follows another in rapid succession, and no one sensation endures continuously for any appreciable period of time. But when these same sensations are projected out of the mind into the external they are viewed to be the attributes of material objects or in philosophical language, as bundles of sensations—they lose their fleeting character and acquire the opposite characteristic of permanency. It is this that requires a full recognition and explanation. And we claim for the Vedānta the clearness of analytical vision to have recognised this residual element in our experience after making the fullest allowance for the fleeting sensations in which it is embodied. Through our consciousness, whether centred in self or directed out of it, there runs in a perpetual current this conviction of perdurability; and the philosopher has therefore to fix his attention on this and to take its bearings as an element of the universe. The Vedāntin declares it to a power of Brahman, that is, he declares that it is an ultimate fact. Whether this declaration amounts to a confession of his ignorance of the Ultimate nature of this fact or whether we can clothe this statement with a realizable significance is another question. But we need not seriously object even to the former alternative, for we may then seek refuge in the observation of Professor Max Müller that :

> there is a point in every system of philosophy where a confession of ignorance is inevitable and all the greatest philosophers have had to confess that there are limits to our understanding the world; nay, this knowledge of the limits of our understanding has, since Kant's Criticism of Pure Reason, become the very foundation of all critical philosophy.

The doctrine of *Māyā* is the Vedāntin's view of cosmogony; Brahman, the supreme, is associated with a certain power called *Māyā* or *Avidyā* to which the appearance of this universe is due. Why is this power called by such same as *Māyā*, nescience, ignorance, illusion? It is because, in the view of the Vedāntin, this power and its effect, that is the world and its belongings, stand in the way of our reaching to a knowledge of the Ultimate Truth. Now knowledge is either of phenomena or of noumena. And engrossed in the former we are unable to rise to a knowledge of the latter; and as a knowledge of the eternal realities affects our destinies most intimately, whatever operates to screen them off from us must be viewed as darkness keeping us away from light. Remember that science in its soberest form has made no declaration hostile to metaphysics; and God has yet a place in the universe. If so, a knowledge of God, of the relation that subsists between Him and ourselves, and also of His relation to the material universe ought to be admitted to be indispensable, or at least desirable. And if the phenomenal, knowledge that comes to us through the senses tends to withdraw us from the search for the underlying principles of existence, we may well term this phenomenal knowledge *avidyā*—ignorance, not because it is valueless in itself, but because of its self-centering hostility to the higher kind of knowledge. The Vedāntin confines his attention to the highest problems of life; and views with disfavour whatever tends to obscure the philosophic vision. And the phenomenal has this tendency, and receives hence such names as *avidyā*, illusion, etc. These names have given offence to many, both in this country and elsewhere, but it will be seen that they have done so without reason. For, in the first place, we must allow that the problems of metaphysics have important bearings on human life. If our life time here is but an instant in the eternity that belongs to us, if, in consequence, our temporal concerns are as nothing in the balance when weighed with our concerns in the hereafter, if these premises, in no way rejected even by agnosticism, be granted, then indeed it follows indisputably that the problems of the future have a higher value than those of the present. This Absolute

Superiority, if once admitted, justifies fully the language adopted by the Vedāntin in respect of the material concerns of life. These concerns are paramount, it is true, to physical science and to us as denizens on this earth. Science endeavours to make the best of the present; and it is but just and proper that it should do so. But that is no reason why we should forget that the concerns of science are after all subordinate to the higher concerns of philosophy. Children when engaged in their engrossing pastimes may not have the remotest glimpse of the serious problems of life that await them in the future, and yet the latter are more important than the former. And we should not quarrel with children for securing the utmost pleasure their pastimes while engaged in them. The same applies to the relation between philosophy and science. The latter engrossing as it is, and, we may say, engrossing as it ought to be, has yet to yield to the other in intrinsic worth; and may be called *Avidyā Māyā*, in comparison. To show that the statement, that even agnostic science has not brought its good sense into peril by a complete negation of metaphysics, is not gratuitous, permit me to refer to a remarkable passage in the writings of Huxley :

'The student of nature, who starts from the axiom of the universality of the law of causation, cannot refuse to admit an eternal existence; if he admits the conservation of energy, if he admits the existence of immaterial phenomena in the form of conciousness, he must admit the, possibility, at any rate, of an eternal series of such phenomena; and, if his studies have not been barren of the best fruit of the investigation of nature, he will have enough sense to see that, when Spinoza says, 'by God we understand an absolute infinite Being, that is an unchangeable Essence, with infinite attributes,' the God so conceived is one that only a very great fool would deny, even in his heart. Physical science is as little Atheistic as it is Materialistic."

The material world then is s recognised reality and has its origin in Brahman. The Vedāntin admits the knowledge of perception to be right knowledge, but such only in its relation to this world and its concerns. But this knowledge and these worldly concerns he distinguishes from the knowledge of philososophy, of God, Creation, etc. This latter knowledge is possible to man, in his view. But to reach it he must not forget the fact of the existence of the varieties of philosophy foreshadowed even in perceptual knowledge. We have already said that these abet us on every side even in our dealings with phenomenal appearance. This recognition of their existence, as distinguished from the knowledge of their manifestations and effects, is the first step in the process that is to lead us up to a knowledge of Brahman. But this recognition is not sufficient by itself for the successful arrival at the final goal. When standing on this side of the vestibule of God, when studying the multiplex manifestations of the complex machine of the universe from the outside, hardly able to enter into its revolving wheels and flying bells, the true spirit of scientific investigation would have felt the insignificance of the inquirer in the presence of the vast conglomeration of energising matter. The man of science may then say with the poet, that he feels,

> *"A presence that disturbs me with the joy*
> *Of elevated thoughts; a sense sublime*
> *Of something far more deeply interfused,*
> *Whose dwelling is the light of setting suns.*
> *And the round ocean, and the living air,*
> *And the blue sky, and in the mind of man."*

If this be the right frame of mind even in regard to the inquiry into the material manifestations of God's *Māyā*, what should be the preparation of mind required to render us fit to approach nearer to the throne of the Eternal? The Vedāntin rightly insists upon renunciation, tranquillity, self-restraint, and *Śraddhā* or faith, as the necessary, conditions antecedent to the commencement of the inquiry into Brahman. For, what is it that he is inquest of? It is not the phenomena of the world which he should observe and examine and dissect with vigilant eyes. It is not simply an enumeration, nor even a classification and analysis of his mental phenomena. This world is the world of action; and in it alone is there room for the play of the senses. If we would get at the truths which lie beyond and behind it, we must suppress our action and suppress our senses. However, valuable these are when dealing with the world and its phenomena, though their work as mild-builders should also be recognised, yet when we go to dissect the contents of the mind, our senses and activities are hindrances and not helps in our researches. Even Professor Max Müller fails to grasp the full import of the logic of the Vedānta when he says that "the object of the Vedānta was to show that we have really nothing to conquer but ourselves, that we possess everything within us, and that nothing is required but to shut our eyes and our hearts against the illusion of the world in order to find ourselves richer than heaven and earth." It is true that the search for the truths of the Vedānta must be into ourselves, and that we must shut our eyes and hearts if we would engage in that search undisturbed by them. But the riches higher than those of heaven which our Self is to reveal, is not to be the exclusive result of this shutting up of our eyes and hearts; nor should it be said that the Vedāntin requires every individual among us to stand unaffected by his sense organs and by his sentiments and emotions. If you seek communion with the Brahman enthroned on your inner Self, you should approach Him with singleness of purpose and exclusive devotion. The Vedānta is jealous of rivals and would stand alone in the intellectual embrace of its devotee. To understand God, to comprehend the process of creation, the nature of the human soul and its past life and future destiny, the Self must be grasped in its entirety and in its inmost nature; and to do this, the student must abnegate whatever is calculated to disturb him in his absorbing subjectivity. The tranquillity, misnamed apathy and quietism, is this indispensable imperturbability by external calls without which the mind cannot possibly soar up the peaks of the Vedānta. This is not any dreamy imagination that the Hindu mind specially, indulges in; it is no indication of any absence of a genius for system and order in the Hindu intellect; nor is it the burling of thought "as a venture into the nature of metaphysical conceptions." It is the only path open for man to win what knowledge he can of the realities that ever elude the grasp of the unthinking mind. The Vedānta ignores the phenomenal, not because the phenomenal is unimportant, but because it is beyond the special sphere of investigation which it marks out for itself; it is subjective, because by being subjective alone can it accomplish its task; and it would forget the world and withdraw the mind from all temporal calls, as then alone there is a chance of man reaching to a knowledge of thing.

The Vedānta requires :—

That blessed mood
In which the burthen and the mystery,
Of all this unintelligible world
Is lightened; that serene and blessed mood
In which the affections gently lead us on.
Until the breath of this corporeal frame,
And even the motion of our human blood
Almost suspended, we are laid asleep.
In body, and become a living soul :
While with an eye made quiet by the power.
Of harmony and the power of joy.
We see into the life of things.

The mind, thus withdrawn from the phenomenal and also from the cravings of the body with which it stands associated, should approach the question of the Vedānta in a spirit of true faith and devotion, and not in that of cavil. The faith here insisted upon may be said to stand at the basis of all religions; and the Vedānta does not stand alone in this respect. But it is no blind faith that is demanded of the student. In that case, there is no room for enquiry or for conviction or knowledge. The demand is negative rather than positive. The Vedānta will have no determined atheist as its disciple, but demands that the inquiring mind should approach it in a spirit of meek reverence. Reason should be the guide, but not the tyrant of the philosopher. "There is so little which Reason, divested of all emotional and instinctive supports, is able to prove to our satisfaction that a sceptical aridity is likely to take possession of the soul." The mental mood should not be that described by Wordsworth in the following lines :—

> *Till, demanding formal proof*
> *And seeking it in everything, I lost*
> *All feeling of conviction; and, in fine,*
> *Sick, wearied out of contrarieties,*
> *Yielded up moral question in despair.*

"In this mood all those great generalised conceptions which are the food of our love, our reverence, our religion, dissolve away."

I said above that the Vedānta demands faith from its disciple. It is only when the student goes to the subject with faith that his eyes open into the vista of divine truth : "A man who is free from desires and free from grief", says the Kaṭha Upaniṣad, "sees the majesty of Self by the grace of the Creator. The Self cannot be gained by the Veda, nor by understanding, nor by much learning. He whom the Self chooses, by him the Self can be gained."

Few there are who feel an inclination for each inquiries; and of these but few understand what they are about. We all know that death is the portion of us all. But how many even of those brought to its very doors can bring themselves to attend to its significance? In the heyday of life, when the blood leaps along our veins, it is, but excusable, nay it is reasonable, that we should make the most of the world for which we are then best adapted. That is then our duty to ourselves and to the past and the future generations. But when the best part of our worldly mission is over, when we have contributed our mite to the smooth flow of life amidst its rugged paths, it is but natural that the phenomenal should loosen its hold upon us and allow us at times at least to look at the fundamental facts of the universe. It no doubt occasionally happens that this philosophic mood comes upon us unexpectedly even when young, as was the case with Nachiketas, of whom it is said that "faith entered into his heart," even when he was a boy.

The faith that we here speak of is not subversive of reason and it is viewed only as a frame of mind that is to lead us up to knowledge. Knowledge, not faith, is, according to the generally accepted doctrine, the ultimate requisite for the true comprehension of the Brahman. The Brahman who is " hidden in all beings," that is, who is to revealed to our vision only by a deep search into our own innermost heart, is seen "by subtle seers through their sharp and subtle intellect." Where the Brahman is not, "the sun does not shine, nor the moon and the stars nor these lightnings, much less, this fire." If he is such that "when He shines, everything shines after Him; by His light all is lighted", how can we apprehend Him but by the light of grace and knowledge shed by Himself on our minds?

I cannot within the short compass of a lecture explain even if I had the necessary ability and knowledge, the doctrines of the Vedānta, regarding the nature of the *Paramātman,* the nature of the *Jīva,* of its life in this world and of its passage to the next, and the other connected questions. I have endeavoured only to offer some reasons to show that the Vedānta deserves our careful attention and that one may set down those dabblers in philosophy who will speak of it in a spirit of supercilious contempt, as persons who have no claim whatever to approach the subject. The Vedānta which gives us a knowledge of the true God, which preaches "as with a voice of thunder" the virtues of self-denial, charity and universal benevolence, which induced powerful sovereigns among us to descend from their thrones and abandon their palaces to meditate in solitary forests on its problems and teachings, and which promises immortality as the final outcome of its knowledge, can this be to the thinking mind a subject for contempt or ridicule? "In the world of nature to reveal things hidden, to sanctify things common, to interpret new and unsuspected relations, to open a new sense in man; in the moral world, to teach truths hitherto neglected or unobserved, to awaken men's hearts to the solemnities that encompass them, to deepen our reverence for the essential Soul, to make us feel more truly, more tenderly, more profoundly, to lift the thoughts upward through the shows of time to that which is permanent and eternal, and to bring down on the transitory, things of eye and ear some shadow of the eternal, till we :—

'feel through all this flushy dress.
Bright shoots of everlastingness'—

this is the office" which the Vedānta should not cease to perform as long as it is approached in the proper spirit. We may say of the Vedānta what the critic has said of the poetry of Wordsworth, that "the more thoughtful of each generation will draw nearer and observe it more closely, will ascend its imaginative heights, and sit under the shadow of its profound meditations, and in proportion as they do so, will become more noble and pure in heart." I feel no hesitation therefore in closing these observations with the appeal addressed to us Hindus by a foreign admirer of the Vedānta :

"So the Vedānta, in its unfalsified form, is the strongest support of pure morality, is the greatest consolation in the sufferings of life and death,—Indians, keep to it!"

Veda and the Vedānta[1]

Prof. Max Müller

To the present day India acknowledges, no higher authority in matters of religion, ceremonial, customs and law than the *Veda*, and so long as India is India, nothing will extinguish that ancient spirit of Vedāntism which is breathed by every Hindu from his earliest youth, and pervades, in various forms, the prayers even of the idolater, the speculations of the philosopher; and the proverbs of the beggar.

For purely practical reasons therefore,—I mean for the very practical object of knowing something of the secret springs which determine the character, the thoughts and deeds, of the lowest as well as of the highest amongst the people in India,—an acquaintance with their religion, which is founded on the Veda, and with their philosophy, which is founded on the Vedānta, is highly desirable.

It is easy to make light of this, and to ask, as some statesmen have asked, even in Europe, What has religion, or what has philosophy, to do with politics? In India, in spite of all appearances to the contrary, and notwithstanding the indifference on religious matters so often paraded before the world by the Indians themselves, religion, and philosophy too, are great powers still. Read the account that has lately been published of two native statesmen, the administrators of two first class states in Sourashtra, Junagadh and Bhavnagar, Gokulaji and Gaurisankara,[2] and you will see

1. From "India : What can it teach us?"
2. Life and Letters of Gokulaji Sampattirama Zala and his views of the Vedānta, by Mannassukharama Suryarama Tripathi, Bombay, 1881.

whether the Vedānta is still a moral and a political power in India or not.

But I claim even more for the Vedānta, and I recommend its study, not only to the candidates for the Indian Civil Service, but to all true students of philosophy. It will bring before them a views of life, different from all other views of life which are placed before us in the History of Philosophy. You saw how behind all the *Devas* or gods, the authors of the Upaniṣads discovered the *Ātman* or Self. Of that Self they predicated three things only, that it is, that it perceives, and that it enjoys eternal bliss. All other predicates were negative : it is not this, it is not that—it is beyond anything that we can conceive or name.

But that Self, that Highest Self, the *Paramātman,* could be discovered after a severe moral and intellectual discipline only, and those who had not yet discovered it, were allowed to worship lower gods, and to employ more poetical names to satisfy their human wants. Those who knew the other gods to be but names or persons—*personae* or masks, in the true sense of the world—*pratīkas,* as they call them in Sanskrit—knew also that those who worshipped these names or persons, worshipped in truth the Highest Self, though ignorantly. This is the most characteristic feature in the religious history of India. Even in the *Bhagavadgītā,* a rather

As a young man, Gokulaji, the son of a good family, learnt Persian and Sanskrit. His chief interest in life, in the midst of a most successful political career, was the 'Vedānta.' A little insight, we are told, into tills knowledge turned his heart to higher objects, promising him freedom from grief, and blessedness, the highest aim of all. This was the turning point of his inner life. When the celebrated Vedāntic anchorite, Rāma visited Junagadh, Gokulaji became his pupil. When another anchorite, Paramahamsa Sakkidananda, passed through Junagadh on a pilgrimage to Girnar, Gokulaji was regularly intiated in the secrets of the Vedānta. He soon became highly proficient in it, and through the whole course of his life, whether in power or in disgrace, his belief in the doctrines of the Vedānta supported him, and made him, in the opinion of English statesmen, the model of what a native statesman ought to be.

popular and exoteric exposition of Vedāntic doctrines, the Supreme Lord or *Bhagavān* himself is introduced as saying : 'Even those who worship idols, worship me.[1]

But that was not all. As behind the names of Agni, Indra, and Prajāpati, and behind all the mythology of nature, the ancient sages of India has discovered the Ātman—let us call it the objective Self—they perceived also behind the veil of the body, behind the senses, behind the mind, and behind our reason (in fact behind the mythology of the soul, which we often call psychology), another Ātman, or the subjective Self. That Self, too, was to be discovered by a severe moral and intellectual discipline only, and those who wished to find it, who wished to know, not themselves, but their Self, had to cut far deeper than the senses, or the mind, or the reason, or the ordinary Ego, All these too were mere *Devas*, bright apparitions—mere names—yet names meant for something. Much that was most dear, that had seemed for a time their very self, had to be surrendered, before they could find the Self of Selves, the Old Man, the Looker-on, a subject independent of all personality, an existence independent of all life.

When that point had been reached, then the highest knowledge began to dawn, the Self within (the *Pratyagātman*) was drawn towards the Highest Self, (the *Paramātman*), it found its true self in the Highest Self, and

1. Professor Kunen discovers a similar idea in the word placed in the mouth of Jehovah by the prophet Malachi, *i.* 14. 'For I am great King, and my name is feared among the Heathens. 'The reference,' he says, 'is distinctly to the adoration already offered to Yahweh by the people, whenever they serve their own gods with true reverence and honest zeal. Even in Deuteronomy, the adoration of these other gods by the nations is represented as a dispensation of Yahweh. Malachi goes a step further, and accepts their worship as a tribute which in reality falls to Yahweḥ,—to Him, the Only True. Thus the opposition between Yahweh and the other gods, and afterwards between the one true God and the imaginary gods, make room here for the still higher conception that the adoration of Yahweh is the essence and the truth of all religion.' Hibbert Lectures, p. 181.

the oneness of the subjective with the objective Self was recognised as underlying all reality, as the dim dream of religion,—as the pure light of philosophy.

This fundamental idea is worked out with systematic-completeness in the Vedānta philosophy, and no one who can appreciate the lessons contained in Berkeley's philosophy, will read the Upaniṣads and the *Brahma-Sūtras* and their commentaries without feeling a richer and a wiser-man.

I admit that it requires patience, descrimination, and a certain amount of self-denial before we can discover the grains of solid gold in the dark mines of Eastern philosophy. It is far easier and far more amusing for shallow critics to point out what is absurd and ridiculous in the religion and philosophy of the ancient world than for the earnest student to discover truth and wisdom under strange disguises. Some progress, however, has been made, even during the short span of life that we can remember. The Sacred Books of the East are no longer a mere butt for the invectives of missionaries or the sarcasms of philosophers. They have at last been recognised as historical documents, aye, as the most ancient documents in the history of the human mind, and as palaeontological records of an evolution that begins to elicit wider and deeper sympathies than the nebular formation of the planet on which we dwell for a season, or the organic development of that chrysalis which we call man.

If you think that I exaggerate, let me read you in conclusion what one of the greatest philosophical critics—and certainly not a man given to admiring the thoughts of others—says of the Vedānta, and more particularly of the Upaniṣads. Schopenhauer writes :

'In the whole world there is no study so beneficial and so elevating as that of the Upaniṣads. It has been the solace of my life—it will be the solace of my death.'[1]

---

1. Sacred Books of the East, vol. I. The Upaniṣads, translated by Max Müller; Introduction, p. lxi.

I have, thus, tried, so far as it was possible in one course of lectures, to give you some idea of Ancient India, of its ancient literature, and, more particularly, of its ancient religion. My object was, not merely to place names and facts before you, these you can find in many published books, but, if possible, to make you see and feel the general human interests that are involved in that ancient chapter of the history of the human race. I wished that the Veda and its religion and philosophy should not only seem to you curious or strange, but that you should feel that there was in them something that concerns ourselves, something of our own intellectual growth, some recollections, as it were, of our own childhood, or at least of the childhood of our own race. I feel convinced that, placed as we are here in this life, we have lessons to learn from the Veda, quite as important as the lessons we learn at school from Homer and Virgil, and lessons from the Vedānta quite as instructive as the systems of Plato or Spinoza.

I do not mean to say that everybody who wishes to know how the human race came to be what it is, how language came to be what it is, how religion came be to what it is, how manners, customs, laws, and forms of government came to be what they are, how we ourselves came to be what we are, must learn Sanskrit, and must study Vedic Sanskrit. But I do believe that not to know what a study of Sanskrit, and particularly a study of the Veda, has already done for illuminating the darkest passage in the history of the human mind, of that mind on which we ourselves are feeding and living, is a misfortune, or, at all events, a lose, just as I should count it a loss to have passed through life without knowing something, however little, of the earth and its geological formation, of the movements of the sun, the moon, and the stare,—and of the thought, or the will, or the law, that governs these movements.

Vedānta toward all Religions[1]

Swami Abhedananda

Hundreds of educated men and women of this country have found in the Vedānta the true foundation of an absolutely unsectarian universal religious which has neither dogma nor creed of any kind, which embraces all the special religions, such as Christianity Buddhism, Zoroastrianism, Mahomedanism, Brahminism, and, like a thread, strings them together into a garland of flowers variegated in their colour and size. Like an impartial judge, the religion of the Vedānta gives the proper place to each of these sectarian religions in the grand evolution of the spiritual thoughts and systems of the world. Having no particular founder, it stands upon the eternal, spiritual laws that have been discovered by various sages and seers of truth of all countries and of all ages and which have been described in the different Scriptures of the world. Those who have studies the religion of the Vedānta in its various aspects have found the spiritual laws which are given in all the different Scriptures. For them it is not necessary to study the Vedas of the Hindus, the Tripitakas of the Buddhists, the Zend Avesta of the Parsees, the Old Testament of the Jews, the Bible of the Christians and the Koran of the Mahomedans in order to understand those spiritual laws, because they can find the essential points, the moral and spiritual laws that govern our lives, through the study of Vedānta. It is not necessary if they can only understand this central point, that truth is universal. If there be any spiritual law, that must be universal and must prevade all the Scriptures of the world. Then there is no

1. A lecture delivered in America.

difficulty—everything will appear to us as simple. Furthermore, the students of the Vedānta find in this religion the ultimate conclusions of the greatest scientific thinkers of the world. It includes all the scientific truths. The religion of the Vedānta therefore is extemely comforting for those who have outgrown the doctrines and dogmas of special religious, and I can assure you that it has brought the greatest comfort and consolation into the lives of those who are earnest and sincere seeker after truth.

The religion of the Vedānta is like a huge structure, the foundation of which is laid, not upon the quicksand of the authority of any particular book or personality, but upon the solid rock of logical and scientific reasoning, and the walls of which are not made up of the clay of superstitious dogmas, but are built with the stones of spiritual experiences, placed one upon another by the artistic hands of the great seers of truth of ancient and modern times. The roof of this superb structure is not confined within the celestial domain of the anthropomorphic God of a personal religion, but it extends beyond all the heavens of different religions, and, rising above all the various planes of relativity, reaches that infinite and eternal abode of being, intelligence, love and everlasting bliss. The gates of this magnificient palace are guarded, not by zealots and fanatics who carry destructive weapons in their hands to prevent the entrance of other sectarians, but by sincerity and earnestness standing like sentinels to welcome with open arms all those who are sincere and earnest seekers after truth, spiritual life and God-consciusness, irrespective of their creed, nationality of religious conviction. There are many storeys in that palatial building, three of which are of great importance. The first floor is for the monotheists, or those who believe in the existence of one personal God whom they worship under a particular name and a particular form. Here is the place for all the monotheistic believers and worshippers in Judaism, Christianity, Mahomedanism, Zoroastrianism, Lamaism,

Brahminism and Theistic Buddhism, with their various sects and denominations. Here are to be found all the doctrines, dogmas, rituals, ceremonials and symbols that are described in these particular religions. The second storey is for those who have outgrown all ritualism, ceremonialism, symbolism and the worship of a God with a particular name and a particular form. It is for those who have understood that God is not far from us, dwelling in a heaven somewhere above the clouds, but that God dwells in nature; He is immament and resident in nature. He is not far away, but He is here, He is the soul of our souls, He is the life of our life; "in Him we live, move and have our being." Those who feel this and those who realise that we are children of God, that our souls are parts of that one stupendous whole, the Infinite Being, worship on the second floor of this superb structure of the religion of Vedānta.

The God of the Vedānta is personal, yet He is not confined to any particular personality. He is impersonal, also, he is above personal and impersonal, beyond both. You cannot confine God by giving Him any particular personality. If you think that he is sitting on a throne somewhere, with two hands,—that will limit Him. That is a phase, but there are other phases. The God of the Vedānta has many, names and many aspects, and these aspects and these names are recognised by the different religions of the world. He is the same Being, but has many names. He has no particular form, yet He assumes many forms in order to satisfy the desires of earnest and sincere devotees; and to fulfil the prayers of the devotee, He manifests Himself in that particular form to which the heart and the soul of the devotee are devoted. His personal aspect is worshipped under different names by different religions. The Christians worship Him as the Father in Heaven, the Mahomedans as Allah, the Zoroastrians call Him Ahura Mazda, the Brahmins give Him various names, the Buddhists call Him Buddha, the worshippers of the Divine Mother call Him the Mother of the Universe. God is sexless and the moment we become sexless, we have become divine. He has no sex. Why should you call Him Father and give Him the masculine sex ? Call Him mother, masculine or feminine, there is no distinction of sex : therefore, He may be called Mother, Father, neuter, it does not make any difference. When you understand this central truth, there is no difference in the expression. But the personal God of the dualistic religions of Semitic origin is masculine, is Jehovah; the same Jehovah again is the Father in Heaven, is Allah, is Ahura Mazda.

The third storey of this structure is for those who have gone beyond all reality, who have transcended phenomenal, existence, and who have reached that state of divine communion which manifests the eternal, absolute oneness of the Supreme Spirit. It is for those who realize the indivisible oneness of that Being. That Being cannot be divided into parts, but He is one stupendous whole, indivisible, finer than space; as space cannot be divided, so God cannot be divided into parts. This is the Absolute Spirit, the infiite Being; It is called by various names. In Vedānta it is called Brahman, *Paramahaṁsa* or Over-Soul; but it the same as the God of Plato, the *Substantia* of Spinoza, the transcendental thing-in-itself (Ding in Sich) of Kant, the Will of Schopenhauer, the Unknown and Unknowable of Herbert Spencer, the Substance of Ernest Haeckle, the Science of Matter of the Materialists, the Real Entity or Spirit of the Spiritualists; It is also the same as Christ. Christ is this being, this Universal Spirit Who is called by other names, and He is also Buddha. Buddha means that Eternal Wisdom, that Truth.

These different names are given by different philosophers, as also by different worshippers. These three phases of the Vedānta,—the dualistic, the qualified non-dualistic and the non-dualistic or monistic,—include all the sectarian religions of the world and impart the highest ideals given in all the Scriptures. What is the highest ideal given in the Scripture of the Christ, or of the Mahomedans, or of the Parsees? The worship of one God; that is the highest ideal. God is personal; He may have some form, He may have a particular name but still He is one. That is the highest ideal. This you find in the dualistic phase of Vedānta. The Vedānta accepts that ideal, and therefore it embraces all the religions that I have just mentioned. As, on the one hand, the religions of the Vedānta embrace the special religions of the world, and the higher ideals of all the scriptures of the world, so, on the other hand, the philosophy of the Vedānta embraces the highest ideals add ultimate conclusions of the greatest scientists, the deepest philosophers, the profoundest thinkers and the best metaphysicians of the world; therefore, this religion is truly universal. Its scope is unlimited and there is no other religion in the world which can be compared to it in its universality and its infinite scope.

The religion of the Vedānta is inseparable from true science and from true philosophy. Why? Because all sciences and all philosophies are nothing but so many attempts of human minds to grasp some particular phase of the Eternal Truth, the Infinite Reality. As truth is the goal of all science and all philosophy, the same truth is the goal of the Vedānta; and, as Vedānta attempts to lead all human minds to the realization of that absolute truth of the oneness, so it embraces all the philosophies of the world. In particular, doctrines, in particular arguments and discussions and particular points, there may be diversity, but the ideal is one, and hence Professor Max Müller said that "the Vedānta is the most sublime of all philosophies and the most comforting of all religions." Why is this? Because it embraces the highest truths given in the philosophy of Plato, of Schopenhauer, of Hegel, Kant, Berkeley, Hume, and others. For this reason we should call the religion and philosophy of the Vedānta absolutely unsectarian and universal. The follower of the Vedānta religion is a true Christian. He is a true Christian, but in spirit he is broader than a Christian. He is a true Mahomedan; also he is a true Buddhist, a true Brahman, a true Hindu; he is a worshipper of truth. He honours and reveres all the great prophets and seers of truth of all countries, accepts their teachings and never fails to separate the essentials of religion from the non-essentials or the crystallized dogmas and doctrines of special religions. He does not belong to any sect or creed of any particular religion, yet in spirit he belongs to all sects and all creeds of all religions because he knows the spirit of all creeds, he understands the meaning of all sectarian doctrines and dogmas. He does not belong to any particular church or any particular temple, but all churches, all places of worship, all temples and mosques, are equally sacred, equally holy. To his all-embracing soul they are all equally great, and so he is able to worship his ideal in a Catholic church or in a Mahomedan mosque. He is not limited. When he sits under a tree, he worships. He may not go to Church on Sunday, he may stay in the park under a tree and worship God in spirit. He feels that each individual soul is the temple wherein dwells the Eternal Being and He must be worshipped in spirit. That is a grand ideal.

The Vedānta accepts the teachings of the great prophets, like Moses, like Zoroaster, Jesus, the Christ, Buddha, Confucius, Laotze and other great prophets and seers of truth who have arisen in other parts of the world, as well as those of India,—such as Krishna, Rāma and others; it recognises Jesus the Christ as the Son of God, as the Incarnation of Divinity, but not as the only one. There have been many other incarnations and will be many in future. God is not limited to any particular tribe or particular nationality, or time, or place. Why should we limit Him? He is the Infinite Being, the Father of all nations. Wherever His manifestation is necessary, He will appear; He loves all mankind equally. He does not think that the Jews are His best friends, while others are heathens. No, they are equal in His eyes. All nations are great before Him. We must not have any national prejudice on account of colour or particular mode of living. All are children of God.

The religion of the Vedānta recognizes spiritual growth and evolution in the path of realization. As in our physical body, there are different stages of growth,—like childhood, youth and maturity,—so in the spiritual life there is spiritual childhood, spiritual youth, spiritual maturity. One leads to the other, one merges into the other, and ultimately leads to God, to Realization. Spiritual childhood begins with the worship of ancestors or departed spirits and ends with the conception of one extra-cosmic personal God, Who dwells outside of nature; that is the limit of spiritual childhood. All primitive religions began with ancestor-worship. In fact, ancestor-worship or spirit-worship was the foundation of all religions in primitive times. Modern spiritism or ancient ancestor-worship is only the beginning of spiritual childhood. In ancient times, when the people came to believe in departed spirits and felt that they had power over certain phenomena or control over certain conditions, they were frightened and they began to revere and honour these spirits. Gradually, this gave rise to another conception,—that of still higher and more powerful spirits who had larger control over the phenomena of nature, and they called these tribal gods. They become nature Gods, and such tribal gods you will find amongst the different tribes of the ancient Jews, as amongst the tribes of ancient India, China, Japan and other countries. They are like chiefs who have control over certain manifestations of nature or certain powers; and this may be called the second stage of spiritual childhood. Gradually, this leads to another step, which is a little higher; that is, that there is one governor over all these tribal gods or chiefs, and this conception is the monotheistic conception of a personal God; that He is the ruler of all, of the sun-god, of the moon-god, of departed spirits, of ancestors and bright spirits,—that is, the ruler of all. This is the beginning of the dualistic conception, and here is the end of spiritual childhood. All those dualistic religions which we call monotheistic religions do not go beyond this. They lead our minds and souls to the worship of one personal God who dwells outside of nature and they make us believe that this is the highest, that there can be nothing higher.

These dualistic religions, therefore, like Zoroastrianism and Mahomedanism, lead to the highest stage of spiritual childhood in the spiritual life. But the spiritual youth begins when we begin to realize that God is not outside of nature but He is in nature; He is not outside of us, He is in us; that He is not extra-cosmic but intro-cosmic; He is immanent and resident in nature; He is the soul of the universe; just as the soul of our body is the internal ruler of the body, so the soul of the universe is the internal ruler of the universe. He governs, not from outside, but from inside. He is the Creator, not in the sense that He sits somewhere and commands and creates the world out of the material which dwells outside of His own being, but He creates, by pouring His spiritual influx in nature and starting the evolution of that cosmic energy which is called *Prakṛti*, or nature. In fact, the cosmic energy forms the body of the Spiritual Being. God then appears to be both of the efficient and material cause of the universe, and therefore He is not only the Father but the Mother of the universe, Father and Mother, both in one. The individual souls come out of His own being like sparks coming out of a huge bonfire. The huge bonfire is Divinity and our souls are like sparks which have sprung out of that bonfire of Divinity. We are immortal by our birthright, because we are parts of that one stupendous whole.

This state gradually leads to spiritual maturity, where we do not think of the world, we do not think of creation; but, rising above all phenomena, we realize the indivisible oneness,—that we are not merely sparks, but we are some thing close to divinity—we are one with God. Then we say, "I and my Father are one." Not one in the sense that an earthly child is one with its father, but it is unity, because God is all in all, and all is God. There is nothing outside of God, everything has vanished, all phenomena have disappeared, all relative existences have disappeared and the whole universe appears to be like a solid mass of infinite and indivisible reality. All phenomenal existences seem to be like dreams. I am talking, you are listening,— this is like a dream; you cannot realize it unless you rise on a higher plane. We are all playing parts on the stage of the world. I have taken some part and you have taken some other part. There is no difference. You are playing the part of a listener; I am playing the part of a speaker, but we are all on the same stage. You may help me and I may help you. Your desires you are trying to fulfil by your thoughts and deeds, so everybody else is doing the same. You may have certain dreams in your life; you may think that if you can accomplish these, you have fulfilled your purpose in life. Then, after fulfilling that, you thing that there is another purpose. Yon must push on and reach that, and so on and on we go until all purposes are fulfilled, all desires are satisfied and all aims are gratified. So in reaching the maturity in spiritual life, we reach the absolutely monistic perception of spiritual oneness. It is not Pantheism. Do not for a moment dream that it is Pantheism. No, it is Absolute monism; there is no other word for it. Pantheism does not express it. Pantheism means, this is God; mother is God, the chair is God. No, in absolute monism, the chair does not exist; the particular phenomenon does not exist, but we reach the background. God is like the eternal canvas upon which the beautiful picture of this phenomenal world is painted by the Divine Hand. Then we realise the canvas. At present we are fascinated and charmed by the colourings of the external; we have forgotten the canvas, the background of the universe. Then we realize the background and we reach the highest.

The religion of the Vedānta teaches that there is one God, but with many aspects. From spiritual childhood we must rise to spiritual youth, and from spiritual youth to maturity; then we shall be one with the Infinite. The same God is worshipped under different names. The religion of the Vedānta is truly catholic and tolerant; it does not dispute, it has no particular form of worship, nor does it ask that you do this or that; but its main theme is that any form of worship which appeals to the sincerity and earnestness of the soul of the devotee is right. If you think that by worshipping any particular ideal, in a particular way, it will help you,—go and do it. Do not hesitate. If you think that it would not help you, do not do it. The worship of God depends upon the attitude of the worshipper, the attitude of the mind, the heart of the worshipper. If you wish to go and pray, go and pray; if you do not believe in prayer, do not pray. What your wish, go and do, but be directed by your highest impulse by your highest desire.

Try to understand the highest purpose of life and then worship the ideal under any form or any name which appeals to you; do not hesitate for a moment. All rituals, all ceremonials, all forms of worship, are only the means to the highest end, to the realization of the divinity, and therefore the religion of the Vedānta embraces all other special sectarian religion, all forms of worship, under the different names that I have given you. Some do not care to worship a personal God, but think of His impersonal nature; they are just as good. They are not going astray. So long as there is sincerity and earnestness and devotion and love for the spiritual ideal, there is no going astray. We make our heaven and hell on this earth by our thoughts and deeds. There is no other external hell or eternal place of punishment. Our own minds dwell in hell when we have performed some wicked deeds, some wrong. Our souls rebel then. But when we are in the path of righteousness, our souls are happy, there is peace, there is the manifestation of divinity; because God manifests when our minds are silent, and that silence comes through peace, and when there is peace, there is happiness and bliss.

The Vedānta in Outline[1]

Pandit Sitanath Tattvabhushan

Two Meanings of 'Vedānta'

The term *'Vedānta'* is a compound of 'Veda' and *'anta'* (end), and means, in its primary significance the latter part of the Veda or Vedas. The Vedic literature is divided by the expounders of the Vedas into two main *kāṇḍas* or sections, the first or *pūrva* portion being called the *karma-kāṇḍa*, that is, the section treating of *karma*, actions or duties; and the second, *anta*, or *uttara* portion the *jñāna-kāṇḍa*, the section on knowledge. The division is not clearly represented by distinct books or even chapters of the Vedas; but roughly speaking, the *Mantras* and the sacrificial portions of the *Brahmanas* represent the *karma-kāṇḍa*, and the treatises called *Upaniṣads*, attached mainly to the *Brāhmaṇas*, represent the *jñāna-kāṇḍa*. This *jñāna-kāṇḍa* of the Vedas is the Vedānta in the original sense of the word. As a part of the Veda, the Vedānta is *śruti* or scripture. As *śruti* or scripture, therefore, the Vedānta is identical with the Upaniṣads. The use of the term 'Vedānta' in this sense will be found in the Upaniṣads themselves, for instance, in the *Muṇḍakopaniṣad* III. 2.6, and the *Śvetāśvataropaniṣad, VI.* 22. Śaṅkarācārya the greatest authority on the Vedānta, uses the word in this sense everywhere in his writings. However, the word *'anta,'* in 'Vedānta,' from meaning 'end' or 'latter part,' came gradually to mean 'conclusion,' 'gist' or 'purport.' The composers of the Upaniṣads claimed that they had discovered the gist or

1. Reprint from the *Indian Review.*

purport of all Vedic teaching in the knowledge of the Absolute, of whom the gods worshipped by the authors of the *Mantras*, as well as all objects in creation, were, they taught, names forms or relative manifestations. The final end of all Vedic disciplines were, they thought, union with Brahman, the Absolute Being. In this latter sense, therefore, in the sense of the gist or purport of the Vedas, it was the Upaniṣads, again, which were called the 'Vedānta' or 'Vedāntas.' But the term came gradually to mean something quite different from, through closely related to, the Upaniṣads. As the Upaniṣads treated of a large variety of subjects, both essential and non-essential to the spiritual life, and as the teachings of the different treatises were apparently, if not really, conflicting, it became necessary to have systematic statements of the main doctrines taught in them,—statements backed by seasonings where necessary, and reconciling apparent discrepancies in the original teaching. Thus arose what is called the Vedānta Philosophy that is, the Philosophy of, or based on, the Vedānta or Upaniṣad. This philosophy, the body of aphorisms which is its chief exponent, oftener goes by the name of 'Vedānta' than the Upaniṣads, the original Vedāntas and the basis of all later Vedāntic teaching. The distinction, however, between the Vedānta as *sruti* or scripture, and the Vedānta as *Darśana* or Philosophy, must never be lost sight of.

The Vedānta-Śruti

The Vedānta, as scripture, consists, as I have said, of the Upaniṣads. Their traditional number in one hundred and eight; but modern scholars have found out that there are no fewer than one hundred and fifty bearing the name. All of them, however, are not genuine parts of the Vedas nor do all truly represent the spirit of the original Vedāntic teaching. Practically, twelve are recognised as forming the Vedāntic canon and the basis of the Vedāntic Philosophy. They are the *Īśa, Kena, Kaṭha, Praśna, Muṇḍaka, Māṇḍūkya, Taittirīya,*

Aitareya, Chāndogya, Bṛhadāraṇyaka, Kauṣitakī and *Śvetāśvatara* Upaniṣads. Of these, the *Aitareya* and the *Kauṣitakī* belong to the *Ṛgveda;* the *Kena* and the *Chāndogya* to the *Sāmaveda;* the *Isa* and the *Bṛhadaranyaka* to the *Śukla* or White *Yajurveda;* the *Kaṭha,* the *Taittirīya* and the *Śvetāśvatara* to the *Kṛṣṇa* or Black *Yajurveda;* and the *Praśna,* the *Muṇḍaka* and the *Māṇḍukya* to the *Atharvaveda.* The other Upaniṣads, such as the *Rāmatāpanīya,* the *Gopālatāpanīya* and *Nṛsiṁhatāpanīya,* are mostly *'Sāmpradāyīka', i.e.,* sectarian, and not content, like the twelve named above with teaching of the Infinite and absolute Being, extol historical or mythical heroes as incarnations of the Deity.

The Vedānta-Darśana

The most honoured exposition of the philosophy of the Vedānta is the body of aphorisms ascribed to Vyāsa or Bādarāyaṇa. Bādarāyaṇa himself is named in these aphorisms as one of several teachers of the Vedāntic Philosophy; so that Vedāntism, as a philosophical system, must have existed and been widely taught long before the composition of these aphorisms, however ancient they may be, and possibly there may have been previous compendiums of the philosophy on which they were based. But, as a fact, we possess none more ancient than they. Some of the names by which these aphorisms are called deserve to be mentioned and remembered by the student of the Vedānta philosophy. They often go by the name of the *Vedānta Darśana,* though all expositions of the Philosophy of the Upaniṣads may claim the name. They are called the *Uttara Mīmāṁsā;* because they are a *Mīmāṁsā* or reasoned exposition of the *Uttara* or latter part of the Vedas, *i.e.,* of the Upaniṣads. They are so called in distinction from the *Pūrva Mīmāṁsā* ascribed to Jaimini, which expounds the *Purva* or earlier parts of the Vedas, *i.e.,* the *Mantras* and the sacrificial portions of the *Brāhmaṇas.* They are called the *Brahma Sūtras,* aphorisms expounding the nature of Brahman, in distinction from the

Dharma Sūtras or aphorisms expounding the nature of *Dharma* or duty, the subject matter of Jaimini's work. They are named the *Śārīraka Sūtras* or *Śārīraka Mīmāṁsā*, because they treat of the true nature of the *Śārīraka*, the embodied soul. Other names are the *Vyāsa Sūtras*, the *Bādarāyaṇa Sūtras*, the *Vedānta Mīmāṁsā* and the *Aupaniṣadi Mīmāṁsā*. This great work, divided into four chapters and sixteen sections, consists of five hundred and fifty-eight pithy utterances many of which contain the concentrated gist of a great deal of meditation and reasoning. This fact makes the book almost unintelligible without a commentary. Various commentaries on it, however, are extant, commentaries which represent the various schools of the Vedānta Philosophy. Of these, I shall speak later on. Besides the *Vedānta Sūtras*, there are various works exponding the Philosophy of the Upaniṣads. But they all belong to some particular school or other, and shall be noticed when I come to speak of these schools.

The Three Vedāntic Institutes

Besides the twelve *Upaniṣads*, and the *Vedānta Sūtras*, another work, the *Bhagavadgītā*, is held by all Vedāntic schools as embodying Vedāntic teaching of an uncertain nature, and this in spite of the apparently sectarian character of the book—in spite of the fact that Krishna, the incarnation of Vishnu, is therein represent as the Supreme Being. So it has happened that ever since the time of Śaṅkarācārya, and perhaps, since a time anterior to him, the *Upaniṣads*, the *Vedānta Sūtras* and the *Bhagavadgītā* have been held to compose the complete Vedāntic canon. They are called the three *prasthānas* or institutes of Vedāntic teaching, the Upaniṣads being called the *Śruti Prasthāna* or scriptural institute; the *Vedānta Sūtras* the *Nyāya Prasthāna* or logical institute; and the *Bhagavadgītā* the *Smṛti Prasthāna* or institute of duty. All the great founders of the various Vedāntic schools have commentaries on these three institutes, and their mutual differences consist in the different ways in which they interpret the fundamental teaching contains in the *Prasthānatrayam.*

Unsectarian Vedāntism

This fundamental teaching, if it could be gathered from the canonical books without the aid of the founders of the Vedāntic schools, or without being biassed by their peculiar views, would be true, uncertain Vedāntism, not identified with the views of any particular Vedāntic teacher of later times. But, as a fact, Vedāntism as a system, does not exist in such a pure and unsectarian form in any of its various representations. As I have already said, all the various works in which the philosophy is expounded, belong to some particular school or other. If an independent exposition were now attempted, it would, no doubt, bear the stamp of the expounder's habitual trend of thought and feeling, and would be set down as sectarian. It would perhaps even be identified with the one or the other of the existing schools. Perhaps this is inevitable from the very nature of things. Realism, Idealism, Monism, Dualism, Hedonism, Legalism, Rationalism, etc., are not so much opinions identified with particular philosophers as they are phases or stages of thought which commend themselves to the mind of man according to the peculiarities of his nature and education. The teachings of the Upaniṣads and the two other Vedāntic institutes are so various, representing so many phases and strata of thought, that it is possible to find authority in them for all the forms of speculation named above. I am indeed far from thinking that the principal teachers of Vedāntic doctrine were not agreed as to a number of fundamental principles or that the highest teaching contained in the three institutes is not uniform. But I must confess that this highest and uniform Vedantism exists, even in the institutes, not to speak of later works, side by aide with a good deal of lower of tentative teaching representing various stages of culture in the teachers. If, however, the latter class of teaching is held by some Vedāntic teacher as essential, and embodied in his system as such, his method may be blamed as defective, but the claim of his system to be called Vedāntism cannot justly be denied. The difficulty of deducing from the canonical books a system that would be recognised as Vedantism pure and simple, is, therefore, patent. But I shall nevertheless try to enumerate a few principles of a most general nature which are to be found in all Vedāntic-systems. It is the less difficult to find out some such principles from the fact that though differing from one another in the interpretation they respectively give of particular Vedāntic doctrines, all Vedāntic schools are opposed as one uniform system to the other schools of the national philosophy, for instance, the Cārvāka, the Buddhist, the Pūrva Mīmāṁsā, the Sāṃkhya, the Yoga, the Nyāya and the Vaiśeṣika school. Their points of difference from these schools are points of agreement among themselves. Thus, then, to begin with, the Cārvāka doctrine of the material and destructive character of the soul is rejected by all Vedāntic schools. The Vedāntic doctrine of the soul is that it is immaterial and indestructible in nature. Then, the idealistic or rather individualistic doctrine of certain Buddhist philosophers, the doctrine that there is no world independent of the ideas of individual minds, is opposed by the Vedānta. It gives to Nature an existence independent of the individual soul, however dependent that existence may be on the Universal Soul. The same opposition is offered to Buddhist Sensationalism, the doctrine that there is nothing more real and permanent than perishing sensations, the Vedāntic doctrine being that the Self, with its permanent ideas, is an unchangeable witness of the past and the present. So, in opposition to the Sāṁkhya Dualism, the doctrine of Puruṣa and Prakṛti as the dual cause of the world, the Vedāntic teaching is that the cause of the world is one, namely Brahman, the Supreme Intelligence, who is both the regulating or occasional (*nimitta*) cause and the material (*upādana*) cause of the universe, having made the world out of his own or will nature without the help of any extraneous substance. In this respect, the Vedānta is opposed to the Vaiśeṣika conception of eternal, uncreated atoms as the material cause of the Universe. Then again, the Yoga doctrine of a God existing apart from the individual soul is rejected by the Vedānta, the Vedāntic doctrine of the relation of the individual and the universal Self being that the Universal exists continually is the individual, sustaining and regulating it. In the same manner, the Nyāya doctrine of Nature, God and the individual soul as independent realities, is refuted by the Vedānta as inconsistent with the infinitude of God, the Vedāntic teaching being that everything is comprehended in the Divine existence. In practical matters the Vedānta holds, in opposition to the *Pūrva Mīmāṁsā,* that ceremonial observances have no absolute value, their importance consisting only in their being disciplines teaching the mind to look beyond the immediate objects of sense and purging it of the grosser desires. The Vedānta attaches great importance to devout meditations on Brahman, of which the *Upaniṣads* contain numerous samples, and the *Bhagavadgītā* lays special stress on the culture of *bhakti,* the reverential love of God. In brief, *karma* or duty devoutly, and disinterestedly performed, and *upasana* or devout meditation carried on with *bhakti* leading to *jñāna,* the knowledge and constant consciousness of the Supreme Being, constitute the ethical scheme of the Vedānta in its essence. The supreme end of existence is indissoluble union with Brahman, which may be realised in this life or another according to the quality of one's spiritual efforts. As to the future life, the Vedānta teaches that the individual soul, which is an eternal, uncreated part or manifestation of the Supreme Soul, goes through a countless series of incarnations till it is freed from the fetters of physical embodiment and blessed with conscious union with God. These fetters are, the Vedānta teaches, five in number, and are called *koṣas* or sheaths, since they hide from the soul, in its ignorant state its true spiritual essence. In the various stages of culture previous to the highest enlightenment, the soul ignorantly identifies itself with one or another of the following : the first or the most gross, the *annamaya koṣa* or the gross material body; the second in order of grossness, the *prāṇamaya koṣa* or the vital powers; the third, the *manomaya koṣa* or the sensorium; the fourth, the *vijñānamaya koṣa* or the understanding; and the fifth, the *ānandamaya koṣa* or the pleasurable emotions. Beyond these, but illumining all with the light of its consciousness, is the pure self, whose true nature and relation to God must be realised before *mokṣa* or liberation can be attained. However, having a subtler body than the visible, namely, that consisting of the subtler sheaths, it is easy to see how the soul passes at death from one body to another or from one region of the universe to a higher or lower one. As to the details of the future life, the Vedānta conceives three very different states for the three classes into which it divides all moral beings. For those who have led vicious or merely natural lives, without subjecting themselves to any disciplines, it anticipates no less horrible a destiny than transmigration into inferior organisms, at best to the bodies of the lowest class of human beings. It seems to consider the lower animals also as moral beings and admits the possibility of their gradual elevation to humanity. The scientific doctrine of the evolution of the higher animals from the lower, seems to favour this view, thought no scientific evidence in the true sense is possible in the matter. As for the pious, the Vedānta awards two different destinations to them according to the nature of the disciplines they have passed through. The followers of the *karma kāṇda*, those whose worship consists in offering sacrifices to the Gods, are destined for the Pitṛloka, the habitation of the manes, where they pass through a way called the *Pitṛyāna*, and figuratively described as consisting of a number of phenomenal objects such as mist, dark nights, clouds, etc. Through this way they pass to the moon, which either contains the Pitṛloka or is associated with it. There they dwell in enjoyment of the fruits of their good works until they, the fruits, are spent out, when they have to retrace their steps to the earth and be re-born according to their merits. On the other hand, the followers of the *jñāna kāṇḍa*, the spiritual worshippers of the Infinite, are destined for the *Brahmaloka*, the world of Brahman. They also have to follow a particular path called the *Devayāna*, the way of the Gods. This also consists of a number of elements which are altogether more auspicious than those composing the *Pitṛyāna*. The most prominent are the rays of the sun, which perhaps represent spiritual enlightenment. Led through this path to the divine regions, painted in gorgeous colours, but in language which is evidently figurative, the spirits of the pious are said to live in perfect beatitude, in constant communion with God and in the company of the *devas*, and never return to any mundane state of existence unless at their own will. Whether this Brahmaloka is the final goal of all rational beings, or there is a higher state of existence, is a matter of controversy among the various schools of the Vedānta Philosophy, of which I now proceed to give a short account.

The Vedānta Schools

It is in the detailed interpretation of the fundamental principles enumerated above, that the Vedānta Philosophy branches out into schools. Of these, three have the largest following, those of Śaṅkara, Rāmānuja and Mādhva, the followers of the first, again, outnumbering by far those of the other two. These three perhaps are the only schools that may be called living, and are also important as representing three poles of thought to one or another of which the mind of man naturally turns. To these, I, as a native of Bengal and knowing more of this province than others, shall add the school of Baladeva Vidyabhushana, to which the followers of Chaitanya belong, and that of Raja Ram Mohan Roy, the founder of the Brahmo Samaj, who, faithful to the instincts of a true Indian reformer, wrote commentaries on the *Prasthānatrayam*, and whose school, though not sticking to traditional methods in all matters is yet important as representing a fusion of ancient Indian thought with the thought of the West. That there were more or less opposed schools of Vedāntic thought even before the foundation of the earliest of the existing schools namely, that of Śaṅkara, appears evident from the mention of Vedāntic teachers in the *Sūtras* with the points in which they differed in their interpretation of the scriptures. That there were at least two main currents of Vedāntic thought before Śaṅkara and Rāmānuja, is also evident from these two teachers professing to follow two ancient traditions—traditional methods I mean—in their respective commentaries, and from the former's anticipating, in substance, the views of the latter, several centuries before his actual advent, and refuting them in his commentaries. To indicate, however, a few lines of difference followed by the different schools. Though agreeing in the opinion that Brahman is the sole cause of the universe, the schools differ a good deal as to the method of creation and the nature of the power with which God creates. Śaṅkara holds that creation is not real in the same sense and in the same degree as the Creator. The creation of a real world, of a world really different from the Creator, would affect his infinitude by placing a reality outside the limits of His existence. Nor could creation be the Creator's assuming a particular form, for that would militate against His perfect and unchangeable nature. Nature and the finite soul, therefore, Śaṅkara concludes, are not real as such, but only passing appearances of the one only Reality, Brahman, and the power of creation, though eternally existing in him and containing in it the germ of all created things, is in fact a mysterious and inscrutable power, called *Māyā* or *Avidyā*, producing the passing illusions of finite intelligences and material worlds without at the same time subjecting the Supreme Being to these illusions. Thus Śaṅkara is a Māyāvādi as to the method of creation and an Advaitavadi or Monist as to the relation of creation to the Creator. As the power of creation is a power of producing illusions and not realities, and as the finite does not really exist, but only seems to do so, Śaṅkara conceives that the Divine nature has no necessary relation to the finite, and is therefore an absolute or unqualified unity. His Advaitavāda is therefore called *viśuddha i.e.*, pure, absolute or unqualified. Very different is Rāmānuja'a idea of creation and its relation to the Creator. If created objects, he says, were independent of the Creator, their real existence would indeed be inconsistent with his infinitude; but though distinct from him, they are dependent on him and are, in that sense, his *Prakāra* or modes, and as such, real and not illusory existences. They are necessarily related to him and exist in him eternally in a subtle form before creation and in a developed form in the state of creation. The method of creation, according to Rāmānuja, is therefore a *pariṇama,* change or evolution of the cosmic form of God from a subtle to a developed state, leaving the extra-cosmic or divine aspect of his nature untouched and unchanged. The necessary relation of the world to God introduces, in Rāmānuja's opinion, an element of difference in the divine nature, which is conceived by Rāmānuja as a qualified unity—a unity not related to anything outside of it but diversified by relation within itself. Hence Rāmānuja's Monism or *Advaitavāda* is called *Viśiṣṭa* or qualified. Mādhva, otherwise called Anandatirtha or Purṇaprajña, was a defender of common sense, and condemned Monism in both the unqualified and the qualified shape. Though holding matter and the individual soul to be dependent on God, he conceived the Infinite in such an abstract manner, that he could see no unity between it and the finite. He put particular emphasis on the expressions of duality and difference in the *Upaniṣads* and the *Vedānta Sūtras,* and explained all utterances of an opposite drift in the light of the former. His system, therefore, is called Dvaitavāda or Dualism, and is really the return of Philosophy from the heights of speculation to the uncritical conceptions of common sense hallowed with a glow of reverential faith. The same remark applies to the system of Baladeva Vidyabhushana. Raja Ram Mohan Roy follows Śaṅkara in the main, but interprets him is a way that modifies to a certain extent some of the features of his system that are repulsive to common sense. Of the systems of Baladeva and the Raja, I shall, however, for obvious reasons, confine myself to this brief mention. Returning to Śaṅkara and Rāmānuja, we find the ethical and spiritual philosophies of these, thinkers deeply affected by their differing conceptions of the world and the Divine nature. Śaṅkara, looking upon all differences as ultimately illusory, regards all actions; even the highest, as consistent only with a passing state of ignorance, since they all proceed upon a distinction of agents, things acted upon and the fruits of action. On the other hand, Rāmānuja, to whom distinctions, when rightly seen by the light of Reason, are real, regards the higher duties of life as of permanent value. For the same reason, while the latter sees no incompatibility between the highest enlightenment and the householder's life, the former extols detachment and regards the anchorite's life as an essential condition of liberation. Again, contemplating Brahman as impersonal Intelligence, Śaṅkara conceives even the highest reverential worship as a transitional stage of culture, and regards a consciousness of absolute unity with the supreme as the goal of all spiritual discipline. To Rāmānuja, on the other hand, Brahman is a Personal Being, and even in the highest stages of communion, the worshipper feels that he is distinct from his object of worship. As regards liberation, likewise, the two schools differ a great deal. The finite soul's ascension to Brahmaloka, as described in the *Śrutis* and the *Sūtras*, is accepted by Rāmānuja as its final liberation, while Śaṅkara, finding that the description of that state of liberation leaves several points of difference between the individual and the Universal Self, teaches that it is only partial or relative liberation that is thus described, and that there is a higher state of absolute liberation, indicated in certain passages of the canon,—a state involving a complete merging of the individual self in the Absolute. Mādhva, the Dualist, agrees with Rāmānuja in the main as regards ethical and spiritual matters.

Later Vedāntic Literature

Besides the commentaries on the three institutes written by the great founders of the schools, a good number of handbooks expounding the philosophy have been written by the founders themselves and their followers. Unfortunately it is only works belonging to the schools of Śaṅkara that are well-known throughout the country. Mādhva's *Tattvamuktāvalī* is read in Bengal, but Rāmānuja's *Vedānta-saṅgraha* and other minor works, and even his commentary on the Upaniṣads are only heard of. Of works of Śaṅkara's school, the *Upadeśa Sāhasrī* and the *Vivekacūḍāmaṇī* ascribed to him are well-known and so are several smaller tracts said to be written by him, but probably composed by later writers belonging to his school. The *pañcadaśī* by Mādhavācharya and the *Vedāntasāra* by Yogindra-Sadananda are among the best known of minor works on the Vedānta, and have been translated into English. Somewhat less known but still important is the *Vedānta Paribhāṣā* by Dharmaraja Adhvarindra. One of the most ancient books of this class, but not strictly philosophical in method, is the celebrated *Yogavaśiṣṭha Rāmāyaṇa.* For English readers, I may mention the translation of the Upaniṣads by Professor Max Müller, by Mr. Roer and others in the Asiatic Society's Edition, by Messrs. Chatterji and Mead of the Theosophical Society, by Pandit Sitarama Sastri and Ganganath Jha and by the present writer. The edition done by the two Pandits last mentioned has the singular recommendation of containing translation of Śaṅkara's commentary. The *Vedānta Sūtras* with the commentary of Śaṅkara have been translated by Professor

Thibaut and the *Bhagavadgītā* by Professor Telang and many others.

The Vedānta as a Basis of Popular Religion

In this article, I have had no opportunity to say what I think, as to the philosophical basis and the logical strength of Vedāntism. My aim has been to give a most general and unbiassed statement, untinged by sectarian predilections, of the fundamental principles of the Vedānta. But as a Vedāntist, I may perhaps be allowed to say at the conclusion of the article that I believe Vedāntism, in its essence, to have a very long life before it, as it has had a long life behind it in the past, as a system of Philosophy and as a basis of popular religions. Every system of Hinduism worth mentioning has been built upon it, for it is opposed to none, and it has been alike the ideal aspired after by the novice and the backward in religious culture, and the solace and delight of the advanced devotee. As I understand the Vedānta, I find no authority in it for image worship as it prevails in the country at the present time. But the early Vedāntists believed in orders of beings higher than man and some of them were in favour of honouring them according to the methods laid down in the ancient rituals, though others regarded such warship to be consistent only with ignorance and worthy of the wise. However, the Vedāntic discipline of concentrating the attention in particular objects of Nature and contemplating them as Brahman, since they are his relative manifestation, seems to have given a sort of countenance to Idolatry, and so we find Idolatry and Vedāntism closely leagued together in various sects both in ancient and modern times. But we also find schools, like the followers of Nanak, who shook off Idolatry but adhered to the Vedānta. The Brahmo Samaj movement of the present day was inaugurated as a purely Vedāntic movement, and if some of its later leaders loosened the Vedānta connection on account of their defective scholarship and denational education, the Samaj seems to be now, in its latest developments, tracing back its way to the old affinity and feeling after the old foundations beneath its feet. The Theosophical movement is largely Vedāntic and the Ramkrishna or Vivekananda movement professedly so. Muhammadanism and Vedāntism meet in Sufism and other esoteric systems of Islam, and there is no reason why the enlightened Mussalman of the present day should be blind to the claims of his Hindu brother's revived Vedāntism. As to Christianity, appearances point to a not very distant fusion of the most liberal form of this faith with the most advanced and reformed forms of Vedāntism—a fusion far more glorious and fruitful than that of Neo-Platonism and Christianity in the early centuries of the Christian era. These appearances are not confined to Europe and America, but are to be seen in this country also in the growing interest of certain Christian converts in the study of the Vedānta and in the attempt made in certain quarters to establish a newly conceived Christian Theology on the basis of the Vedānta Philosophy. There is nothing to prevent the success of such an attempt. The Vedāntic doctrine of incarnation, rightly conceived, is so rational and liberal, that if the holy Jesus can be historically proved to have said and felt, as well lived in the consciousness of the truth—'I and my Father are one,' no true Vedāntist can refuse to accept him as an incarnation of the Deity, as much as Vamadeva of the Vedic days and Sri Krishna of the *Bhagavadgītā*.

The Vedānta Religion[1]

Prof. M. Rangachariar, M.A.

Vedānta is a name which is generally given to the *Upaniṣads.* In this connection, it is interpreted to mean the *end of the Vedas,* that is, the last portion of the revealed scriptural literature of the Hindus. It is also used as the name of a well-known system of Indian philosophy which is mainly based on the teachings of the *Upaniṣads.* The word may, however, be more appropriately understood as *the end of all knowledge.* What, then, is really the end of all knowledge? Even the physical sciences have been said to be like the kind mother who, when asked merely to give bread, gives also the invigorating milk of ideas. So, the immediate practical utility of knowledge is certainly not the best part of it. In that transfiguration of man's mind, which is brought about by means of grand, noble and all-comprehending ideas, consists largely the value of knowledge as an aid to human progress. "The ultimate problem of all thought is," it has been well remarked by a writer in the latest number of *Mind,* "the relation of the Finite to the Infinite, of the Universe to the Primal Source of Being from Whom all existence proceeds." There is certainly nothing higher for the human understanding to try to know than the nature of this relation. It is an "open secret" which very few persons are able to read intelligently at all; and even among the gifted few, who read it in one way or another, there is much room for wide differences of opinion. This relation between the Universe and its Primal Source has not been, at all times, understood

1. Reprinted from the *Brahmavadin*, September, 1895.

anywhere in the same way; nor have the different peoples of the earth looked at it from time to time in the same light. Nevertheless, man has had, all along in the course of his history, to live out his life from day to day relying upon some sort of belief in regard to this all-important relation between the Finite and the Infinite. Indeed, the history of man's apprehension of this relation everywhere determines the history of his religion; for, religion is nothing other than the knowledge of this relation and the consequent adjustment of human thoughts, feelings, and activities in accordance with that knowledge.

While the *Upaniṣads* and the *Bhagavad Gītā* form the spiritual foundations of Vedāntic thought in India, the formulation of the Vedānta-philosophy is to be found in the Aphorisms (*Sūtras*) of Bādarāyaṇa : and therein it is declared that the object of the Vedānta is to know the *Brahman*, which is the cause of the birth, existence, and dissolution of the Universe. It is clear from this that the Vedānta does not at all question the existence of the Infinite, and also that it derives the Finite itself from the Infinite. Materialism is beginning to be already so completely discredited even in the West as almost not to deserve the name of philosophy; and in the history of Indian thought, it never had any really serious and important place assigned to it. The Indian mind has been too logical and too contemplative to assert that the Finite is all in it. It cannot be denied that a few Indian men of learning have occasionally played with materialism : but India as a whole has never been able to shake off the awe-inspiring and ever-present steadying weight of the Infinite. Therefore the Vedānta, while taking into consideration the relation between the Finite and the Infinite, has had only the choice between three alternative views to adopt, which views may be characterised as : (1) mechanical, (2) organic, and (3) monistic. The first view holds both the Finite and the Infinite to be real, and conceives the relation between them to be more or less akin to that between an engine and its maker who is also its driver. This may be said to be the view of the *Dvaita Vedānta*. The second view also holds both the Finite and the Infinite to be real, but fuses them together into a single organic whole by conceiving the relation between them to be like that between an organism and its life or 'vital force.' This is the *Viśiṣṭadvaita Vedānta*. The third view holds the Infinite to be the only reality, and conceives the Finite to be merely an illusory reflection or representation thereof. And this is the *Advaita Vedānta*. In none of these schools are we led to apprehend the Infinite merely as a distant God; in all of them we may easily notice the belief in what has been aptly called the inter-penetration of the spiritual and the material worlds, for the God of the *Upaniṣads* is all-pervading and is both far and near at the same time. Further, the Vedānta, however understood, knows only one God, only one Infinite; and man is called upon to see that the purpose of life is to help to fulfil the purpose of universal creation by himself realising, and enabling others to realise, the divineness of human nature and its goal in the God-head. There is, however, no agreement between the various schools of the Vedānta as to the details of the exact nature of the ultimate condition of the liberate human soul. There is no exclusiveness about the religion of the Vedānta; the gates of its temple are open for all to enter. The enlightened Vedāntin is expected to make no-distinction between a Brahmin and a Chandala, a cow and a dog, between friends and foes, as well as between the virtuous and the sinful. One of the excellent features the Vedānta is its open recognition of the ethical and spiritual one-ness of man's nature.

To the Monistic Vedāntin, the way of knowledge is the way to *Mokṣa*—to liberation from the trammels of ever-recurring births and deaths. According to him, God is altogether inaccessible to human thoughts and words, and all forms of worship and prayer only go to make the unconditioned appear as conditioned. Nevertheless, *Upāsanā* or worship is recognized as s necessity even to him, as he holds it to be of great value in preparing the human soul to receive with calm illumination the great truth of its one-ness with the Divine. The followers of the other two schools of the Vedānta see in God the harmonious synthesis of the most perfect ideals of truth, goodness, and beauty. To them, religious worship, is an inviolable duty, and the way of worship is the way to *Mokṣa*. Then, what is the kind of worship that is enjoined on all those who follow in some way or other the teachings of the Vedānta? The old Vedic way of worship consisted in offering prayers and sacrifices to the deities. "It is no exaggeration to state that no nation appears at the dawn of history so full of prayer and praise as the Hindu Aryans," says a Christian Missionary in a recent work of his on Vedic religion. When, however, this profusion of prayer ceases to flow from the abundance of genuine feeling in the heart, and when sacrifices lose their original significance in the way of establishing the wished for kind of communion between the worshipper and the deity, then prayers get petrified into mere formulae, and sacrifices become altogether meaningless rituals. Worship, which is, on the practical side, the essence of religion, becomes the shield of hypocrisy and deceit. This does not take place before the old ideal of religion and of man's duties is felt to be more or less inadequate in the new circumstances, and a new one is slowly beginning to get itself established. We find clear signs of such a change even in the *Śatapatha-Brāhmaṇa* wherein it is said :—He who sacrifices to the *Ātman*, or the Self, is superior. One should say, 'There is he who sacrifices to the gods and also there is he who sacrifices to the *Ātman*.' He who understands that by such and such a means, such and such a one of his members is rectified, and that by such and such another means, such and such another of his members is restored,—he is the person who sacrifices to the *Ātman*. He is freed from this mortal body and from sin in the same way in which the serpent is freed from its worn-out skin; and acquiring the nature of *Ṛk*, *Yajus* and *Sāman*, and of the Sacrifice, he attains to heaven. On the other hand, he who understands that gods are to be worshipped with such and such an oblation, and offers it up to them, is like an inferior who pays tribute to a superior, or like a *Vaiśya* who pays tribute to the king. This person does not conquer for himself so great a world as the other does." Do we not here see that the religion of self-discipline and self-culture is already trying to assert itself as against the old religion of sacrificial rituals? It is indeed far better for a man to fortify himself against temptations, and subdue the evil that is in him, than perform rites and offer numberless sacrifices of various kinds to various deities. The object of all true worship must be not so much to please God as to make man worthy of His love. Even in the Code of Manu, which distinctly enforces caste, ceremonial laws and ritualistic religion, we find evidence enough to indicate the existence of a strong partiality in favour of the Vedānta. "The man," says Manu, "who, recognising himself in all beings and all beings in his own self, sacrifices to the *Ātman*, enters into absolute freedom." In all probability, the freedom that is referred to here is the freedom from the bondage of the Law, that is, from being subject to the operation of ceremonial and ritualistic regulations concerning society and religion. It may mean *Mokṣa* as well.

In the *Upaniṣads*, there are many passages which clearly set forth this very change in the ideal of worship. The second *Khaṇḍa* of the *Muṇḍakopaniṣad* emphatically declares that all those, who believe in the saving efficacy of sacrificial rituals and perform them, are foolish, ignorant, and self-sufficient men, going to ruin and destruction like the blind that are led by the blind. In the place of elaborate rituals, it enjoins austerity, faith, peacefulness, retirement into the forest, and living by the begging of food. In the very last *Anuvāka* of the *Nārāyaṇīya* portion of the *Taittirīyopaniṣad,* we have a passage in which the various elements of the sacrificial ritual are replaced by the elements required for character-building, obviously with the object of pointing out that Vedāntic Worship is far different from Vedic Worship. The same *Nārāyaṇīya* portion of the *Taittirīyopaniṣad* speaks of truth, austerity, temperance, peacefulness, liberality, duty, upbringing of children, worship in the way of kindling the sacred fire, etc., mental contemplation, and resignation, as things of the highest importance without which no man would be able to realise for himself the glory of God. The Vedāntic religion is distinctly not a religion of mere rituals but one of righteousness; and in another *Upaniṣad*, self-restraint, charity, and mercy are naturally regarded as being very much better materials of worship than forms of rituals. In this age of individualistic self-assertion, the Vedāntic discipline of self-denial may appear too rigorous, cold, and uninviting; but the seeds of salvation for individuals, as well as for communities of individuals, are always to be found only in the faithful practice of difficult self-denial. Self-assertion strengthens the bond of *Karma*, while self-denial leads to the freedom of the soul—that blissful freedom from the bondage of matter which comes to man only when he deserves it. Every soul that is bound to matter has to work out its own liberation, and nothing can show better than the Vedāntin's theory of *Karma*, how what a man does here makes or mars his hereafter. The unborn and immortal part of man, namely, his soul, is alone responsible for the acquisition of *Mokṣa* either through the knowledge of truth or by deserving the grace of God. The soul alone is the friend of the soul, the soul alone is the foe of the soul. Man's sense of moral responsibility can in no way be made stronger. It is but proper to point out that with the Vedānta, self-denial does not necessarily mean either quietism or asceticism. According to the *Gītā*, it implies the willing performance of the duties incumbent upon us without attachment to the result flowing therefrom, whatever may be the rank in which we are placed to fight out the battles of life. All forms of worship are good, according to the author of the *Gītā*, so far as they go to aid us in combining, in the conduct of our lives, honest and earnest work with sincere resignation and disinterested self-sacrifice : and indeed one of the best forms of worship is declared to be the worship of silent contemplation.

The *Gītā* recognises that all are not capable of having the same knowledge of truth and of submitting to the same discipline of self-denial and adopting the same menner of worship, and thus takes it for granted that all cannot be of the same religion. " The religion of the many must necessarily be more incorrect than that of the refined and reflective few, not so much in its essence as in its forms, not so much in the spiritual idea which lies latent at the bottom of it, as in the symbols and dogmas in which that idea is embodied." This remark of a thoughtful English writer is so true that it needs no corroboration, and our own Vedāntic Scriptures wisely refrain from all particularisation of forms, symbols, and dogmas. "In whatever way people come to me," says Sri Krishna, "in that same way do I accept them." Forms and symbols and dogmas, are not at all essential to the true Vedāntic Religion. But it does not despise them, seeing that many of us cannot do without them, even when they are not of the best kind. It is said again in this our Divine Lay— "Those who are devoted to other gods, and offer worship with faith, even they, Arjuna, worship me in reality in a way that is not law-ordained. I am indeed the Lord and receiver of all worship : those who do not know me as I am, fall in consequence. The worshippers of the gods go to the gods, ancestor-worshippers go to the spirits, and those that worship me go to me. Whosoever with devotion offers to me a leaf, or a flower, or a fruit, or water, *that* I accept as an offering brought to me with devotion by one who has a well-disciplined soul. Whatever you do, whatever you eat, whatever you offer as sacrifice in the fire, whatever you give, or whatever austerities you practice, O Arjuna, purpose it for me."

The Vedāntic Religion, accordingly, believes in one and only one God, in His omni-penetrativeness, as it has been aptly termed, and in the spirtual oneness throughout of human nature and human destiny. It is not exclusive, and has no peculiar rites and symbols and dogmas. But it does not object to any form of worship, as long as such worship is in harmony with the aspiring heart of the worshipper. It enforces self-discipline and self-culture, and teaches man to realise the life of righteousness as the best means of worshipping God and of obtaining deliverance and bliss. It is in this manner truly catholic and wisely tolerant.

The Ethics of the Vedānta[1]

I

Swami Saradananda

He, who has tried to penetrate the dim vistas of time in the history of India with a fair and candid heart, must have been impressed with the wonderful systems of philosophy, and ethics, and religion, which the Indian mind produced even at a period when the rest of the world was sleeping in darkness and ignorance. All along the way, he may see signs of the tidal waves of spirituality which from time to time covered the length and breadth of the land of mighty religious tornadoes which swept away everything that stood as an obstacle before them, and of great religious upheavals which raised the country higher and higher, till it reached the highest point of development in spirituality to which man has ever risen, and probably can ever rise, in the principles of the Vedānta,—principles wide as the heavens, and embracing all the different particular religion which have already come, or will ever come in the future Reason stands aghast at finding that all the difficult problems in religion and metaphysics with which it has been grappling for a solution through all these years have already been solved by study old minds; and not only solved, but carried into practice in daily life. It can at first scarcely credit that Kapila propounded the Sāṁkhya theory of cosmic evolution and involution thousands of years before the Christian era, that the doctrine of *Karma* goes further in explaining the diversities of human life than the theory of heredity, that the Vedānta has proved beyond the least shade of a doubt

1. From the *Brahmavadin*.

the ultimate unity of all individual souls is the One indivisible Ocean of Knowledge, Existence, and Bliss, and that all the different religions are so many different ways leading to that One, call it God, or the Absolute, or the Brahman, or by any name you please. But our duty is not to deal with these high flights of Indian thought, but to see what effect it has had in developing the moral and ethical side of the Hindu mind. And, at the very outset, the question meets us—is any high philosophy, or religion (for philosophy and religion are synonymous in India) possible without a high standard of morals? The answer which the Vedānta gives to this question is always in the negative. No one can rise to the highest stage of spirituality without being perfectly and absolutely pure and high in point of morality. Look at the founders of the different religions; were they pure, or impure? Examine the lives of the Vedic *Ṛṣis* ("the seers of thought") who attained to super-consciousness; or of Buddha, or Christ, or Śaṅkara, or Chaitanya, or even of the founders of the lesser sects in India or elsewhere, as Nanak, or Kabir, or Knox, or Calvin—were they pure or impure men? Has God ever manifested Himself through an impure channel? Never. These founders have always been men, pure in thought, word, and deed; and what did they teach, every one of them? That morality must be the basis, the foundation, upon which spiritual life should stand; it must be the corner-stone of the spiritual building. Here the Vedic *Ṛṣis*, and all the Prophets of other religions, are at one. This has been beautifully expressed in the *Kaṭha Upaniṣad*, where Nachiketas, the son of a king, goes to Yama, the God of Death and the controller of all, to know the way to perfection. Yama teaches him first how, by fulfilling all duty, and being moral, he will go to the higher spheres, and have, the exalted enjoyments which those spheres afford. But Nachiketas is not satisfied until he is taught the secret or death,—which part of us is eternal and which dies. He values knowledge far higher than the enjoyments even in other and higher spheres. So Yama enters upon that beautiful discourse on soul, and on the attainment of the higher spiritual life which transcends the sphere of morality and duty, which we find in our famous *Kaṭha Upaniṣad*.

Examining into Buddhism, we find there also the same thing. The teachings of the Buddha have been divided into two main parts, one, the *Hīna-Yāna* (the lower way, or the preparatory way, to be followed by householders, and men living in society), and the second, the *Mahā-Yāna* (the great way, which directly leads to Nirvāṇa, and which is to be followed by the monks, or those who, though living in society, are practically out of society). In the first way, duty and morality have been particularly expounded and insisted upon; and in the other, it is taught that, when a man is perfectly established in them, when morality has become as natural to him as breathing itself, he may attain to that highest stage which is beyond all morality and immorality, because it is beyond all relativity. Looking into Christianity, we again find the same thing there again. When a young man came and asked of Jesus the way to perfection, He told him to live according to the laws (and what are laws but morals?). The young man was not satisfied and said he had been living according to the laws from his childhood; to which the Son of Man replied in those deeply impressive words : "If thou wilt be perfect, go and sell all that thou hast and give it to the poor, and thou shalt have treasure in heaven; and then come and follow me."

But to return to what the Vedānta says on this point. The Vedānta insists that the one condition that is essentially necessary in the man who is trying to attain to the superconscious state by following its principles is that he should be perfectly established in the "fourfold ways." These fourfold ways are :—1. The conviction that absolute truth is outside the pale of all, phenomenal existence. 2. That the enjoyments which this life, in other spheres, affords, are trifling indeed, and not worthy to be aimed at. 3. The possession of these six treasures :—(*a*) the control of mind;

(*b*) control of body and the organs; (*c*) the bearing of heat and cold, pleasure and pain, and all the duals, to a certain extent without feeling disturbed; (*d*) the gathering of the mind from external objects at will, and directing it to the internal; (*e*) the faith in the fact that there is a stage and a better stage of life beyond, of which the sages speak—and they speak the truth; (*f*) the holding of the mind to one chain of thought, and forgetting all others. 4. An intense desire to gain liberation by knowing the truth. We can see from this how highly morality is regarded by the Vedānta; and indeed it teaches from the beginning that the man who has not established himself in morality can never attain to high spiritual truths. Then again, according to the Hindus, a man is born with the four following kinds of duties, and he must fulfil them first, before he can pass on to any higher stage of spirituality. The duties are described as so many debts which every man owes by the circumstance of his birth. The first is the debt to his fellow-beings, or all humanity; and this is to be paid by men becoming good members of society, by charity; and by doing unselfish good to all. The second is the debt to all the Ṛṣis, or seers of truth. How is this to be repaid? By believing in them, by studying the Vedas, of such books as contain the revealed knowledge which these Rishis discovered, and by trying to realise the high spiritual truth taught by them and by trying to live up to them. The third is the debt to the forefathers. This is to be repaid by becoming a good and dutiful son, by keeping up the line of the family unbroken by begetting children in marriage and by bringing them up in the path of truth and religion. The last debt is the debt to the gods or the bright ones, and this is to be repaid by worshipping them by means of sacrifices. These fourfold debts were, in ancient days, repaid in the first three of the four stages into which the life of a man was then divided, namely (1) *Brahmacarya* the life of a student, in which absolute continence was kept up; (2) *Gārhasthya* or family-life, into which the student entered by marriage after finishing his studies; (3) *Vānaprasthya* or forest-life, which the man took upon himself after fulfilling the duties of family-life by bringing up his children and doing his duties as a member of society; (4) *Sanyāsa* or monk-life, in which he gave up all ceremonials and devoted all his time and energies to realising his own oneness with the one infinite ocean of knowledge and Bliss. This was the general way in which men passed from stage to stage of their lives in olden times. But there were special laws for those who were exceptionally spiritual. They passed from the student-life at once to the life of a monk, as was the case with Sukha, the son of Vyāsa and with Vāmadeva and some others. In Modern India, the life of a Hindu man is practically made up of only two stages :—*Gārhasthya* or house-hold-life covers the first three divisions of the old arrangement, and then there is *Sanyāsa* or monk-life. Even now the married man cannot take upon himself the duties of monk-life unless he has performed and fulfilled all the duties of married life. In the *Maha-Nirvāṇa-Tantra,* it is said,—"He, who forsakes a devoted wife and young children and takes to monk-life, will never be able to realise God, and will incur sin;"—and this law has not at all become a dead letter. Marriage in India has ever been regarded as a sacrament and a very holy bond; it has never been intended to serve as a charter for unbridled display of passion. The name for wife there is *Sahadharmaṇī, i.e.,* one who practises religion with her husband, or a partner in religion. This word itself shows, how highly the marriage-relation between man and woman is looked upon. Man and wife were regarded as forming one whole, one unit, as is expressed in the term *ardhāṅgī*, another name for the wife, meaning the half of the body. The gods could not be pleased, no prayers would be heard, if worship was not performed jointly by husband and wife in their family-life. A beautiful story illustrating this is related in the *Śaṅkara-dig-vijaya,* or the *Conquests of Śaṅkara,* the greatest metaphysician the world has ever produced, whom the Hindus regard as a divine incarnation. It is said that, when he was travelling all over India and converting the country back to Vedantism after the downfall of Buddhism, he met a very learned man, a great leader of men, who was teaching the ritualistic portion of the Vedas to a large body of pupils. He was of opinion that the one end and aim of human life was to go to higher spheres of enjoyment by performing meritorious works here on earth, and that all the Vedas and all the seers (*Ṛṣis*) taught to the same effect, and that to gain the superior enjoyments which the higher world afforded, was one end and aim of the life of man. Śaṅkara, when he met this man, told him that he was teaching a false doctrine, which the Vedas never advocated. So they entered into a discussion, making the wife of the man the umpire between the two, and with this condition, that the man defeated would become the disciple of the other. Days and nights were passed in discussing the question, and both sides held their ground very well; till, on the seventh day, the man was defeated by Śaṅkara and had to admit that not enjoyment but knowledge was the end of life, not going to the heavens but becoming one with the infinite Ocean of Knowledge and Bliss was the gist of the whole teaching of the Vedas. According to the condition with which they started, the man was called upon by Śaṅkara to enter the monk-life by becoming his disciple. But the wife, who decided impartially in favour of Śaṅkara, interfered and said "My dear sir, don't be overjoyed. You have conquered only the one-half of my husband. Here is the other half; you will have to conquer this before you can make a monk of him". And Śaṅkara had to defeat the learned lady before he could make the man his disciple. Those who have read the book know that he met with very hard work in his argument with the wife. This man eventually became one of the greatest of the disciples of Śaṅkara, the best commentator on the writings of his teacher, and a great leader of the monks of India.

The one great point of the teachings of Vedānta is that man's spiritual evolution does not stop with the evolution of a high code of ethics alone, but there is another higher step to which he reaches, another link in this process of evolution and involution which completes the circle. And this step is to be gained, not by denying, but by the fulfilling of all laws,—not by throwing overboard all duties, but by the right performance of all duties, not by discarding society, but by being useful members of it, not by contracting the self, but by expanding it to its farthest limit, not by a man's thinking of himself as a cut-and-dried entity separate from the universe, but by feeling and realising that he is one with this universe. This universe, according to Rāmānuja, the great leader of the qualified Monists in India, has been produced by the contraction of the knowledge of the soul, by the soul's forgetting that it is the store-house of all knowledge and bliss, and that it is one with the Infinite Ocean of Knowledge which forms the background of the universe, and called God, or the Absolute, or Brahman, or Ātman, or by so many different names. And liberation is to be attained by the expansion of the knowledge of the soul, when it will feel its union with the Divine and with the universe which is nothing but a projection out of the Divine. Monism goes only a step further than the position of Rāmānuja, and teaches that perfect liberation is to be attained when the individual soul will not only feel this union and see the unity in the sum-total of all these differentiations, but will feel its identity with the Deity. This stage the Vedānta describes as the state of realisation, or the super-conscious. The three states of the human mind, the sub-conscious, conscious, and the super-conscious, are not three distinct minds, but the three different stages of the one and the same mind. Modern science has discovered the process in the theory of evolution, how the sub-conscious develops into the middle plane, the conscious existence, and the Vedānta is one with it as far as it goes, but it says further that this leaves the evolution (or as the, Vedānta says the involution) incomplete; the conscious will have to develop into the super-conscious, and then alone will the process be complete. All our struggles individual, social and human, are for that end trying to gain that higher stage. There alone will man find the permanant basis of ethics, of religion, of everything. There, if an illiterate man enters, he will come out a sage, a prophet. The founders of the different religions, the religious giants whom the world has produced, and will produce in the future, have been and will be men who raise and will raise themselves to this higher stage. This is the stage which was described by Buddha as Nirvāṇa, by Christ as being one with the Father, by the Mahomedan Sufis as Analhak, union with the truth, and in the famous aphorisms of the Vedānta as "Thou art that Infinite Ocean of Knowledge and Bliss" or "I am that Absolute Brahman."

The universe, according to the Vedānta, is one indivisible whole. It is by mistake that we think ourselves separate from the rest of the world. In the external world, our bodies represent so many different points in the one vast ocean of matter, in which there is no break. Behind that lies expanded the one universal ocean of mind, in which our minds but represent so many different whirlpool, and behind that even, is the Soul, the Self, the Ātman, the store-house of all knowledge, power and bliss. So though there is but one soul shining above, there are so many millions of reflections on the millions of whirlpools in the mental ocean, and these reflections are nothing but so many individual ages. So that when a man raises himself to the super-conscious, he sees the One Sun that is shining above the mental ocean, he knows that he is not a particular reflection but the Sun himself, who has given rise to all the reflections in the ocean of fine matter, called the mind. And where lies the basis of all ethics? In the fact that I am one with, and not separate from, the universe, that in injuring you I injure myself, in loving you I love myself. In the fact that behind this manifold diversity, there is unity, or, as the Vedāntist says, behind these names and forms, there is that one eternal, unchangeable Ocean of Knowledge, and Bliss, which is our real nature. "This universe has been projected out of that Ocean of Bliss Absolute". That Divine is trying to manifest itself through these names and forms, and the evolution of nature into higher and higher forms is caused by this struggle of the Divine within, to manifest itself better and better. Or as Patanjali says in his Yoga Aphorisms, "The change of one species into another is by the infilling of nature."

Every form or organism is a conduit through which the Divine is trying to manifest itself and all that we need to do is to remove the barriers, which obstruct this flow of the Infinite within. With every act of love and sympathy, every performance of duty, every observance of morality, man is trying to go beyond himself by feeling himself one with the universe. He is abnegating his lower self, and does not in this self-abnegation lie the basis of all ethics? Examine all the ethical codes which the world has ever produced and you will find this one great fact taught,—to live up to the higher self by denying the lower. Consciously or unconsciously, every code of ethics is leading to that. They may not give you adequate reasons why a man shall be moral and deny himself, but are we not thinking according to the laws of logic with every act of reasoning, though we may not have read a single page of logic ? The Vedānta supplies the reason why we should be moral, why we should do good to others why we should love all humanity as ourselves. Behind all these varied codes of ethics lurks that one great truth that we are one with the Universe. He who lives up to that one central truth has truly renounced himself. He who does not know this truth but tries to become a perfectly moral man, in thought, word, and deed, he too is unconsciously living up that truth. The word *renunciation* has got a very bad name now-a-days. Yet every religion has enforced it often and often. It is the corner-stone upon which all religions, all ethics have been built. Nay we are practising it every day of our lives consciously or unconsciously. A man loves his wife, his children, his country, what is he doing all the time? Is he not renouncing himself? True renunciation, which every religion teaches, does not consist in isolating one's self from everything and every being, but in expanding one's self more and more widely, embracing the whole of the universe in one's self by love. For not in isolation or contraction, but in expansion, consist life and progress; this is the teaching of the Vedānta.

Examining the different standards of ethics in different countries and different religions, we find that they vary from one another in many particulars. What is regarded as moral in one country and religion is not regarded so in another. In short, take the most general principles and you will find them almost identical with one another, but go to the particulars and you will find them to differ from one another, more and more widely. What makes this difference? Does the Vedānta give any answer to it? Yes. In order to understand this, we shall have to examine a little what the Sāṃkhya says about the origin of cosmos, and the supplement of the Vedānta upon it, Māyā, or Prakṛti, or the creative principle of Īśvara, the ruler, is made up of the harmonious and even flow, of the three qualities or particles [for they are synonymous] of *Satva* [the bright and effulgent], *Rajas* [or active], and *Tamas* [or dull and opaque]. This even flow is disturbed at the beginning of the cycle, when creation starts afresh, and the three begin to act upon, one another. They produce first the Prāṇa [the cosmic or primal energy] and the Ākāśa [the primal matter]. Then the Prāṇa begins to act upon the Ākāṣa and produces or evolves first the mental ocean (or the universal consciousness) and the individual whirlpools (which represent the individual minds). Then out of this mental ocean is evolved the gross ocean of matter and the gross individual forms. So that as individual whirlpools in the ocean of mind and as gross manifestations we shall always vary. Look at the particular differentiations and you will never, find any two of them exactly alike. But there is unity behind the diversity, there is a centre to all these radii. Grasp it and you grasp the whole thing. Nothing which is true for one mind exactly fits another. What is law then? It is the method or manner in which our minds grasp and connect a series of mental phenomena. It is also internal and not external, and what is known as general or universal laws, such as gravitation, etc., which apply to all individual minds, are the methods by which our minds connect themselves with one another and with the whole of this mental ocean. These universal laws are also relative, and apply only to those minds which are in the same degree of vibration, or, in other words, in the same plane of existence. But to beings whose minds represent matter in a different degree of vibration, these laws will not hold good. They have different laws for their plane of existence, different methods by which they perceive the connection between themselves and the whole mental ocean. So we see that if we pay attention to particulars, we shall find that every particular differentiation has its own laws. If we rise a little higher in generalisation, we shall find different laws for different planes of existence, and when we rise to the highest, to the Ultimate Unity we go beyond the province of all law; for how can there be any law where there is no differentiation, no two, not even the subject and the objects. There alone the law-maker, the law, and the objects of law become one, and this is the highest point of evolution. Law is only possible in the realm of relativity.

This wonderful system of ethics, and the philosophy of ethics, was not built in a day. It must have taken ages for the Hindu mind to evolve it. It is very difficult to determine the exact date when it was found out. But this at least can be said, that the Hindus were the first to discover it; and from the day of its foundation, it has helped and still is helping almost all the great religions of the world. It influenced Buddhism, the first missionary religion of the world, directly. Through the Gnostics and the Alexandrians, it influenced

Greek philosophy. It said that Pythagoras went to India and the influence of Hindu ethics is distinctly traceable in his doctrines. And lastly, this system of ethics influenced directly or indirectly Zoroastrianism and Christianity.

In order to trace the gradual evolution of ethics, and the philosophy of ethics, it is necessary that we should consider a little of the history of India. The one great pecularity of India that the student of history find, is that the Hindus never regarded anything as unnecessary to be thrown away; they believe that man travels from truth to truth and not from error to truth. What is truth for one mind under some circumstances might not appear as truth when one arrives at a higher stage in the process of evolution; yet that apparent error helped him to come up to the higher truth, and there will always be found minds which have arrived only at that point in the appreciation of truths. For is not truth as we know it as much relative as any thing else, and have we arrived at any truth which will always remain unchanged, however much the environment may vary? So the Hindus always preserved the lower truth which helped them to come up to the higher ones. For instance, starting from Dualism when they discovered or evolved the higher truths of qualified Monism and ultimately Monism, they did not throw away dualism, or qualified Monism, but regarded them as stages in the process of development. They had no quarrel with them, for they knew that in order to come up to Monism, man must rise through the other two stages. And so on with all other physical, social, and moral truths. For instance, they knew writing thousands of years ago, and yet committing the Vedas to memory and not depending upon the books is regarded as sacred even now, and there are many who do it up to the present day. The production of fire by friction with two pieces of dry wood was probably the primitive method pursued thousands of years ago, and yet it is done by the priests even now in performing some of the sacrifices. These instances will suffice to convince that if there is any country in which the greatest number of links in the process of evolution in any department can be found, it is India, for in other countries men have always considered that they are travelling from error to truth and have thrown away as unnecessary all the lower steps of the ladder by which they have come up to the higher. This extreme veneration for the past has preserved many things as they were thousands and thousands of years ago.

The first great positive fact that comes before us in the early history of India is that Vyāsa, a great sage, divided and classified the Vedas into the four great divisions, the Ṛk, the Sāma, the Yajus, and the Atharvan, and that he collected all the historical narratives up to that time and called them the *Mahābhārata*, or the history of the great descendants of the king Bharata. This Vyāsa was a contemporary of Sri Krishna, whom the Hindus regard as the greatest of all divine incarnations. Vyāsa divided each of the first four divisions into three parts, the Saṁhitās [the hymn portion], the Brahmanas [the application of the hymns to different sacrifices and the directions how the different sacrifices are to be performed], and the Upsaniṣads [the knowledge portion]. So each of the Vedas was divided in fact into two great portions, the sacrificial or work portion, which included the Saṁhitās and the Brāhmaṇas, and the knowledge portion, or the Upaniṣads. After classifying the Vedas, Vyāsa wrote also the famous Aphorisms of the Vedānta, or the philosophy of the Vedas, based on the knowledge portion of them. He had a great disciple, who supplemented his master's works by writing a philosophy of the work-portion of the Vedas, known as the Pūrva-Mīmāṁsā. It is difficult to determine the age of Vyāsa and Krishna, but Hindu scholars are one in their opinion that the age of Krishna preceded the age of the Buddha, and that Rāma, the hero of the great Epic Rāmāyaṇa, was born before Krishna. So the early history of India before the advent of Buddhism may be divided into those three great periods :

1. The earlier Vedic period, before the Vedas were classified.
2. The period of Rāmāyaṇa, the age of Rāma and Vasiṣṭha.
3. The period of Mahābhārata, the age of Krishna and Vyāsa.

The first of these three periods must have covered many thousands of years, and all that we know and can know of the period is from the narratives in the Vedas themselves. The facts that we gather from those narratives show that the Aryans have already come to the rich valleys of the Indus and the Ganges, and have already settled there by conquering the aborigines. They were a nation of growing people, with young blood in their veins, highly moral, and religious. They were pushing their inquiries into every department. Truthfulness and morality were regarded very highly. The marriage system had already been introduced, and chastity, in women was highly honoured. The caste system was already growing naturally amongst them, and they had divided themselves into the two castes, the Brahmins and the Kṣatriyas (or the warriors). Those who were highly advanced in spirituality in society and were devoting all their energies towards that end were regarded as Brahmins, and the rest, who were devoting their energies to conquest and war and other affairs, were the Kṣatriyas. We find that this caste system was not regarded as very rigorous—the best men in society were regarded as Brahmins, and the qualities of a man made him a Brahmin and not the circumstances of his birth. We find that men from the lower ranks were continually coming up and being regarded as Brahmins, and that Brahmins were not only teachers of spirituality and performers of sacrifices, but that they were joining the armies in times of necessity, and some of them were great generals and teachers of the art of war, down to the time of the Mahābhārata, where it was related that almost all the famous warriors of the age had learned the art of war from Brahmin teachers. Everywhere, we find the trace that the caste system arose naturally on account of social conditions, as in every other nation, and had nothing to do with their religion. Then again, we find that they had already made considerable advances in material civilization. Grammar, Astronomy, and Music, were regarded as essentially necessary for a man's education, and for the reading of the Vedas. In reading the Upaniṣads or the knowledge portion of the Vedas, which must have evolved long after the Saṁhitās, or the hymn portion, we find that the Hindu mind had evolved with long strides. They had already found out a great system of philosophy, the Saṁkhya system, for we find mention of the founder of this system [the sage Kapila] in one of the Upaniṣads.

"Thou who gavest birth to the great seer of truth, Kapila, in the beginning," etc. The Polytheism of the Saṁhitās has already come to Monotheism; nay, some of the great sages have already arrived at the truths of monism and the unity of the soul. The Devas, or the bright ones of the Saṁhitas, have come to be regarded as so many positions in the universe which good and righteous men go and occupy for a certain number of years, by performance of meritorious actions here, and the higher spheres or heavens were regarded as being as much subject to change and destruction as this earth. The theory of the cosmology of Kapila, that nature is evolving and involving from all eternity, has been universally adopted. Looking at material civilization, we find descriptions of the courts of good and great kings, as Janaka in the Chāndogya, of female education, and institutions of female monks, who were discussing abstruse metaphysical questions with the men in the courts of kings, the description of Āraṇyakas, or men who with their wives were living the latter part of their lives in beautiful forests or by the sides of rivers, and devoting themselves entirely to religion and meditation. All along we find traces of the fact that the development of a high spiritual life, by becoming moral in thought, word, and deed, end by fulfilling all the duties in the family and in society, has become the end of the life of man.

Another curious fact comes to our notice in reading the Upaniṣads. The Brahman caste we have seen is highly extolled in the Saṁhitās, or the hymn portion, as in the hymn to the Puruṣa, or the Supreme Being, in the Ṛg Veda Saṁhitā, where the evolution of all nature, or all the particular manifestations from the infinite being, have been described. The Brahmin caste is described as having come out of the mouth of the Supreme Being, thus showing its supremacy over all others. But in reading some of the Upaniṣads, we find the Kṣatriya, or the warrior caste, extolled above all. The Kṣatriyas are described as the founders and teachers of the great truths of monism. This shows plainly that the word Brahmin, applied to men originally in its literal sense of the knower of the Brahman, or the infinite being, has become degenerated, and the word Brahmin has come to be applied to the priests, who have made the church and religion their profession. Coming to the age of Rāmāyaṇa and the Mahābhārata, we find that the Brahmin caste has again risen to the top. The caste must have produced some very great seers, as Vasiṣṭha and others, whose noble lives helped to bring the caste forward again. This went on very well for some time, till, long after the influence of Krishna and the *Bhagavad-Gītā* had gone down, we find the Brahmins degenerated again into priest-craft, trying to shot out the real religion of the Vedas from the mass of the people and preaching to them only of sacrifice, and going to heaven, as the end of man's existence. But before we pass to the consideration of the reform and life brought back again to the people by the mighty heart of Buddha, we shall have to trace the evolution through the two ages of Rāmāyaṇa and the Mahābhārata.

The ages of Rāmāyaṇa and the Mahābhārata are

interesting to the student of history inasmuch as they show the effect which the high ethics and philosophy which the Hindu mind evolved during the time of the Upaniṣads, had on the daily life and progress of the people. High ideals of character in the social and religious field come before us one after another. Great men in every department of life attract our attention, and women who were ideals of chastity and virtue. The family relations and the social relations were based on as good a ground of morality as we have now, at the present day, in any country or society. Nay even more so; judging from the records of the period, we find that the people of that age obeyed the moral laws far more than we do at present with all our boasted talk of ethics and ethical standards. Mark the truthfulness, the self-control, the love of what is good and noble in Rāma, or Yudhisthira, how many of us come up to that to-day? or the noble self-sacrifice of the great hero Bhishma; is it any way inferior to the sacrifice which the noblest of us has made to-day for love of our parents?

Looking to society we find that with the extension of kingdoms and the growth of a high order of civilization, the caste system has grown side by side. The people have been divided into the four castes, and the caste laws have grown more rigorous than in the time of the Upaniṣads. The lower castes are fast becoming in a way hereditary trade-guilds, but between the two higher castes we find communication, and intermarriages; and it was not until after the age of Krishna and the Mahābhārata that we find the two upper castes absolutely separated. The battle of Kurukshetra marks a great change in the social and political life of India, and not only of India but the adjacent countries of Afghanistan and Persia, and the kingdom of Bahlika or Balkh; for in the Maha-Bharata we find that all these countries belonged then to the Hindus; the people intermarried with one another and the kings of these countries fought in the same field, either on one side or the other. Of course, the whole of India and the adjacent countries were divided then into little states, and the ruler of each state was called the king of that state, and the king who conquered in battle all the others was recognised as the emperor of all. Almost all the kings who joined in the fight at Kurukshetra were killed. One great factor of society, the warrior caste, became thus almost annihilated. The result was that the other half, the Brahmins, suddenly rose to great power. The high spiritual teachings of Sri Krishna and the *Bhagavadgītā*, went on very well for some time. But the disturbed balance in society was never restored, and the conservation of power grew more and more on the side of the priests. Education, which was up to this time in the hands of the upper classes, fell entirely into the hands of the Brahmins. The Brahmins thus forgetting their real aim in life became more and more selfish and tried to obtain more and more power in society. They began to preach that pleasing the gods, the bright ones, by means of sacrifices and going to heaven is the end of man. The real religion of the Vedānta was practised by a few only, and those few left society and took to the forest life, or the life of a monk, and the great mass of people in society had become more ignorant and superstitious, day by day, when the great Buddha, "the ocean of light and compassion", took his birth. He joined the order of monks in his thirtieth year and by means of his pure life and courageous preachings, succeeded in bringing back the true Vedānta religion to the people. He preached against the caste system, the killing of animals in sacrifices, and against sacrifices in general. Before the birth of the Buddha, the people of India were a great race of meat-eaters and wine drinkers. He preached against both, and drove these vices from the country; and the influence of his teaching is still there inasmuch as the Indians even at the present day are a nation of vegetarians and teetotallers. Buddhism was in fact a great social reform. It broke down the caste system and freed society from its evils, and it brought education and religion from the forest back again into society; for the religion which Buddha taught is nothing more nor less than the Karma-Yoga of the Vedānta, which teaches that unselfish work will lead men to the highest stage of development, the super-conscious state.

Freed from the trammels of ignorance by the powerful touch of the Buddha, society and the people rose again to a high stage in progress. The condition of India of this period can best be seen by reading the accounts which the Greeks have left of the country and the inscription of the Buddhist king, Asoka. In the Greek accounts, we find that the people are strong and brave and highly moral, so much so that in many places there was no use for any law-courts. Truthfulness is natural to them. The women are all chaste and beautiful and educated. They are a very kind people and extremely hospitable

In the inscriptions of Asoka, we find that India is the first country which sent missionaries of religion to Persia, to China, to Antioch, to Alexandria, and to various other countries. The root of all religions, so runs the inscription, consists in this—"to reverence one's own faith and never to revile that of others. Whoever acts differently injures his own religion, while he wrongs another's. Duty is in respect and service. Alms and pious demonstrations are of no worth compared with the loving-kindness of religion. The king's purpose is to increase the mercy, charity, truth, kindness, and piety of all mankind. Good is liberality; good it is to harm no living creature; good is the care of one's parents, kindness to relatives, children, friends, servants."

In time, Buddhism got mixed up with phalla'a worship and other symbols and ceremonials prevalent in Tibet and other parts of Asia, and degenerated India more than elsewhere. The Buddhist preachers began to teach that total extinction or annihilation was the meaning of Nirvāṇa and the end of life, and that there was no soul, no after-state of existence. The result was the people became degenerated day by day as is shown in the mass of writings of the period, the later Puranas and the lower Tantras. But nowhere has been the truth of the saying of the Bhagavad-Gītā, so much illustrated as in India, "When virtue becomes corrupted, and irreligion prevails, I take my birth, and establish religion again." The birth of the great teacher, Śaṅkara, at this time saved the country again from the bondage of vice and corruption. He is perhaps the greatest philosopher that India has ever produced. His pure life and great genius enabled him to guide the country safe through the period of religious anarchy which prevailed at the downfall of Buddhism. He wrote his famous commentaries on the Vedānta aphorisms while he was only sixteen, the study of which made Schopenhauer predict "that the study of Vedānta will produce as great a revolution in the West as the Renaissance did during the Middle Ages." He joined the order of monks early in his life and spent the last sixteen years of his life—for he lived only up to his 32nd year—in converting India back to Vedantism from the corrupted form of Buddhism.

The ethics and the philosophy of all ethical standards according to Śaṅkara, we have already seen. It remains now only to see what effect the teachings of Śaṅkara had on the life of the people. The date of Śaṅkara is, like the chronology of most other things in India, wrapped up in mystery. The Hindus place him nearly as far back as the first or the second century after the birth of Christ, while modern scholars place him between the 6th and 7th centuries of that era. In any case, the Mahomedan conquest of India took place long after the birth of Śaṅkara and the account which the Mahomedans give of the country and the people will suffice to show the high ethical conditions in India brought about by the teaching of Śaṅkara's philosophy. The Mahomedans, when they first came to India, found the people brave, loyal, truthful, kind, and hospitable. They would not be false to their enemies or use any unfair means even in the battle-field. They would not march their soldiers over their enemies' corn-fields or poison the wells, which the Mahomedans did often. The women were very chaste, and the men were perfectly moral and peaceful. The women had an almost equal position society, as the laws as regards property and inheritance show. Then again, reading the history of the Mahomedans period, we find that almost all the great generals and politicians were Hindus. Names as Man Singh and Jaya Singh and Todar Mull were the great supports of the empire. The immortal bravery of Rāma Pratap of Chitore, and Shivaji in the south shows that the nation had not died out. The immortal names of many noble women, who shed their blood for the country confront us. The heroism and wonderful military genius of Chand Bibi, the bravery of the women of Chitor and the calm and well-balanced political abilities of Ahalya Bai, strike us with admiration. But the general effect of the Mahomedan rule was deteriorating to progress. The caste system grew more and more rigid as the Mahomedans tried to force their religion on India. The Zenana system was a copy of the conquerors in some places, and in others a natural outgrowth of their persecutions. But the conquerors gained much. The study of Hindu philosophy and ethics calmed their fanaticism, produced amongst them the order of the Sufis and brought them to a high condition of moral development. The change which has been produced in them bycoming in contact with the Hindus is well seen when we compare the Mahomedans outside of India with those who are living there.

One more influence remains to be traced. It is that of Christianity. Those who believe that Christianity will supply India with a higher system of ethics or a higher religion are mistaken indeed. The student of history knows well the fact that the high system of ethic which Christianity teaches evolved in India long before the birth of Christ and not only evolved but was carried into practice in the daily life of the people. But the one great thing which Christian people have done in India is revival of free thought. Before the English arrived, the country was too much tied up with the old authorities, and liberty of thought was almost abolished. Western education has helped progress by bringing back again the liberty of thought. Then again, trade competition with Western nations is breaking down the trammels of the caste system every day. Comparative study of the different religions has brought home the conviction that the ethical standard of Vedānta, if not superior to all is inferior to none. But the one bad thing which the Christians have done and still are trying to do is to belittle and destroy the high ideals of the nation. If India knows anything and has anything to give to the world, it is her religion, and she knows only too well how to judge of a system of ethics and religion, if it is not carried out in the daily life of its preachers. Day by day, it is coming out clearly that India will accept Christ as one among her many high ideals but will never become Christian by giving up her own.

The one strong fact which shows the strength of the Vedānta and its ethics is that it has survived and triumphed in its turn over all the numerous invasions of the existing great religions. It does not require a strong centralised government to push its ethics and religion which many other religions do as shown in history. Where is the old religion of Zoroaster, now that the political supremacy of the Persians has gone down? Or of Islam? Going down every day. But the principles of the Vedānta religions have survived and triumphed above all, though India has been in political bondage for many hundreds of years. The religions of the Huns, the Goths, the Parsis, the Mahomedans, and of the Buddha, and Christ too, have tried and are trying to assert their influence, backed by strong centralised governments. But the Vedānta has incorporated them all within itself and will ever do the same, because it is based on principles broad as the heavens, which underlie every particular religion, because it teaches that the whole universe is one indivisible unit, so that by loving you, I love myself, and by hating and doing injury to you, I am doing the same to myself, and because it teaches the grand truth that all the different religions are true; they are so many different ways to attain to that infinite Ocean of Knowledge, Existence, and Bliss.

The Ethics of the Vedānta
II

Mr. N. Vythinatha Aiyar, M.A.[1]

The doctrine of *karma* is, in all its essential features, the same for the three systems of the Vedānta philosophy. Whatever may be the conception formed of the ultimate nature and lot of the individual *Jīva*, whether they regard it as the supreme soul in temporary obscuration, or as a distinct entity now and for ever, and whatever view they may hold regarding its relation to the *Brahman*, Hindu philosophers are in entire accord on the question of the force that determines for the individual his career upon this earth. The life of each man is shaped for him in the main by *karma* or conduct. But what is this *karma*, which is so potent over our lives? A bare statement of the theory in its extremest outlines seems to bring it perilously near to fatalism. But the two are quite distinct and even diametrically opposed. The latter is destructive of all responsibility in man; it reduces him to a mere automaton moving along grooves cut out from him by an inexorable power. The Hindu conception of the human will and human responsibility is far different from this. The question of the Liberty of the Will, originating in most part in the unfortunate application to the Will of the term Liberty, a term that has no more connetcion with it than any other term like whiteness, sweetness etc.,—this controversy seems to be unknown to Hindu Philosophy. But the doctrine of *karma* leaves to the individual will the maximum amount of freedom that may be claimed for it; it makes the individual and the individual alone responsible for the whole of his

1. Reprinted from the *Brahmavadin* for October 1895.

career here. He is not under the control, in his voluntary actions, of any irresistible power external to him; he has not to suffer vicariously for the sins of others; and he cannot hope for redemption through the various expiation of another. He knows that he has to bear the whole burden of his conduct himself.

Yes, all the deeds that men have done,
In light of day, before the sun,
Or veiled beneath the gloom of night,
The good, the bad, the wrong, the right,
These, though forgotten, re-appear,
And travel, silent, in their rear.

This escort of *karma,* which thus ushers the individual into this world, is the aggregate of his deeds, good and bad, in his past lives. This is his *Sañchita karma,* the aggregate of past deeds. Of this total aggregate, each particular deed works out its results on the individual in its due course. When a *Jīva* enters upon its career of life in a particular animal frame, it does so in expiation of some one of its deeds in the past. This, of which each one of us is now experiencing the result and which has given us this particular physical and mental configuration, is known as *prārabdha karma*—the commenced deed. The deeds which we may perform in the future form the *Āgāmī karma.* The entire exhaustion of the aggregate *karma* of the individual would be tantamount to final liberation from the bonds of life and death, and hence would mean salvation. To this exhaustion the individual has to work his way; and destroy the accumulated *karma* of the past with the aid of his conduct in the present and his future. But the course, already entered upon by him under the influence of what is known as *Prārabdha karma;* must be gone through to the end. Our present life belongs to it; and we cannot shake, it off in the middle. But while undergoing the effects of this much of our deeds in the past, we may also be working our way to the final liberation from the sway of *karma,* and to salvation, by means of a virtuous life.

Here, at this stage of the argument, arises the question as to the nature of virtue. To a life of virtue, the Vedāntin ascribes the important result of relieving the human soul from its burden of *karma*. Virtue or good works lead to knowledge, and knowledge leads to salvation. A blind observance of the dicta of religion is useless; and knowledge without works is still worse : All (who worship what is not real knowledge, who are engaged in works, good though they be) enter into blind darkness; those who delight in real knowledge [without the practice of virtue] enter into greater darkness."[1] It is only those who know "at the same time both knowledge and non-knowledge"[2] [virtuous.works] that can overcome death and secure salvation. We should realise in the first place the fact that this body is perishable and that virtue along can lead to "true knowledge." But we must also remember that attainment of true knowledge does not take away the need for a virtuous life. Sages like Janaka did not deem it proper to abandon their duties and responsibilities even though they had ascended up to the highest steps of wisdom. "My body ends in ashes. Oh ! Mind, remember; Remember thy deeds!"[3] Such is the solemn adjuration of the Vedāntin to his mind. It is not to forget himself; nor is it to forget its deeds; and all the while, it should also remember that the "body ends in ashes".

What are the deeds which the mind is thus adjured to remember and the man to perform? The believers in a personal God have an easy answer to this question. The commandments of the Divine Ruler of man form the basis for the distinction of right and wrong. The followers of Śaṅkara, on the other hand, to whom the *Brahman* is not a personal entity distinct from the individual soul, may be supposed to be in a fix in answering this question. Where

1. Isa. Up. 9.
2. *Ibid* 11.
3. *Ibid.* 17

are they to seek for the foundation of ethical distinctions? The world is an illusion; the human soul is but a temporary sojourner in the physical surroundings of its own creation. But the bonds of *karma* must be served; and this can be done only with the help of knowledge, and knowledge can be attained only by good deeds. And it becomes incumbent on them to explain how this is to be accomplished.

We confine our remarks in this article to the teaching on this subject in the *Īśāvāsya Upaniṣad,* which gives a brief statement of the Vedānta doctrine of ethics. It consists of but 18 verses; but in this short compass it gives a clear account of the ethics, acceptable equally to all the three branches of the Vedāntic school of thought. It is unnecessary, as we have said, to dwell upon the ultimate foundation of ethical distinctions in the case of the believers in a personal God. Let us see how the Advaitin also can secure an efficient basis for the inculcation of virtuous conduct in life.

The *Īśāvāsya Upaniṣad* teaches that men should live, work, know and attain salvation. Life is not to be thrown away by him. The human soul has a goal to win; that goal is, in the view of the Advaitin, the recognition of its oneness with the *Brahman.* Though the *Jīva* is to all appearance only a deluded and shackled toy of the phenomenal world and of *karma,* it is yet the all-embracing and all-pervasive spirit of the Universe. Into the logical basis of this doctrine, it is not our purpose to enter at present. Its ethical aspect alone concerns us here. There is an aspect of the *Advaita* theory that places it in a position of advantage ethically. It is the eminence of towering grandeur to which it raises the human soul. It is not simply a spiritual entity exalted above the Universes to the region of eternal bliss. It stands alone and has no second; it is greater than the greatest, and smaller than the smallest. We shall quote here a few of the expressions in which the Hindu philosopher endeavours to express his conception of the self : "That one moves not; but is swifter than thought. The senses never reached it. It walked before them." Each man may say unto himself : "I am the generator and the destroyer of the entire Universe. Than me there is nothing higher. On me all this Universe is woven, as gems are strung on a string. I am the flavour in the water, the light in the sun and moon. By me the Universe is pervaded. I am the Supreme, the Highest, the Eternal, Unborn and All-pervading." Man is not the mere creature of a God; he is God Himself. He has not simply the image impressed upon him of his Creator; he is himself the Creator. He is the Lord of creation in a sense higher and nobler than that assigned to this expression by the religions of the West.

Will one imbued with such a lofty conception of his soul, condescend to contaminate it with evil in thoughts, word or action? Will he defile his *Ātmam* with base deeds? Nobility of character cannot but come of necessity to a man with so noble an ideal of himself. But as man is constituted at present, before his eyes are opened by true knowledge, when he is not fully conscious of the true glory of his soul; and when "the door of the True is covered with a golden disc," how is he to get into the other side of the gates of Heaven? How is he to see the nature of the True ? He believes in a good path which would lead him to the attainment of true knowledge; and he believes that virtue and knowledge would lead him on ultimately to *Brahma-Sākṣātkāra*. But this life into which the *Jīva* is thrown by its *Karma* is not to be despised as it furnishes us with a sphere for the practice of good works, and hence for the destruction of the aggregate of past *karma*.

The injunction to the mortal is that "ever doing works here," he should "desire to live a hundred years."[1] But he performs the works not for his own benefit. "Works will not cling to a man" when be performs them in the right spirit. He secures enjoyment, not by seeking it by means of works, but only by a complete surrender of himself and of his works.

---

1. Īsā. Up. 2.

"When thou halt surrendered all this, then thou mayest enjoy."[1]

The Vedāntin "beholds all beings in the self, and the self in a beings;"[2] and the human race, nay, all animate existence, has its true being in *Brahman.* The self should, therefore, be merged in this conception of the oneness or solidarity of all beings.[3] "Verily, a husband is not dear, that you may love the husband; but that you may love the self, therefore a husband is dear. Verily, a wife is not dear, that you may love the wife; that you may love the self, therefore a wife is dear". Here is a basis for the practice of virtue in universal love, before which the injuction that we should love our neighbours as ourselves dwindles into insignificance.

But the main source of ethical light to the *Advaitins* is his own inner self. In himself he has an infallible guide along the right path. "Whosoever knows that persons whose dwelling is love, whose sight is the heart, whose mind is light,—the principle of every Self, he indeed is a teacher."[4] The heart of every man is tuned to the promptings of righteousness; he needs no light other than what fills his own mind, and so a teacher in virtue, other than his own self. Here is the ethical basis in the innermost conscience of the individual for the Vedāntin. But human conscience full of self-enlightenment as it is, is yet capable of being thwarted by the bodily environment of the soul. The True abides in the heart. "With the heart we know what is true.... The heart indeed is the Highest Brahman."[5] But knowledge is not virtue. The *Jīva,* self-enlightened as he is, is yet entangled in the trammels of *Avidyā.* The *Jīva* consists of desires. And as

1. Īśa. UP. 1.
2. *ibid.* 6.
3. Bṛhad. Up. 2, 4.
4. *ibid.* 3, 9.
5. *ibid.* 4, 3.

his desire, so is the will; and as is will, so his deed; and whatever deeds he does, that he will reap."[1] Self-abnegation, the sacrifice of what binds or individualizes the *Jīva*, the undoing of desires which enter the heart, this is the road to immortality. "When all desires which once entered his heart are undergone, then does the mortal become immortal, then he obtains *Brahman*.."[2] The subjugation of the misleading impulses in us enables us to overcome evil. Without this self-discipline, knowledge and virtue cannot be possible for us, and evil is not destroyed. "He therefore that knows it, after having become quiet, subdued satisfied, patient, collected, sees Self in self, sees all as Self."[3] The perception of the oneness of human nature which is to the *Advaitin* the ultimate basis of universal love and hence of ethical conduct, is impossible to the man who is not subdued and collected. "Evil does not overcome him, he overcomes all evil. Evil does not burn him, be burns all evil. Free from evil, free from spots, free from doubt,"[4] he attains to the *Brahman*.

The innate guidance relied upon by the *Advaitin* should not be taken to mean a disregard of our sacred writings. Those are the outward embodiments of the breathings of the Soul; and, as such, serve to help the blinded *Jīva* to an easy realisation of its own self-contained light. The fire is there; but it is obscured by the covering of ignorance. And the contact with the light that burns eternally in the *Śāstras* imparts an electric stimulus to the inner spirit of man, and rouses it up to the height of its intrinsic greatness. "As clouds of smoke proceed by themselves out of lighted fire, thus verily, O Maitreyi, has been breathed forth from this great Being what we have as the Vedas, etc."[5]

1. Bṛhad. Up. 4,4.
2. *ibid.*
3. *ibid.*
4. *ibid.*
5. *ibid.*

The life as a whole should be regarded as a "sacrifice." The conquest over temptations, which have root in our bodily cravings, is man's *Dīkṣa*,—his preparation to enter upon the life-sacrifice. Its fruits are penance, liberality, righteousness, kindness and truthfulness. And the *yajña* is completed with death, which is the *avabhritha*, the closing ceremonial of the sacrifice. A person who enters upon the path laid down in our sacred books, even though he begins with faith alone, is eventually led up to knowledge. And when good works and knowledge are combined, he is in the right road to salvation.

This is the ethics of the Vedāntin built upon the solid foundation of his inner self, strengthened as it may be by a knowledge of the *Śāstras*. The Vedānta philosophy "has not neglected," to quote the words of Prof. Max Müller, "the important sphere of Ethics, but, on the contrary, we find Ethics in the beginning, Ethics in the middle, Ethics in the end, to say nothing of the fact that minds so engrossed with divine things as the Vedānta philosophers, are not likely to fall victims to the ordinary temptations of the world, the flesh and other powers".

The Ethics of the Vedānta

III

Vasudeva J. Kirtikar[1]

Part I

The ethical ideal of the Vedānta is at least as high as the Christian ideal, if not higher, and occupies an importance place in the Indian system which recognises the doctrine of *tattvamasi* as containing the highest philosophic truth.

The greatest error which Christian writers commit (and this can never be too often repeated) consists in their ignoring the distinction which the Vedānta has emphasised and which Philosophy ought always to emphasise in all its teachings. I mean the distinction between the two kinds of knowledge—spiritual and empirical—called in the Vedānta, higher and lower, *parā* and *aparā-vidyā*. The lower knowledge has reference to the world of sense-experience, while the higher one is spiritual in its character. Both are recognised as essential to the development of man—one as a step to the other. But it would be absolutely unphilosophical to apply considerations which are true in one sphere to the other where they look obviously absurd.

Now, Ethics and Morality admittedly belong to the world of sense-experience, having for their object the development of man in practical life, which necessarily presupposes the dualism of Man and Nature, finding their ultimate reconciliation and explanation in the Highest Reality, by whatever name that Reality may be called.

---

1. Reprint from *The Indian Review*.

Man's relations to the Reality and his social and other relations are all recognised and rightly recognised in this sphere of Relativity; all these relations reign supreme in this sphere. And it is ordained that man must first learn to do the duties which those relations imply and attain, by course of moral discipline, the ethical ideal, before he can become fit for spiritual enlightenment.

In the ethical system which the Vedānta has formulated, it recognises a principle which is of the highest practical importance, that though religious truth as philosophic truth is and must be one that can only be reached by a course of life and study leading to spiritual enlightenment, and though the religious ideals of individuals in a community may and do necessarily vary with the degree general culture and aptitude for grasping spiritual truth still, while thus differing in degree, they must have as their basic truth, the highest ideal which is justified by Philosophy and Theology and is capable of realisation at the highest stage.

All considerations which introduce an element of variety in Ethics and Morality are thus subordinated to the highest ideal of *tattvamasi* as to which it is always insisted on that it must be the aim of every individual to reach it, if possible.

In this view of the matter, the Advaita is as practical in its religious and ethical aspects, as it is speculatively profound in its philosophy. I even venture to think [as I shall show later on] that its teachings, if correctly understood, would be found to be capable of a very wide application and be of practical value as much to the king, to the statesman, to the patriot, and to the citizen, as to the individual in every walk of life. They furnish an excellent foundation for corporate political action and liberty.

The key-note to the practical ethics of the Vedānta is *abheda*, as the key-note to its philosophy and theology is *advaita*. As *advaita* means Oneness without a Second, so *abheda* means Oneness without any distinction of I and Thou, Mine and Thine.

This word *abheda*, when correctly understood, means Love in its purity and fulness, and the manifestation of the principle denoted by it consists in altruistic action and not in selfish inaction or passivity, as is generally supposed.

In no system has this principle of Altruism been so well appreciated and emphasised as in the Indian Vedānta. The entire life of the Vedāntin; it is ordained, must be one of disinterested self-sacrifice.

This idea of sacrifice had its origin in the earliest Vedic literature, where the entire creation was explained as an act of supreme self-sacrifice—the sacrifice of the, Supreme Being (*Puruṣa*) that He might "call into existence and contemplate and commune with these dependent images of Himself which form the object of His thought and love (Māṇḍūkya). This He did by sacrificing a fourth part of Himself (Puruṣa Sūkta). "Let me sacrifice myself [He said] in living things and all living things in myself," and He thus acquired greatness, self-effulgence and lordship [*Śatapatha Br.*] He thus limited Himself by this partial sacrifice, that His life might produce and sustain a multiplicity of separate lives.

What is essentially suggested by this conception is the pouring out of life for the benefit of others—a truth underlying all evolution, physical as well as spiritual.

Advaita philosophy has thus led to the ethics of Universal Love—a disinterested sacrifice of the heart in the service of all.

The principle of *abheda* teaches man that though he himself is an independent individual apparently, there is the universal principle in him, in common with all other beings, which has made him what he is and binds him to them all as parts of one organism, "as being all moving on one wheel [of universal life,"] as "jewels threaded on a string."

It teaches him a most important lesson that he is not a solitary being on earth but his very existence and well-being are tied up with those of others. Wherever he may be, whether alone by himself or otherwise, he is at one with them and bound to help them as they help him. He lives *on* others, and he must, in common honesty, live *for* them.

Another lesson insisted on with equal stringency is that, while Self-sacrifice and Altruism are the guiding rules of conduct, they must be practised without any personal attachment or hope of reward. Care should always be taken that there is no tinge of egoity in either thought or deed. Duty must be done for duty's sake and dedicated to God [Bhagavad Gītā, ix. 27, 28].

The practical value of Kant's categorical imperative is thus fully appreciated as a rule of conduct by the Indian Advaitin, whether he be a householder or a recluse [Śaṅkar's Introduction to *Ait. Up.*]. Never flinching from the path of duty, one should try to gain the calm which is unruffled by the guests of fortune and find a home in any scene and live a life of "heaven on earth."

The sentiments presupposed and involved in this conception of *Abheda* are—an absence of all egoity, an absence of all distinction between friend and foe, and between Mine and Thine; an absence of all attachment to earthly possessions and earthly ties. No room is thus left for bad passions to exercise their sway, and, in their place, come self-abnegation, self-contentment, renunciation, resignation, equanimity, truthfulness, sense of justice—a desire to injure none; love, compassion, forgiveness, charity, humility and peace.

A certain amount of preparation is necessary to discipline the mind for a correct observance of this principle in practice. The most disquieting or disturbing element in human nature is the element of egoity. It is the most fruitful source of desires for self-satisfaction, and these desires bind man to things earthly, and give rise to passions when they are not satisfied.

Hence the necessity of insisting on the practice of self-denial; hence also the necessity of the teachings that nothing on earth is man's except his own thoughts and deeds, which ought always to be pure, good and great; that he should disentangle himself from sense objects; that his happiness or misery is dependent on himself alone, that he gets only what he has earned, and that, accordingly, he himself is the architect of his fortune and destiny.

He is taught that a life of self-restraint and self-surrender, with indifference to all that is "of the earth, earthly," brings in its train the virtues I have above mentioned, culminating in happiness which no one can take away.

These virtues have necessarily the effect of purifying the heart and making man righteous and religious. But their sphere of influence is not confined to this mundane existence; they elevate man to higher and higher planes. In every step that he takes towards the attainment of these virtues, he goes through the process of "dying to live"; at every step he goes on living a larger and larger self.

He learns first to identify himself with his kith and kin, next his friends and relations, then his caste and country, and so on. In other words, he gradually goes on including within his Self the 'Self's of others, realising the truth that their happiness is his happiness, and their misery his own misery, and having faith in the assurance that such expansion of the Self is sure ultimately to prove to him its own identity with the Divine Self.'

Such is the analysis of the sentiments involved in conception of *Abheda* and such exactly is the ethical ideal insisted on in the Vedānta.

One has only to read the *Bhagavad Gītā* to see how wrong it is to suppose that Indian philosophers were simply soaring high in the regions of speculation and cared little for the practical concerns of life.

That little Book,—whether a Revelation or not, in the sense in which orthodox Christians consider their Bible to be—is, indeed, a sacred book in the fullest sense of the term and richly deserves the reverence which is paid both in Europe and America.

This is what one reads in Sir Edwin Arnold's preface to his translation of the Bhagavad Gītā:—

> "In plain but noble language, it unfolds a philosophical system which remains to this day the prevailing Brahminic belief, blending as it does the doctrines of Kapila, Patañjali and the Vedas. So lofty are many of its declarations, so sublime its aspirations, so pure and tender its piety, that Schiegels, after his study of the poem, breaks forth into this outburst of delight and praise[1] towards its unknown author :—'Reverence to the great (teachers) is counted by the Brahmins among the most sacred duties of piety. Therefore, thou, Oh, most holy Poet, favoured of the Deity, whatever, at length thou art called among mortals, (thou) the author of this Lay, by the prophetic strains of which the mind soars to an eternal and divine height, with a certain unerring pleasure to thee, foremost, I say, I offer my salutation and constant adoration to the vestiges thou hast left."
>
> "Lassen re-echoes this splendid tribute; and, indeed, so striking are some of the moralities here inculcated and so close the parallelism—oftentimes actually verbal—between its teachings and those of the New Testament, that a controversy[2] has arisen between

1. The original is in Latin.
2. See the learned introduction by Mr. (afterwards Justice) Telang to his translations of the Gītā in verse. Mr. Telang's view that the date of the Gītā was anterior to the Christian era is not acceptable to the generality of Christians, who believe that they *wish* to be true. The wonder is they do not say that Laotze and Buddha, too borrowed from the New Testament, for their teachings present surprising analogies with Christian thought and sentiment.

Pandits and Missionaries on the point whether the author borrowed from Christian sources or the Evangelists and Apostles from him."

Another writer whom we all esteem as one of the truest friends of India, Mrs. Annie Besant, says of this, our precious treasure, as follows :—

"Among the priceless teachings that may be found in the Hindu poem of the *Mahābhārata*, there is none so rare and precious as this, 'The Lord's Song' * * * how many troubled hearts; has it quieted and strengthened, how many weary souls has it led to the Lord? It is meant to lift the aspirant from the lower levels of renunciation where objects are renounced to the loftier heights, where desires are dead, and where the Yogi dwells in calm and ceaseless contemplation, while his body and mind are actively employed in discharging the duties that fall to his lot in life. That the spiritual man need not be a recluse, that union with the Divine Life may be achieved and maintained in the midst of worldly affairs, that the obstacles to that union lie not outside us but within us—such is the central lesson of the *Bhagavad Gītā*." (Preface).

The *Gītā* is at once a code of ethics, holding forth the highest spiritual ideal, a code of religion, inculcating a loving devotion to God, and a philosophy of Advaita beautifully expounding the scientific truth that the dualism involved in the idea of *bhakti* begins to fade with the intensity of the devotional element and ultimately culminates in Unity, where all differentiations must disappear with the development of the altruistic element and the complete realisation of the principle of *Abheda*.

The whole ethics of the *Gītā* may be briefly summed up thus—

(a) Renounce things earthly, so that your thoughts and deeds might be free from the tinge of egoity and free also from earthly desires and attachments, which arouse bad passions and lead one astray.

(b) Forbear injuring any being.
(c) Treat all alike.
(d) Help the needy even at a sacrifice to yourself.
(e) Do all your duties in a disinterested spirit and as an offering of love to the Supreme Being, in purity of heart.

Even that unsympathetic translator of the *Gītā*, Mr. Thompson, exclaims, "would that in the present selfish and this northern active clime, it ['the sensible and religious doctrine' of the *Gītā*] could be applied and successfully carried out by Christians, as we call ourselves.* * * We, too, should have *our* final emancipation, our salvation ever as our only desire, and *our* Supreme Being,—so far superior, so far more lovable than the imperfect deity of the Hindu philosopher[1]—ever as our chief object of love. We, too, should do our duty in this world without self-interest and attachments, and morally renounce the world in the rejection of all interest in it." [Introduction, p. cxxx.]

When such a presentment of the Indian ethical ideal was possible, we had reasons, to expect that the attitude of Christian writers generally would be one of admiration, first, because the Buddhistic ideal which is derived from that of the Indian Vedānta and which practically is identical with it[2] has become attractive to the Western mind; and secondly, because of the "strong parallelism—often times actually verbal" between the teachings of the *Gītā* and those of the New Testament.

---

1. Of course, our deity must be imperfect, and what not, besides! We here are without a Divine Guide! There is only one unerring Preceptor (p. 90) and with that only Christians have been blessed! So none of the other nations in the world dare claim any Divine guide among their own people, and Mr. Thompson warns his readers that no more praise should be accorded to the author of the *Gītā* than is due "to a clever reformer and a wise ethical philosopher" (Introduction, cxxx).
2. No doubt Buddhism is less metaphysical and leas mystical, but this makes no difference in the *practical* ethics of the two systems.

But, unfortunately, objections have been seriously made to our ideal, and others, too, are possible, of a character similar to what Christian writers are wont to take to the Stoic standard of morality.

It might, for instance, be objected that this ideal is too high and impracticable, or that it is too cold and unemotional, there being an utter absence of religious fervour; it might be said that it improperly advocates indifference to family ties and to matters concerning the practical life of man, that it discourages the virtue of patriotism and leads to a life of Quietism based upon a pessimistic view of nature, and as such, is of no practical value at all.

The first of these objections has been taken to Stoicism which is much akin to the Indian system in this respect. It is said that the ideal is one of "unapproachable perfection", "unpractical and even impracticable," and that if any one professed himself to have realised it, he would justly expose himself to ridicule.

This is not a matter on which any argument could be usefully employed. Whether such a life as is portrayed in the Bhagavad Gītā and other sacred writings of the Hindus possible, can be best answered by another question whether such a life has, as a matter of fact, been lived or not; and if the answer to this last question be in the affirmative, that ought to settle the other question. The Indian literature—both ancient and modern—teems with instances of complete self-sacrifice and devotion to truth and jutsice under the most trying circumstances. And I feel "washed in better moral air" in mentioning with reverence and pride on the names, for example, of Bali, Janaka, Dasharatha, Rāma, Harischandra, Bharat, Bhishma and Karna, of Chaitanya, Nanak, Guru Govind, Janardhan, Eknatha, Ramdas and Tukaram, and referring generally to other saints who flourished between the 14th and 18th centuries of the Christian era.

Even in the present degenerate age, instances of saintly

characters would not be found wanting, I expect, if one were to take the trouble of travelling in India as Count Tolstoy did in his part of the country in search of instances of Christ life actually lived.

"The best fruits of religious experience [says Prof. James] are the best things that history has to show. [To recount them], to call to mind a succession of such examples [of genuinely strenuous and religious life] is to feel encouraged and washed in better moral air. The spirit of peity and charity * * * of love and humility * * * of severity for one's self, accompanied with tenderness for others—[these] have the same savour in all countries under distant suns and in different surroundings. * * * These devotees have often laid their course so differently from other men, that judging them by worldly law, we might be tempted to call them monstrous aberrations from the paths of nature," [Varieties of Religious Experience, 259-261].

Here, then, are instances of saintly characters having, as a fact, actually lived such a life as is portrayed in the highest ethical ideals.

Turning now to the teachings of the Bible itself, we find Jesus telling his disciples, 'Be ye perfect, even as your Father Which is in heaven is perfect,'; and Mr. Clifford Harrison observes, "If the great words of Jesus of Nazareth are true, true on all planes, as such words of such a speaker must ever be, an ideal for the whole entity of man is proclaimed in them, nothing short of perfection. *** * *If man once realises his present state and has faith in what the Great Ones of the world have told him and will put it into action, the advancement lies before him.* [Notes on the margin 214.]

"In the past—and most of all in the far past—there seem to have been individual cases of the faith received and the will exercised into triumphant expression. (*ib.*)

"We will not fear to take the highest possibilities that can be announced to man, nor call them impracticable, because his present condition seems so far removed from them. The first step out of that condition is the admission that it is not final. 'We are near waking when we dream that we dream.' (*ibid.*, 210).

"The longing of a soul is the prophecy of its fulfilment [Emerson].

As to the second objection above noted, it is generally supported that the idea of Divine Love is unknown to the Indian Vedānta and the ideal it presents is too severely abstract to touch the heart and the imagination.

> "Having convinced himself by rigorous logic of his oneness with Brahma, the Vedāntin (says Max Müller) knows, no raptures no passionate love for the Deity."

In other words, *premal-bhakti* is said to be an idea of modern growth.

If the Advaitin is taught that he is one with Brahma, if it is also said that, among the aims of self-realisation in this life, Universal love is one [*Jīvan Mukti Viveka*], it is obviously wrong to suppose that he has no love for Brahma, unless one is prepared to say of him that he does not love himself. In fact, unflinching devotion is laid down as one of the necessary, means of acquiring a knowledge of Brahman and of one's identity with it. But, says Prof. Upton :—

> "Both in Brahminism and Buddhism, man's ethical ideal is not regarded as a real revelation of the essence and character to the Eternal Self; for, in their view, the *end* of Ethics is not to realise in increasing fulness a sense of *personal relationship* to the Divine Self or the Father within us, but either to so fuse the human self with the Eternal Brahma as to virtually destroy all distinct sense of individual personality, or else, as in the case of Buddhism to achieve that total extinguishing of the desire to live which appears to be equivalent to personal annihilation. The tendency of these systems of Hindu thought is to weaken and efface all personal

passions and affections and so to destroy that distinct consciousness of individuality which, in their view, was not a privilege but rather an undesirable condition from which they sought redemption." (*Hibbert Lectures*, 1893, 241-2).

I have quoted this page in *extenso*, for it fairly represents the views generally entertained by Christian writers on Indian Vedānta and Indian Theology.

The whole of this passage, however, is misleading, and the error consists in the confusion of the two standpoints, which the Vedānta again and again insists on being always borne in mind—I mean the moral and spiritual—the stand point of the individual who is moving in this world of relativity—the world of the One and many and the other, the standpoint of the Absolute where all relations lose their significance in the One Eternal life.

To those who cannot transcend the former, the relation of a devotee to his God is the highest fact in their religious experience and this is no doubt the experience of the masses. In their case there is no effacement at all of either the individual *ego* or of the passions and affections of the devotee.

But as to the philosopher in search of the highest variety, his philosophic sense tells him that the highest ethical ideal is but a means for the attainment of something still higher. Where man has begun "to realise in increasing fulness a sense of personal relationship to the Divine Self," where is this to culminate if such culmination be ever possible, if not in a complete self-surrender of one's own personality?

Is this "fusion of the human self with the Divine Self" to be condemned as virtually destroying all distinct sense of individual personality? If Love means the feeling and consciousness of identity. "I in thee and thou in me" [2 Hald 241]; if love is implied in our desire to realise unity [D' Alviella], is not that love the greatest and truest, when the lover entirely forgets himself to *become* the beloved?

In other words, is not the progressive self-surrender to the immanent and self-revealing Divine Being pre-supposed as an accomplished fact in one who has reached the highest ethical ideal; and what value would such an one, at that stage, attach to his individual personality? Are his passions and affections weakened and effaced or purified and ennobled? Why did Jesus teach man "to deny himself to hate father and mother and wife and children and brothers and sisters, yea, his own life also?" What is the meaning of the Christian saying "He that *loses* life shall *have* it"? Are not the same sentiments re-echoed by Christian divines. "The Self, the I, the me, and the like, all belong to the Evil Spirit. * * Be simply and wholly bereft of Self " (*Theol. Germ.* 73).

The Bishop of Ripon, in *The Hibbert Journal* for April, 1905, writes :—

"Christ is born, and the Christ spirit must be formed in men; Christ dies, and so *the self in man must be crucified,* for how can love live alongside the life of Self? Christ rises, and the true Self is only found *when the old self been crucified*".[1]

Is there no virtual destruction of all distinct sense of individual personality in any of the above utterances?

It may at once be conceded, however, that *passionate* love there is not and could not be at a stage which pre-supposes the possession of true knowledge [Gnosis, *jñāna* but love it certainly is,—only ennobled by *jñāna* by which is understood spiritual enlightenment. It is spiritual, but it is not the less love because there is no display of emotion in it.

1. The italics in the above passage are mine. It is gratifying to find Christian theologians are willing now to interpret the Christian dogma by sentiments like those which the Vedānta has always entertained. The Supreme Self-surrender, the Neo-platonic idea of the Logos, God's descent unto him and love for him, the Crucifixion of Jesus, that is, of the lower egohood in man, his Resurrection or the rise of the Christ, that is, of the true Self in him, and his ascension or union with the Godhead—all these become intelligible when thus interpreted.

"Love must be guided and taught of knowledge. This love so maketh a man one with God that he can nevermore be separated from Him" [Theol. Germ. 159.] It is Love in its purity and fulness.

Devotional or what is called emotional Love is considered by the Vedānta as a means of acquiring spiritual knowledge. [Śaṅkar, B. *Gītā*, XIII. 10, etc.]. And there cannot be the slightest doubt that devotion, practised in the attitude and under the conditions prescribed in that behalf, must bring in spiritual enlightenment and ultimately of a surety lead to salvation [see, for instance, B. Gītā, Chap. XII].

Nor is our belief in such salvation a vain one. "The Gītā [says Barnett] has a gospel to deliver, telling of a consecration of life's every work to the selfless service of God and an Infinite Love that at every place and every time pours forth its illimitable grace to all that seek after it."

The next objection noticed above his reference to the indifference which the Vedānta advocates to things earthly, to earthly attachments, etc.

It is said that a philosophy or theology which insists on the abandonment of all earthly concerns, on the killing of all passions and desires for the purpose of obtaining union with God, simply means an attempt to go empty-handed into an empty house, to be there "left as it were alone with God without any world to meditate" between the two, with the result that "in the ecstatic vision of the Absolute, the light of reason is extinguished. This is what Dr. Edward Caird has said of the Stoic system.

We in India also consider it a true and a noble lesson that nothing on earth is ours except our own thoughts and deeds, which we carry with us; that all things pertaining to our empiric consciousness are "of the earth, earthly," transient and ephemeral— wealth, fame, honours, even our domestic affections and bonds of friendship—that all these have no doubt their limited aims and ends and serve as steps in our progressive development and enlightenment; but for higher and spiritual ends they have to be left behind.

This is, indeed, our ideal; but the question is, whether, in following it, we strip ourselves of all that we had and try to reach an abstract emptiness and delude ourselves into the belief that we have attained the goal or that we are possibly on the way to it, when, in reality, we are only in a state of spiritual nudity and physical nothingness.

If spiritual enlightenment pre-supposes the transcendence of the ethical standpoint as an accomplished fact, if man at this stage has already transcended the world of sense-experience, if, at this stage, as Fichte says, "all wrappings disappear and the world passes away for him with her dead principle"[1] or if, as Śaṅkar says, the world appears as "melting away like the imagery of a dream," of what value is the meditation of such a world at that highest stage? Of what value is a toy-elephant to one who understands that it is only a toy? Of what value as a diagram [and that too an inaccurate one] to one who is face to face, so to speak, with the original Reality?

Again, what is the meaning of the remark that "the light of reason is extinguished?" The question here raised can only be answered with the help of what Principal John Caird terms 'the hidden logic of a spiritual process.' If what the learned Master of Balliol calls reason is extinguished, he may be answered that something better and nobler is acquired in this process of transformation. But why assume the extinction of reason, when it is admitted that nothing is annihilated in the process of development but all is assimilation and transformation? Why not say that the potential universality of reason becomes a realised and accentuated fact in such a case?

Similarly, as to Passions and Desires, when the Vedānta

---

1. See Vedānta Sūtras, III, 2, 21; 2 Thib-163.

advocates Self-denial as a virtue, it does not ask us to destroy the senses or the sense-objects; but to keep the senses under proper control, while moving among sense-objects (*B. Gītā* II, 64). Nor are we asked to demolish all the desires, as is popularly believed; for this is impossible in the very nature of things. To demolish all desire would mean the cessation of all activity, which is absolutely impossible. (*B. Gītā*, III, 4 to 7).

No doubt, the senses are described as very powerful, trying impetuously to carry away the heart of even a prudent man who strives to restrain them (*B. Gītā*, II, 60). No doubt, also, that desires and passions are said to be the greatest enemies of man [*B. Gītā*, III, 37-39].

But all these are a part of our nature, though only a perverted part, and cannot be eradicated or plucked out as thorns, in one's body. They are not at peace with man, it is true, but yet they cannot part company, and virtue considers in man's victory over them not by killing but by converting these enemies into friends.

In other words, what is meant is, that what constitutes the lower nature of man should be made to do higher and nobler work. As was well said by a celebrated poet, let the object of *Kāma* [desire] be devotion to God, let *Krodha* [anger] be employed to control the senses, etc., and when so employed, they are "purified and idealised by being made the natural basis of a higher spiritual satisfaction"; they are brought in harmony with the true and assimilated with it. This is exactly the idea which the *Bhagavad Gītā* means to convey in VI, 5-6.

उद्धरेदात्मनात्मानं नात्मानमवसादयेत्।
आत्मैव ह्यात्मनो बंधुरात्मैव रिपुरात्मनः।।६।।

बंधुरात्मात्मनस्तस्य येनात्मैवात्मना जितः।
अनात्मनस्तुं शत्रुत्वे वर्तेतात्मैव शत्रुवत्।।६।।

Even the utterances of Śaṅkar, the greatest Advaitin, may well be referred to as showing what, according to him also, is meant by the "lifting up of the Self by the Self."

It is the *mana* which creates objects of desire, and give rise to egoity and attachment to things earthly and these make man a ceaseless wanderer in the phenomenal world (*saṅsāra*). Pursuit of external objects being checked, desires are also checked, tranquillity of the mind thus results, and from this arises the vision of the *Paramātman* Purify, therefore, the *mana* and strengthen it for its fitness for *mukti*. This is attainable by the performance of one's duties and this world would then be to such an one as naught. [*Viveka Cūḍāmaṇī*].

But why should the indifference, advocated in the Indian systems, to things earthly, to earthly attachments, etc., find no sympthetic response from modern Western thought? Is it in any degree worse than the indifferent advocated in the sacred writings of Christianity and by Christian saints in the name of Jesus?

> "If any man will come after Me, let him deny himself' * * * and follow Me" (Matt. XVI. 24). If he hate not his father and mother and wife and children, yea, and his own life also, he cannot be My disciple" (*Luke*, XIV. 26).

"So long as a man clingeth unto the elements and fragments of this world, [and, above all, to himself] and holdeth converse with them, and maketh great account them, he is deceived and blinded." (*Theol. Germ*, 66). "A man must begin by denying himself and willingly forsaking all things for God's sake* * He who will have the one must let the other go." (*ibid*. 45-46).'

> "Eschew bodily pleasures and rest in Me alone* * * Desire to despite thyself, break thy appetites, and crush out all thy pleasures and desires" (Suso). "Disengage thyself so completely from all creatures in all things

which might hinder all creatures in all things which migh hinder thine eternal salvation. ** There is no other way, however hard this may appear. * * * We must divest ourselves of external occupations and establish ourselves in a tranquil stillness of soul by an energetic resignation, as if we were dead to self and thought only of the honor of Christ and his Heavenly Father" (*ibid*).

It is difficult for Christian writers to escape the criticism which they are pleased so freely to pass on others. Mr. Thompson, who has translated the *Bhagavad Gītā*, feels that some of the passages above quoted come "from the mouth of the only unerring preceptor," meaning Jesus Christ, and he explains in his note to *B. Gītā*, XIII. 9., where similar sentiments [but couched in much milder language] occur, that such passages should not be construed literally; "they only mean that where one's salvation requires it, even the nearest earthly ties must be disregarded." [Thompson's *B. Gītā*, p. 90].

This explanation is only superficial. The meaning of such teachings involving indifference to family ties, to earthly attachments and objects lies much deeper. When a person has learnt the lesson of "dying to live," his self in the process goes on becoming larger and larger, and in the end it includes within itself the selfs of all other beings. The individual identifies himself with all. With him, humanity is a big brotherhood, (*Vasudhaiva Kuṭumbakam*), so that the particular relation-ships of father, mother, etc., fall in the shade; there is here exclusion of the relations *as such* no doubt, but there is their inclusion in the larger whole. He dies to them as he dies to himself, to live a larger self. He thus rises "above all considrations connected with the mere *personality* of those around him, and so is free from all the injustice and partiality which ordinary love so often brings in its train."

This is exactly what the Vedānta means when it desires the extinction of the *ahaṁvṛtti* [egoity]; what is aimed at is not the destruction but the elevation or transformation of the individual Self, which brings with it the spiritual capacity of looking upon all alike *samadṛṣṭi* [*B. Gītā*. II. 54-71 etc.]. It means the expansion[1] of the Self to become the Self of all. There is no "emptiness" in such a conception, where the Self is conceived as becoming, in the course of its development, so far expanded as to embrace within it the self's of all beings. The language of one who has reached this state, says Vasiṣṭha, is :—

> "Self fills the whole universe * * within, without, below, above, everywhere all is Self, here and there; there is no Not-Self anywhere * * There is nothing which is not in me. What should I desire, when the whole world is one web of Universal Consciousness." (See *Jīvan Mukti Viveka*, 140.)

Similarly, says Śaṅkar :—

> "He who knows the Oneness of the Self has no desires because for him there is no object to be desired; as his Ātman is himself, he cannot desire it. The being centred in Self is emancipation. This proceeds from [spiritual] knowledge alone * * No doubt the variety of *Karma* prescribed in the *Śāstras* are useful as aids to knowledge" (*Tait. Up.*, I. 12.1.)

It is interesting to read the following description of the Indian Sage given in the *Mahābhārata* :—

> "He who behaves towards all creatures as if he is their kinsman, who has acquired the knowledge of the Supreme Spirit, who is free from all passions and is absorbed in the knowledge of the Self, he who is compassionate, whom all creatures have ceased to fear,

1. I have advisedly adopted the above mode of expression to make any meaning intelligible to those who are not Advaitins. From the Advaita point of view, it is not the Self that is expanded for the Self is eternal and changeless; the expansion here referred to means the gradual removal of the veil of Nescience

who abstains from injuring others in thought, speech or deed, he who is free from the bondage of desire, he into whose mind all sorts of desires enter like diverse streams falling into the ocean without being able to transcend its limits by their discharge—it is such an one who gains Peace—not he who cherishes desire for earthly objects."

And those who have studied the psychic constitution of man tell us that the powers of such a personage become so far developed that while they are far-reaching, they are also so very tender and sensitive, that they are capable of responding to "every thrill in the outside universe." The person, who has reached this degree of enlightenment, "feels and answers to everything and, just because he desires nothing for himself, is able to give everything to all." Such an one, it is said, "becomes more and more a channel of Divine Life to the world; he asks nothing save to be a channel with wider and wider bed along which the great Life may flow, and his only wish is that he may become a larger and larger vessel with less of obstacle in himself to hinder the outward pouring of the Life; working for nothing save to be of service."

[Annie Besant's *Karma*, p. 69].

So, too, says Śaṅkara in his Viveka Cūḍamaṇī :—

"The great and peaceful ones live regenerating the world like the coming of spring; and after having crossed the ocean of embodied existence, help those who try to do the same thing, without the personal motives. It is the innate character of the great ones to remove the sufferings of others, as it is the character of the moon to allay the pains of those who are suffering from the intense heat of the sun."

Every great man is a living power; he is a most impressive personality, while living and is, in a sense, and his influence on mankind continues even when he is physically dead.

> "Such men (says Dr. E. Caird) seem still to grow beyond the end which hides them from our eyes. * * * The great man in his lifetime stands before his contemporaries as an external image of excellence which may, indeed, awaken a new spirit in those who are able, even partially, to appreciate it; but when the outward presence is removed, the awakened spirit reproduces the inmost reality of fact in an idealised vision, which is truer than anything seen with the eyes of sense * * * and this new idealised image, in turn reacts in further developments of the same spiritual energy which produced it" (2 Evol. Rel. 227; see also Tiele and D'Alviella),

And why is it that such men command such an influence over people among whom their lot is cast? What, it that makes them the pioneers of religious movements? It is the *life they live*; it is the spiritual light which shines forth through their life [their aura, as an occultist might say] which directly touches the vision and pierces the heart of every man who comes within its all embracing radiating influence. Their very presence "changes sorrow into joy, fear into courage, despair into hope, weakness into power." [See Trine : also *Jivan Mukti Viveka*.]

Inspired with the Divine Spirit, full of the Infinite Ātman and *Ātman* alone, endowed with a vision which pierces through things visible to things invisible, realising the Infinite everywhere in this finite existence, these men live the life of the Infinite, and what they think, will and act is what the Infinite thinks, wills and acts through them. [Tiele.]. They embrace within their fold universe and all that is contained within it. It is this life which makes their impressive personality a living one; it is these who have really conquered death.

It is these who, though they may appear to be doing little, in reality do much—much that is good and noble and of everlasting interest. In India, the Upaniṣads Āraṇyakas, etc., are a living monument of the work done by such "choice specimens of humanity."

Such is the ideal of the Indian Sage and the Asceticism of the Indian Vedānta is no other than what the sage's life represents.

But unfortunately, as said of the Greek Cynics, many sturdy beggars, and ill-conditioned vagrants take up, as a convenient disguise, "the ascetic's staff and mantle" and bring into disrepute the entire scheme of Hindu society and with it the wisdom that has planned that scheme.

Part II

There is undoubtedly a good deal of misconception about Indian asceticism, and this misconception is due partly to the degenerated form in which it is at present observable in practice and partly to the garbled accounts of unsympathetic and prejudiced Christian writers, who pose themselves as authorities on this question.

These writers invariably associate with asceticism the ideas of mortification of the flesh and retirement into solitude with no really noble end in view. The Indian ascetic is always represented as a person who renounces the world as a pessimist and seeks refuge in a jungle from the vicissitudes of life, as a discontented soul, and ekes out his existence there, doing nothing really useful. He is sometimes described as "a bundle of negations."

Now, this is not a correct view of Indian asceticism. The Hindu system in its pristine purity did not enjoin either mortification of the flesh or bare retirement into solitude, any more than Christianity in its pristine form did.

The Indian ascetic is called a *tapasvin* or *sannyāsin*, *yogin* but none of these words connotes the notions so freely accredited to Indian asceticism by foreign writers.

No doubt, rigorous practices involving mortification of the flesh etc., are prescribed in what is called *haṭha yoga*, but these practices are generally resorted to by the uncultured and have always been severely condemned by right-minded thinkers.

It is only *Rāja Yoga* that is countenanced and recommended, and here what is said about the life of a *tapasvin* or *sannyāsin* or *yogin* is that it is one of self-sacrifice, that is, of a sacrifice of the heart by self-surrender and self-abnegation for the good of others. A true Yogin is described as "becoming delightfully satisfied in the fulfilment of all duties, and self-realisation of the truth, "I am Brahma, the eternal source of all transcendent bliss." The whole practice of *Rāja Yoga* breathes a spirit of moderation in exercise, such as might, instead of causing bodily pain and distraction of attention, be helpful to concentration of the mind and a proper meditation on the Ātman. A Yogin, says Vivekanand, must always avoid the two extremes of luxury and austerity.

Then as to retirement into solitude, that, too, could be justified by the laws of psychic phenomena. If any individual reached an exceedingly high degree of spiritual development, rendering his constant presence in society hurtful, he, in his wisdom, would naturally shift his residense and retire into solitude, both for his own sake and for the sake of his brethren whom he is bound to help. This is not, however, a matter which we, on the lower plane, could understand or appreciate.

But this much we must admit that the kind of development above-mentioned is possible only in the case of a person who has passed through all the lower stages of social development, fulfilled all his duties to his kith and kin, to his caste and country. At this stage, therefore, he would naturally turn his attention to the investigation and solution of the most important problems of Life, and the attainment, by practice in spiritual devotion, of the spiritual end, which is our goal.

The scheme of Hindu society wisely, ordains retirement

into solitude, not for a life of inaction; as is erroneously supposed, but for work in the interest of philosophy and the gratification of man's highest aspirations here. What useful work our forest hermits did in ancient times, our Upaniṣadas and Āraṇyakas amply testify.

At the same time, it must be borne in mind that if any one took this step of retirement before having fulfilled the duties attached to his station in life, and before having passed through a proper course of moral discipline and become fit for spiritual enlightenment, he was liable, as a rule, to be condemned as a hypocrite, just as a false *tathāgata* was, in the Buddhistic system; for no man could become a *sannyāsin* or *yogin* merely by abandoning his duties and retiring into solitude. In every true *sannyāsin*, the first essential is the performance of one's duties in a spirit of devotion and complete selflessness. (*B. Gītā*, xviii. 7, 9, 10, 11).

It must no doubt be admitted that passages do frequently occur in our sacred writings to the effect that the highest stage of spiritual enlightenment is that of a *paramahaṁsa* and, in the case of such a person, it is often said that "for him all *karma* has ceased."

And because such a high ideal is placed before man, some writers think that the teachings of the Vedānta might "fail to call out and strengthen the many qualities required for the practical side of life, and that it might raise the human mind to a height from which the most, essential virtues of social and political life might dwindle away into mere phantoms."

Yes, there might be this danger, if one ignored the distinction between the two paths, which the Vedānta considers as most essential to be borne in mind as a key to a correct reading of its teachings—the two paths, *viz.*, of *pravṛtti* and *nivṛtti*-the one as a preparation for the other.

If one fully realised to oneself the fact that one who wants to go to the top of a hill must *climb* and not fly to reach it, there would be no danger of the social and political virtues dwindling away into mere phantoms. All these virtues have to be exercised and exercised as "a consecration of life's work to the selfless service of God," before the highest point could be reached, at which eternal Bliss and Peace reign supreme and from which there is no longer any return to earthly life for one's own personal development and perfection.

यस्मिन्गता न निवर्तन्ति भूयः। यद्गत्वा न निवतन्ते तद्धाम परमंमम।

–Gītā, 15.4-6

If this condition is deemed unattainable, and if, therefore, the position itself condemned by Christian writers as meaning a useless life of Quietism, the teachings of Jesus, too, would have to be condemned on that ground.

> "The Kingdom of God, set forth by Jesus, is (says Professor Pfleiderer) in sharpest contrast to the kingdoms of this world and their glory; which must be renounced by whoever would win the Kingdom of Heaven."—the renunciation here referred to being of all earthly ties and earthly possessions (Matt. xix 29; Luke, xiv 25).

And Jesus adds, as to one who wins the Kingdom of God :—

"I will make him a pillar in the temple of my God and he shall go out no more." [Rev. III, 12].

The truth is that when it is said that "*Karma* for the spiritually perfect has ceased," it does not mean that he, from that time, becomes a cypher or a block of stone. It means that action in his case and for *his* own individual enlightenment has ceased; having reached the highest condition, he has nothing to desire for *himself*, nothing to do for *himself*; but for that very reason, as stated before, there is much which he has to do, and that is, in helping those who are on the lower planes and need an uplifting hand.

If God acts thus for the good of His creature [*B. Gītā*, III

22-25], why should not man do the like? If all are dependent upon each other as parts of an Organism, and if the spiritually enlightened one has realised to himself his identity with all that forms this universal brotherhood it would be a contradiction in terms to say that he has, by the very reason of his spiritual culture, become a useless member of that brotherhood.

The *Bhagavad Gītā* emphasises this lesson in Chap. III, 17-25.

It must, indeed, be conceded that the highest stage, contemplated by the Vedānta, is beyond the reach of ordinary mortals. The path of the *Paramahaṁsa* (परमहंस) is, indeed, very difficult. It is said to be "sharp as a razor" '[Kaṭh. Up. III. 14] and hardly one that the masses can be expected to tread.

Sri Krishna tells Arjuna :—

> Among thousands of men scarce one striveth for perfection; of the successful strivers scarce one knoweth Me in essence.
>
> मनुष्याणां सहस्रेषु कश्चिद्यतति सिद्धये।
> यततामपि सिद्धानां कश्चिन्मां वेत्ति तत्त्वतः ।।
>
> [*B. Gītā*. VII 3.]

Nor is one life enough for the purpose. As Suso, the German Mystic, puts it :

> Be sure thou wilt have to endure many deaths before thou canst put thy nature under the yoke.

But ultimate success is assured to us as being, within our reach.

The religious and ethical truths which are of immediate practical value to men belong to the lower plane—the plane of the One and Many—the sphere of Relativity, as I have elsewhere often termed it, and here all is activity and no Quietism.

But one must not forget that the activities implied in

this sphere, if well directed, with the ideals of *Advaita* and *Abheda* always present to the mind, prepare the way for a higher and holier life. "Our lower civilisation is but a preparation for the higher."

These ideals of *advaita* and *abheda* are as useful to social and political progress as they are to the progress of the individual. The idea of 'dying to live' and of 'living a larger and larger self' are sufficiently suggestive of higher and nobler aspirations.

As stated by Rev. Charles Kingsley in connection with European Mysticism, I might, with equal truth, assert that the great spiritual laws, upon which the Vedānta has founded its practical Ethics.

> hold just as good in the family, in the market, in the senate, in the study, aye, in the battle-field itself; and teach (man) the way to lead, in whatever station of life he may be placed, a truly manlike, because a truly Godlike, life.

The teachings of the Vedānta are as practical as they are speculative. There is a vast amount of sacred literature intended to convey truths of a practical character to the popular mind. Of this I may here mention only the two grand Epics—the Mahābhārata and the Rāmāyaṇa. These two Epics contain a great deal of practical teaching with practical illustrations, founded on the Vedāntic ideals of *advaita* and *abheda*. Great ideals are placed before the people in such a popular form, that very few, indeed, could be found who are unfamiliar with the episodes of the great personages related in them or with the truths intended to be conveyed by them. They furnish topics for *kirtanas* and *bhajanas* in every Hindu temple; they are in the mouth of every rustic, young and old, whose whole life is influenced thereby. It is impossible to estimate this influence on their daily life, but it cannot be denied that it is wide and far-reaching.

The *Bhagavad Gītā* is another sacred book which I ought

to mention in this connection, as being one of the best exponents of the practical aspect of the Vedānta.

To begin with, the practical character of the Gītā is prominently observable in its lessons on devotion. While recognising to the fullest extent the philosophical ideal of *tattvamasi*, it takes note of the broad fact that all men are not of the same intellectual calibre to be able to grasp this ideal and appreciate and realise it, all at once.

Man is, accordingly, told that the Absolute and Unrelated cannot at once be intelligible to him, for it requires the most abstract contemplation and elevation of thought, which is beyond the ordinary powers of his intellect to accomplish; that till that stage of intellectual and spiritual attainment is reached, he must content himself with contemplating and worshipping, as God, the Supreme Essence as a differentiated entity in Its manifestations in Its own works throughout the Universe, taking any of such manifestations as a *symbol*, through which to reach It in a proper, moral and religious attitude.

Some of our Christian critics denounce this as a "conscious alliance with falsehood, the deliberate propagation of lies."

I will deal with this objection in my article on "Hinduism and Its strength." It is enough, for the present, to say that, if the use of symbols to explain truths, which cannot otherwise be grasped, be hypocrisy, we must bid farewell to all the methods of teachings which we have adopted in Schools, and hold the teachers as so many liars, when, for instance, in teaching Geometry, the points and lines drawn on the School board, they represent as the Geometrical points which are without magnitude, and Geometrical lines which are simply length without breadth! Euclid himself, too, would be a huge liar, in this view of the matter.

If these critics think that Christian Churches have done well in trampling down and destroying the lower worships, instead of explaining them, and in insisting upon one uniform standard, irrespective of whether it is suited to men of every grade of culture, we wish them joy.

We here think differently. If we provide food to human beings according to their physical capacity to digest it, if we regulate the education of the people according to their intellectual capacities and needs, we think we ought to observe the same law in respect of their religious and, spiritual culture.

A writer in the *Hibbert Journal*, in July 1906, (p. 747), very pertinently says :—

> "Children are compelled to say, by heart, sentences the meaning of which they cannot possibly know. Can one wonder at the slow progress of Christianity, or at the lukewarm interest of laymen in the Church, when, as babes, they are fed with the strongest meat, and their appetite and digestions ruined?"

We here make "our abstract religious conception popular by means of symbols, pictures and images; never forgetting, at the same time, to impress the truth that these are but symbols and pictures, and that the various beliefs and worships and divinities are but manifestations of Brahma—the only Eternal Verity in the Universe. So that, when a Hindu worships his divinity by symbols, pictures or images, he does not worship the symbol, picture or image hut the metaphysical verity underlying it, all these being but manifestations of that Eternal Verity.

As suggested by an educated Hindu, the analogy of a ladder with innumerable rungs well and correctly represents our position. Each individual soul stands on the rung suited to itself; and no person has a right to say that the rung on which he himself stands is the only true one and the others, false; there is a germ of truth even in the lowest layers of superstition, and each one must climb the ladder by stages and not jump over the intermediate rungs to go to the top.

This very fact has rendered the religion of the Hindus elastic and tolerant; it adapts and assimilates the lower forms of worship; instead of endeavouring to destroy them [Lyall].

The roles about *Loka-saṅgraha* given in the *Bhagavad-Gītā* are also suggestive of profound wisdom. Of these, the first and foremost is, "Let no wise man unsettle the mind of ignorant people attached to action."

It is wisely ordained that the wise must take the ignorant masses on and on *with* them, being always *with* them and *of* them; that they should act prudently and try to purify their conduct, first improve their moral character and aptitude for grasping and appreciating higher truths; well remembering that it would be most imprudent and useless to force higher truths on them, without preparing the ground for their reception.

All our readers are probably not aware of the story of Moses and the Shepherd. The shepherd in his prayer was using the language of an anthropomorphic God, and offering to serve him with food, clothing, etc., when Moses rebuked him saying that God was a spirit, and needed no such ministrations. The effect of this rebuke was that the shepherd lost his God and had none other given him, whom he could devoutly worship.

> A voice from heaven was (then) heard, saying, 'O Moses, wherefore have you driven away my servant? Your office is to reconcile my people with me, not to drive them away from me. I have given to each race different usages and forms of praising and adoring me. I have no need of their praises, being exalted above all such needs. I regard not the words that are spoken, but the heart that offers them. I do not require fine words, but a burning heart. Men's ways of showing

devotion to me are various, but so long as the devotions are genuine, they are accepted.

The above is a complete echo of the sentiments contained in the *Bhagavad-Gītā*.

With every advance in intelligence and moral culture, each one is sure to find explanations which will satisfy him, and there will be a corresponding improvement in his religious attitude.

Thus, with the backbone of the philosophical ideal, the religion of the Vedānta, in a thoroughly tolerant spirit, opens the path to every one who is desirous of salvation. Mr. Rajam Aiyar rightly calls it "a grand Religious Republic of the Vedānta."

Then as to social relations and the duties those relations impose, throughout the book, when it speaks of *duties*, the *Bhagavad-Gītā* tells us that we are bound to do the duties attached to the position in which we are placed.

It first tells us that man's mission on earth in his embodied existence is *action* (कर्मण्येवाधिकारस्ते–*Gītā*, 2.47)—not one single moment of his life can anybody pass without it. (न हि कश्चित्क्षणमपि जातु तिष्ठत्यकर्मकृत्–*Gītā*, 3.5).

The entire humanity is divided into four classes according to the kind of *Karma* and the degree of development which have determined the situation each one occupies in this life (गुणकर्मविभागश:). The duties thus assigned to man constitute his *Dharma* and these must be religiously observed. One who has the *sāttvika* element pre- ponderating in him is bound to do the work of spiritual instruction and the elevation of man's character in every thing that pertains to his moral, religious and spiritual welfare. One who has the *rājasika* element pre-ponderating in him must do all that requires activity : all political activities belong to this sphere. Commerical activity belongs to the third class; and the last and lowest class represents the people in whom the *tāmasa*-

guṇa predominates, and who, therefore, stand by far in the greatest need of protection from the higher classes, while in a state of serfdom and bondage.

Each man, says the *Gītā*, must actively do the duties peculiar to his station in life, and these he cannot well neglect, for any neglect on his part would create a hindrance in the way of his further development in the right direction. This would constitue his sin, bringing its own punishment with it.

"Fight and conquer or die in the struggle against iniquity and wickedness" is the teaching rung into Arjuna's ears at the end of every Discourse. Fight in the interests of dethroned Virtue, and recover the crown for her by conquest, or die in the attempt.' Unmindful of earthly ties, fight bravely, not for bread nor for money nor for fame; in the same of Duty which is thy allotted lot.

Nor is this teaching in the least inconsistent with the other teachings which enjoin Non-Resistance to evil, the return of good for evil, etc. It is only in the India Vedānta that such teachings, though apparently inconsistent with each other, are found side by side; and the key to their correct interpretation consists in a strict observance of the distinction which I have repeatedly emphasised in my writings.

All social duties necessarily imply relations and active conduct for the maintenance and development of those relations. Sri Krishna's advice to man to fight is perfectly intelligible and proper, from the social point of view. Man must fulfil his duties in his mundane existence, before he can become fit to enter the region, wherein all relations lose their significance.

Society as a whole can never be expected to enter this region, all at once or simultaneously. This world of sense-experience, wherein man has to struggle for existence and for his supposed happiness, cannot be transformed into a "Kingdom of God" all at once. It contains beings of various degrees of culture, and, though they all may be on their onward march, they cannot be expected to reach the goal, all simultaneously.

Activity must, therefore, continue to be their watchword and a *sine qua non.*

It must also be remembered that our life in this world is one of probation and difficulties—difficulties arising from wickedness and evil; fighting to conquer this wickedness and evil must, therefore, be one of our first duties to society.

Each individual has to pass through this struggle and become fit, by a course of moral discipline, for spiritual enlightenment. He has to form his character, which implies the improvement of himself as well of his environment, and, for that purpose, resistance to evil becomes a necessity and has to be practised.

But in practising it, he ought not to forget the higher teachings, 'Resist not evil,' 'Return good for evil,' etc.

Man's duty, accordingly, is to resist evil and resent injury, if the interests of any member of society, including himself as such member, are jeopardised or affected by such injury; but in doing so, he should try even to reclaim the evil doer, remembering that he, too, is a member of that organism.

In other word, while non-resistance to evil ought to be the ideal before man and is insisted on, as a rule of *individual* conduct, so far as possible, the exigencies of society would seem to require an adjustment, from time to time, of the several relations involved in it and, therefore, justify resistance to evil for such adjustment.

In this view of the matter, it is through Resistance that man has to go to the higher plane, where Non-Resistance to evil is the rule. There is therefore in reality no antagonism between the two principles of Resistance and Non-Resistance to evil, just as there is none between Egoism and Altruism. They are only two stages in Evolution.

Duties, says the *Gītā*, must be performed by man in a spirit of complete 'selflessness' with the fact ever present to his mind that the good of all is his own good. Duties, begun on the lower rungs of the ladder may go on expanding and embracing what are generally known as the duties of citizenship and patriotism and eventually duties to the entire humanity and to all other beings and things, the principle of *abheda* being the truth underlying them all.

Even a whole nation can become s model nation, if this principle of *abheda* were rightly apprehended and correctly reduced into practice. The individualism and self-seeking, which the present materialistic age unfortunately fosters, must give way before a life of altruism; the people under proper culture must begin to feel that each one lives not for himself but for the common good of all; their sense of egoism must become so far expanded that the interest of the people may become the interest of each one individually. In such a case, the people would identify themselves with their king "merging their will in the will of their monarch, and ascribing their virtues to the virtue of the king." The king, on the other hand, would realise "the nation, as it were, within himself, as a company of souls grouped with mutual bonds into an ordered host for the higher purposes of divine economy."

Nor is this a mere fanciful picture of a model nation, impossible of actual realisation. History has furnished only recently an excellent illustration of such a nation. I mean Japan; and the words I have quoted in the preceding paragraph from the *Theosophical Review*, for October, 1905, refer to that country.

Here, again, is an interesting statement bearing on the point in an article in the *Hibbert Journal* for October, 1905, contributed by Prof. Anesaki, of the Imperial University of Japan. After referring to the teachings of his spiritual teachers which enjoin altruism and the sacrifice of everything to the *Dharma*, the learned Professor observes :—

> These were no mere teachings but the morality inculcated by them has tuned the actual life so deeply, that self-sacrifice for the sake of one's ideal has become the spirit of our national life. Applied to the morality of the warrior class, it has caused many warriors to die gladly for the sake of their lord of the nation. The spirit of self-sacrifice is the vital force of our morality and has manifested its power during the present war most remarkably.

Here is an instance highly suggestive of more than a bare possibility of realisation of the Vedāntic ideal—an instance in which we find conquest going on "hand in hand with gentleness and self-control."

The *Bhagavad Gītā* itself gives instances of Kings leading an active life even after their spiritual enlightenment. King Janaka is mentioned by name in III. 20. "He fought battles, improved commerce and industry, and is reported to have been one of the justest kings of the world, and withal, one of the greatest Indian Vedāntins." (*Rajam Aiyar*). Rāma, the hero of the Rāmāyaṇa, is another instance; and a number of other instances might also be found showing that *kingly duties were not considered to be in any way incompatible with spiritual culture.*

"Rulers ought to be philosophers," says Plato; and some of our Upaniṣads show that Kṣatriya kings were the custodians of philosophical knowledge, and Brahmins went to them for acquiring it.

There is also abundant evidence to show that, side by side with the high ideals which the Indian Vedānta placed before man, there existed institutions in India, even in the pre-Buddhistic period, for the education of the young—male and female—in which all the most noble and heroic virtues were taught, both in theory and practice—institution intended for philosophical, moral, religious and political instruction, for the elevation of the disciples 'in spirit and in action'—'institutions somewhat similar to those which were founded by Pythagoras in Crotona and other places in the sixth century B.C.

And, what is more important still, the teachers, who volunteered their services in this mission, without any pecuniary gain to themselves, were the very men whom European writers are wont to condemn as so many 'bundles of negation'—I mean; the sages and ascetics, who had renounced the world and who, having nothing to desire for themselves, were ever devoted to serve others, in order to elevate them to their own heights.

How literally true was it that the Great Ones, instead of being the Masters, were the servants of the people among whom their lot was east.

If institutions, sixth as I have above mentioned, existed as a fact in ancient India, it might-safely be inferred that they had a most salutary effect on the society in which they flourished and the government which tolerated and encouraged them. If members of the royal household were among the disciples attending these institution, if the sons of the nobility and commonalty; so to speak, all received instruction on one common ground—instruction based on the broad ideals of *advaita* and *abheda*, such instruction must naturally have had a good effect upon both the rulers and the ruled.

The relations between the two must naturally have been all that could possibly be wished—the ruler acting with wisdom like an unselfish and loving father towards his children, and the ruled serving him in a right loyal spirit with devotion and love. Filial piety and loyalty would, in such a case, be completely united; as they are seen united in Japan at the present day [*Hibbert Journal*].

We have thus in the Vedānta a philosophy which has never been "excelled in its spiritual heights or in speculative profundity," and an ethical and religious ideal which is eternally and universally true and capable of *practical* application.

It has a power to strengthen the souls of the noblest man for "action and endurance." Owing to its "firm grasp of the central idea that there is a rational principle in the world, which is one in nature with the self-conscious intelligence within us," it has been able to make every thing bend to it. It recognises a principle of a highly practical character, which is legitimately deducible from it. The noble idea of the entire universe being one big brotherhood *Vasudhaiva-kuṭuṁbakam* finds its justification and explanation in that central idea—a brotherhood, in which all distinctions of Mine and Thine lose their significance, and in the interests of which all are held bound to co-operate, sinking their individual personality altogether.

How grand is this conception of *Vasudhaiva-kuṭuṁbakam*. In the words of Principal J. Caird, it is not a fantastic dream of the theorist but a noble ideal.

If both the Rulers and the Ruled were only to realise the importance of the truth implied in it and shape their conduct accordingly, what a tremendous revolution in the religious and political attitude of both would result!

Our country would, then, be veritably a "Heaven on Earth."

Is India destined ever to experience such a blissful condition?

The Philosophy of the Vedānta[1]

Dr. Paul Deussen

On my journey through India, I have noticed with satisfaction, that in philosophy till now our brothers in the East have maintained a very good tradition, better perhaps, than the more active but less contemplative branches of the great Indo-Aryan family in Europe, where Empiricism, Realism and their natural consequence, Materialism, grow from day to day more exuberantly, whilst metaphysics, the very centre and heart of serious of philosophy, are supported only by a few ones, who have learned to brave the spirit of the age.

In India, the influence of this perverted and perversive spirit of our age has not yet overthrown in religion and philosophy the good traditions of the great ancient time. It is true, that most of the ancient *darśanas* even in India find only an historical interest; followers of the Sāṁkhya System occur rarely; Nyāya is cultivated mostly as an intellectual sport and exercise, like grammar or mathematics,—but the Vedāntic is now, as in the ancient time, living in the mind and heart of every thoughtful Hindu. It is true, that even here in the sanctuary of Vedāntic metaphysics, the realistic tendencies, natural to man, have penetrated, producing the misinterpreting variations of Śaṅkara's Advaita, known under the names *Viśiṣṭādvaita*, Dvaita, *Śuddhādvaita* of

1. An address delivered before the Bombay Branch of of the Royal Asiatic Society, Saturday, the 25th February 1893.

Rāmānuja, Mādhva, Vallabha,—but India till now has not yet been seduced by their voices, and of hundred Vedāntins (I have it from a well-informed man, who is himself a zealous adversary of Śaṅkara and follower of Rāmānuja) fifteen perhaps adhere to Rāmānuja, five to Mādhva, five to Vallabha, and seventy-five to Śaṅkarācārya.

This fact may be for poor India in so many misfortunes a great consolation; for the eternal interests are higher than the temporary ones; and the system of the Vedānta, as founded on the Upaniṣads and Vedānta Sūtras and accomplished by Śaṅkara'a commentaries on them,—equal in rank to Plato and Kant—is one of the most valuable products of the genius of mankind in his researches of the eternal truth,—as I propose to show now by a short sketch of Śaṅkara's Advaita and comparison of its principal doctrines with the best that occidental philosophy has produced till now.

Taking the Upaniṣads, as Śaṅkara does, for revealed truth with absolute authority, it was not an easy task to build out of their materials a consistent philosophical system, for the Upaniṣads are in Theology, Cosmology and Psychology full of the hardest contradictions. So in many passages, the nature of Brahman is painted in various and luxuriant colours, and again we read, that the nature of Brahman is quite unattainable to human words, to human understanding;—so we meet sometimes longer reports explaining how the world has been created by Brahman, and again we are told, that there is no world besides Brahman, and all variety of things is mere error and illusion;—so we have fanciful descriptions of the *Saṁsāra*, the way of the wandering soul up the heaven and back to the earth, and again read that there is no variety of souls at all, but only one *Ātman*, who a fully and totally residing in every being.

Śaṅkara in these difficulties created by the nature of his materials, in face of so many contradictory doctrines, which he has not allowed to decline and yet could not admit altogether,—has found a wonderful way out, which deserves the attention, perhaps the imitation of the Christian dogmatists in their embarrassments. He constructs out of the materials of the Upaniṣads two systems; one esoteric, philosophical (called by him *nirguṇa vidyā*, sometimes *pāramārthika avasthā*) containing the metaphysical truth for the few ones, rare in all times and countries, who are able to understand it; and another exoteric, Theological (*saguṇa vidyā, vyāvahārika avasthā*) for the general public, who wants images, not abstract truth, worship, not meditation.

I shall now point out briefly the two systems, esoteric and exoteric, in pursuing and confronting them through the four chief parts, which Śaṅkara's system contains, and which every complete philosophical system must contain :—

I. Theology, the doctrine of God or of the philosophical principle.

II. Cosmology, the doctrine of the world.

III. Psychology, the doctrine of the soul.

IV. Eschatology, the doctrine of the last things, the things after death.

I. Theology

The Upaniṣads swarm with fanciful and contradictory descriptions of the nature of Brahman. He is the all-pervading *ākāśa*, is the *puruṣa* in the sun, the *puruṣa* in the eye; his head is the heaven, his eyes are sun and moon, his breath is the wind, his footstool the earth; he is infinitely great as soul of the universe and infinitely small as the soul in us; he is in particular the *Īśvara*, the personal God, distributing justly reward and punishment according to the deeds of man. All these numerous descriptions are collected by Śaṅkara under the wide mantle of the exoteric theology, the *saguṇa vidyā* of Brahman, consisting of numerous "*vidyās*" adopted for approaching the Eternal Being not by the way of knowledge but by the way of worshipping, and having each its particular fruits. Mark, that also the conception of God as a personal being, an *Īśvara,* is merely exoteric and does not give us a conform knowledge of the Ātman;—and indeed, when we consider what is personality, how narrow in its limitations, how closely connected with egoism the counterpart of Godly essence, who might think so low of God, to impute him personality?

In the sharpest contrast to these exoteric *vidyās* stands the esoteric, *nirguṇa vidyā* of the Ātman! and its fundamental tenet is the absolute inaccessibility of God to human thoughts and words :

यतो वाचो निवर्तन्ते अप्राप्य मनसा सह। Tait. Up. 2.9

and again :

अविज्ञातं विजानतां विज्ञानमविजानताम्।

and the celebrated formula occurring so often in Bṛhadāraṇyaka-Upaniṣad; *neti ! neti !*, viz., whatever attempt you make to know the Ātman, whatever description you give of him, I always say : *na iti, na iti,* it is not so, it is not so! Therefore, the wise *Bhava,* when asked by the king Vashkalin to explain the Brahman, kept silence. And when the king repeated his request again and again, the *ṛṣi* broke out into the answer : "I tell it you, but you don't understand it; *kuto yam ātmā,* this Ātma is silence"! We know it now by the Kantian philosophy, that the answer of *Bhava* was correct, we know it, that the very organisation of our intellect [which is bound once for ever to its innate forms of intuition, space, time, and causality] excludes us from a knowledge of the spaceless, timeless, Godly reality for ever and ever. And yet the Ātman, the only Godly being, is not unattainable to us, is even not far from us, for we have it fully and totally in ourselves as our own metaphysical entity; and here when returning from the outside and apparent world to the deepest secrets of our own nature, we may come to God, not by knowledge, but by *anubhava*, by absorption into our own self. There is a great difference between knowledge, in which, subject and object are distinct from each other, and *anubhava* where subject and object coincide in the same. He who by *anubhava* comes to the great intelligence, *"aham brahma asmi,"* obtains a state called by Śaṅkara *Samradhanam*, accomplished satisfaction; and indeed, what might he desire, who feels and vows himself as the sum and totality of all existence.

II. Cosmology

Here again we meet the distinction of exoteric and esoteric doctrine, though not so clearly severed by Śaṅkara as in other parts of his system.

The exoteric Cosmology according to the natural but erroneous realism [*avidyā*] in which we are born, considers this world as the reality and can express its entire dependency of Brahman only by the mythical way of a creation of the world, by Brahman. So a temporal creation of the world, even as in the Christian documents, is also taught in various and well-known passages of the Upaniṣads. But such a creation of the material world by an immaterial cause, performed in a certain point of time after an eternity elapsed uselessly, is not only against the demands of human reason and natural science, but also against another important doctrine of the Vedānta, which teaches and must teach (as we shall see hereafter) the beginninglessness of the migration of souls," *saṁsārasya anaditvam*. Here the expedient of Śaṅkara is very clever and worthy of imitation. Instead of the temporary creation once forever of the Upaniṣads, he teaches that the world in great periods is crested and re-absorbed by Brahman (referring to the misunderstood verse of the Ṛgveda (10.190.3) : सूर्यचन्द्रमसौ धाता यथा पूर्वमकल्पयत् this mutual creation and re-absorption lasts from eternity) and no creation can be allowed by our system to be a first one, and that for good reasons, as we shall see just now. If we ask : *Why* God has created the world? The answers to this question are generally very unsatisfactory. For His own glorification? How may we attribute to him so much vanity!—For his particular amusement? But He was an eternity without this play-toy!—By love of mankind? How may He love a thing before it exists; and how may it be called love, to create millions for misery and eternal pain!—The Vedānta has a better answer. The never-ceasing new-creation of the world is a moral necessity connected with the central and most valuable doctrine of the exoteric Vedānta, the doctrine of Saṁsāra.

Man, says Śaṅkara, is like a plant. He grows, flourishes, and at the end, he dies but not totally. For as the plant, when dying, leaves behind it the seed, of which, according to its quality, a new plant grows;—so, man, when dying, leaves his *Karma*, the good and bad works of his life, which must be rewarded and punished in another life after this. No life can be the first, for it is the fruit of previous actions, nor the last, for its actions must be expiated in a next following life. So the *Saṁsāra* is without beginning and without end, and the new creation of the world after every absorption into Brahman is a moral necessity. I need not point out, in particular here in India, the high value of this doctrine of *Saṁsāra* as a consolation in the distresses, as a moral agent in the temptation of life;—I have to say here only, that the *Saṁsāra,* though not the *Absolute Truth,* is a mythical representative of truth which, in itself, is unattainable to our intellect; mythical is this theory of metempsychosis only in so far as it invests in the forms of space and time what really is spaceless and timeless, and therefore beyond the reach of our understanding. So the *Saṁsāra* is just so far from the truth, as the *saguṇa vidyā* is from the *nirguṇa vidyā;* it is the eternal truth itself, but [since we cannot conceive it otherwise] the truth in an allegorical form, adopted to our human understanding. And this is the character of the whole exoteric Vedānta, whilst the esoteric doctrine tries to find out the philosophical, the Absolute Truth.

And so we come to the esoteric Cosmology, whose

simple doctrine is this, that in reality there is no manifold world, but only Brahman, and that what we consider as the world is a mere illusion (*māyā*) similar to a *mṛgatṛṣṇīkā*, which disappears when we approach it, and not more to be feared than the rope, which we took in the darkness for a serpent. There are, as you see, many similes in the Vedānta, to illustrate the illusive character of this world, but the best of them is perhaps when Śaṅkara compares our life with a long dream :—a man whilst dreaming does not doubt of the reality of the dream, but this reality disappears in the movement of awakening, to give place to a truer reality, which we were not aware of whilst dreaming. The life a dream! This has been the thought of many wise men from Pindar and Sophocles to Shakespeare and Calderon de la Barca, but nobody has better explained this idea, than Śaṅkara. And indeed, the moment when we die may be to nothing so similar as to the awakening from a long and heavy dream; it may be, that then heaven and earth are blown away like she nightly phantoms of the dream, and what then may stand before us? or rather in us? Brahman, the eternal reality, which was hidden to us till then by this dream of life !—This world is *māyā*, is illusion, is not the very reality, that is the deepest thought of the esoteric Vedānta, attained not by calculating *tarka* but by *anubhava*, by returning from this variegated world to the deep recess of our own self (*Ātman*). Do so, if you can, and you will get aware of a reality, very different from empirical reality, a timeless, spaceless, changeless reality, and you will feel and experience that whatever is outside of this only true reality is mere appearance, is *māyā*, is a dream!—This was the way the Indian thinkers went and, by a similar way, shown by Parmenides. Plato came to the same truth, when knowing and teaching that this world is a world of shadows, and that the reality is not in these shadows, but behind them. The accord here of Platonism and Vedāntism is wonderful, but both have grasped the great metaphysical truth by intuition; their tenet is true, but they are not able to prove it, and in so far they are defective. And here a great light and assistance to the Indian and the Grecian thinker comes from the philosophy of Kant, who went quite another way, not the Vedāntic and Platonic way of intuition, but the way of abstract reasoning and scientific proof. The great work of Kant is an analysis of human mind, not in the superficial way of Locke, but getting to the very bottom of it. And in doing so, Kant found, to the surprise of the world and of himself, that three essential elements of this outside world, *viz.*, space, time and causality, are not, as we naturally believe, eternal fundaments of an objective reality, but merely subjective, innate, intuitive forms of our own intellect. This has been proved by Kant and by his great disciple Schopenhauer with mathematical evidence, and I have given these proofs [the fundament of every scientific metaphysics] in the shortest and clearest form in my "Elemete der, Metaphysik"—a book which I am resolved now to get translated into English, for the benefit not of the Europeans [who may learn German] but of my brothers in India, who will be greatly astonished to find in Germany the scientific substruction of their own philosophy, of the Advaita Vedānta! For Kant has demonstrated that space, time and causality are not objective realities, but only subjective forms of our intellect, and the unavoidable conclusion is this, that the world, as far as it is extended in space, running on in time, ruled throughout by causality, in so far is merely a representation of my mind and nothing beyond it. You see the concordance of India, Grecian and German metaphysics; the world is *māyā*, is illusion, says Śaṅkara;—it is a world of shadows, not of realities, says Plato;—it is "appearance only, not the thing in itself," says Kant. Here we have the same doctrine in three different parts of the world, but the scientific proofs of it are not in Śaṅkara, not in Plato, but only in Kant.

III. Psychology

Here we convert the order and begin with the esoteric Psychology, because it is closely connected with the esoteric Cosmology and its fundamental doctrine; the word is *māyā*.

All is illusive, with one exception, with the exception of my own Self, of my Ātman. My Ātman cannot be illusive, as Śaṅkara shows, anticipating the *"cogito, ergo sum"* of Descartes,—for he who would deny it, even in denying it, witnesses its reality. But what is the relation between my individual, soul the *Jīva-Ātman* and the highest soul, the *Parama-Ātman* or Brahman? Here Śaṅkara, like prophet, foresees the diviations of Rāmānuja, Mādhva and Vallabha and refutes them in showing that the *Jīva* cannot be a part of Brahman [Rāmānuja], because Brahman is without parts [for it is timeless and spaceless, and all parts are either successions in time or co-ordinations in space,—as we may supply],—neither a different thing from Brahman [Mādhava], for Brahman is *ekam eva advitīyam,* as we may experience by *anubhava,*—nor a metamorphose of Brahman [Vallabha], for Brahman is unchangeable [or, as we know now by Kant, it is out of causality). The conclusion is, that the *Jīva,* being neither a part or a different thing, nor a variation of Brahman, must be the *Paramātman* fully and totally himself, a conclusion made equally, by the Vedānta in Śaṅkara, by the Platonic Plotinos, and the Kantian Schopenhauer. But Śaṅkara in his conclusions goes perhaps further than any of them. If really our soul, says he, is not a part of Brahman but Brahman himself, then all the attributes of Brahman, all-pervadingness, eternity, almightiness [scientifically spoken; exemption of apace, time, causality] are ours; *ahaṁ brahma asmi,* I am Brahman, and consequently I am all-pervading [spaceless] eternal (timeless,) almighty [not limited in my doing by causality]. But these godly qualities are hidden in me, says Śaṅkara, as the fire is hidden in the wood and will appear only after the final deliverance.

What is the cause of this concealment of my godly nature? The *Upādhis,* answers Śaṅkara, and with this answer, we pass from the centric to the esoteric psychology. The *Upādhis* are manas and *indriyas, prāṇa* with its five branches, *sūkṣmaṃ śarīram,*—in short, the whole psychological apparatus, which, together with a factor changeable from birth to birth, with my *karman*, accompanies my *Ātman* in all his ways of migration without infecting his Godly nature, as the crystal is not infected by the colour painted over it. But wherefrom originate these *Upādhis*? They form, of course, part of the *māyā*, the great world illusion, and like *māyā*, they are based in our innate *avidyā* or ignorance, a merely negative power and yet strong enough to keep us from our Godly existence. But now, from where comes the *avidyā*, this primeval cause of ignorance, sin, and misery? Here all philosophers in India and Greece and everywhere have been defective, until Kant came to show us that the whole question is inadmissible. You ask for the cause of *avidya*, but she has no cause; for causality goes only so far as this world of the *Saṁsāra* goes, connecting each link of it with another, but never beyond *Saṁsāra* and its fundamental characteristic, the *avidyā*. In enquiring after a cause of *vidyā* with *māyā*, *Saṁsāra* and *Upādhis*, you abuse, as Kant may teach us, your innate mental organ of causality to penetrate into a region for which it is not made and where it is no more available. The fact is, that we are here in ignorance, sin and misery, and that we know the way out of them, but the question of a cause for them is senseless.

IV. Eschatology

And now a few words about this way out of the *Saṁsāra*, and first about the exoteric theory of it. In the ancient time of the hymns there was no idea of *Saṁsāra*, but only rewards in heaven and [somewhat later] punishment in a dark region [*padaṁ gabhiram*], the precursor of the later hells. Then the deep theory of *Saṁsāra* came up, teaching reward and punishment in the form of a new birth on earth. The Vedānta combines both theories, and so he has a double expiation, first in heaven and hell, and then again in a new existence on the earth. This double expiation is different [1] for performers of good works, going the *Pitṛyāna*, [2] for worshippers of the *Saguṇa Brahma*, going the *Devayāna*, (3) for wicked deeds, leading, to what is obscurely hinted at in the Upaniṣads as the *Tṛtīyam Sthānam*, the third place—[1] the *Pitṛyāna* leads through a succession of dark spheres to the moon there to enjoy the fruits of the good works, and, after their consumption, back to an earthly existence. [2] The *Devayāna* leads through a set of brighter spheres to Brahman, without returning to the earth (तेषां न पुनरावृत्तिः). But this Brahman is only *Saguṇa* Brahma, the object of worshipping, and its true worshippers, though entering into this Saguṇa Brahma without returning, have to wait in it until they get *mokṣa* by obtaining *samayogadarśanam*, the full knowledge of the *Nirguṇa* Brahma. (3) The *Tṛtīyaṃ Sthānam*, including the later theories of hells, teaches punishment in them, and again punishment, by returning to earth in the form of lower castes, animals, and plants. All these verious and fantastical ways of *Saṁsāra* are considered as true, quite as true as this world is, but not more. For the whole world and the whole way of *Saṁsāra* is valid and true for those only who are in the *avidyā*, not for those who have overcome her, as we have to show now.

The esoteric Vedānta does not admit the reality of the world nor of the *Saṁsāra*, for the only reality is Brahman, seized in ourselves as our own Ātman. The Knowledge of this Ātman, the great intelligence : "*ahaṁ Brahma asmi*," does not produce *mokṣa* [deliverance], but is *mokṣa* itself. Then we obtain what the Upaniṣads say :

मिद्यते हृदयग्रन्थिः छिद्यन्ते सर्वसंशयाः।
क्षीयन्ते चास्य कर्माणि तस्मिन्दृष्टे परावरे।

–*Muṇḍakopaniṣad*, 2.2.8

When seeing Brahma as the highest and the lowest everywhere, all knots of our heart, all sorrows are split, all doubts vanish, and works become nothing. Certainly, no man can live without doing works, and so also the *Jīvanmukta*; but he knows it, that all these works are illusive, as the whole world is, and therefore they do not adhere to him nor produce for him a new life after death. And what kind of works may such a man do?—People have often reproached the Vedānta with being defective in morals, and, indeed, the Indian genius is too contemplative to speak much of works; but the fact is, nevertheless, that the highest and purest morality is the immediate consequence of the Vedānta. The Gospels fix quite correctly as the highest law of morality : "love your neighbour as yourselves." But why should I do so, since, by the order of nature, I feel pain and pleasure only in myself, not in my neighbour? The answer is not in the Bible [this venerable book being not yet quite free of Semetic realism], but it is in the Veda, is in the great formula *"tat tvam asi,"* which gives in three words metaphysics and morals altogether. You shall love your neighbour as yourselves,—because you are your neighbour, and mere illusion makes you believe, that your neighbour is something different from yourselves. Or in the words of the *Bhagavatgītā* :—he, who knows himself in everything and everything in himself, will not injure himself, by himself. This is the sum and tenor of all morality, and this is the standpoint of a man knowing himself as a Brahman. He feels himself as everything,—so he will not desire anything, for he has whatever can be had; he feels himself as everything—so he will not injure anything, for nobody injures himself. He lives in the world, is surrounded by its illusions but not deceived by them; like the man suffering from *timira,* who sees two moons but knows that there is one only, so the *Jīvanmukta* sees the manifold world and cannot get rid of seeing it, but he knows that there is only one being, Brahman, the Ātman, his own Self, and he verifies it by his deeds of pure uninterested morality. And so he expects his end, like the potter expecting the end of the twirling of his wheel, after the vessel is ready. And then, for him, when death comes, no more *Saṁsāra* : न तस्या प्राणा उत्क्रामन्ति। He enters into Brahman, like the streams into the ocean : he leaves behind him *nāma* and *rūpam*, he leaves behind

यथा नद्यः स्यन्दमानाः समुद्रे
अस्तं गच्छन्ति नामरूपे विहाय।
तथा विद्वान् नामरूपाद्विमुक्तः
परात्परं पुरुषमुपैति दिव्यम्॥

–*Muṇḍakopaniṣad*, 3.2.8

individuality, but he does not leave behind him his *Ātman*, his self. It is not the falling of the drop into the infinite ocean, it is the whole ocean, becoming free from the fetters of ice, returning from his frozen state to what he is really and has never ceased to be, to his own all prevading, eternal, all mighty nature. And so the Vedānta, in it unfalsified form, is the strongest support of pure morality, is the greatest consolation in the sufferings of life and death,—Indians, keep to it!—

The Vedānta Philosophy[1]

Swami Vivekananda

The Vedānta philosophy, as it is generally called at the present day, really comprises all the various sects that now exist in India. Thus there have been various interpretations, and to my mind they have been progressive, beginning with the dualistic or *Dvaita* and ending with the non-dualistic or *Advaita*. The word *Vedānta* literally means the end of the Vedas,—the Vedas being the scriptures of the Hindus.[2] Sometimes in the West, by the Vedas are meant only the hymns and rituals of the Vedas. But at the present time these parts have almost gone out of use, and usually by the word *Vedas* in India, the Vedānta is meant. All our commentators, when they want to quote a passage from the scriptures, as a rule, quote from the Vedānta, which has another technical name with the commentators—the Śrutis.[3] Now all the books

1. The above address was delivered before the Graduate Philosophical Society of Harvard University, in March 1896.
2. The Vedas are divided mainly in two portions : the *Karmakāṇḍa* and the *Jñānakāṇḍa*,—the work-portion and the knowledge-portion. To the *Karmakāṇḍa* belong the famous hymns and the rituals or Brāhmaṇas. Those books which treat of spiritual matters apart from ceremonials, are called Upaniṣads. The Upaniṣads belong to the *Jñānakāṇḍa* or knowledge-portion. It is not that all the Upaniṣads came to be composed as a separate portion of the Vedas. Some are interspersed among the rituals, and at least one is in the Saṁhitā or hymn-portion. Sometimes the term *Upaniṣads* is applied to books which are not included in the Vedas,—*e.g.*, the Gītā; but as a rule it is applied to the philosophical treatises scattered through the Vedas. Those treatises have been collected, and are called the Vedānta.
3. The term *Śruti*,—meaning "that which is heard,"—though including the whole of the Vedic literature, is chiefly applied by the commentators to the Upaniṣads.

known by the name of the Vedānta were not entirely written after the ritualistic portions of the Vedas. For instance, one of them—the Īśa Upaniṣad—forms the fortieth chapter of the Yajur Veda, that being the oldest part of the Vedas. There are, other Upaniṣads[1] which form portions of the Brāhmaṇas or ritualistic writing; and the rest of the Upaniṣads are independent, not comprised in any of the Brāhmaṇas or other parts of the Vedas; but there is no reason to suppose that they were entirely independent of other parts, for, as we well know, many of these have been lost entirely, and many of the Brāhmaṇas have become extinct. So it is quite possible that the independent Upaniṣads belonged to some Brāhmaṇas, which, in course of time, fell into disuse, while the Upaniṣads remained. These Upaniṣads are also called Forest Books or Araṇyakas.

The Vedānta, then, practically forms the scriptures of the Hindus, and all systems of philosophy that are orthodox have to take it as their foundation. Even the Buddhists and Jains, when it suits their purpose, will quote a passage from the Vedānta as authority. All schools of philosophy in India, although they claim to have been based upon the Vedas, took different names for their systems. The last one, the system of Vyāsa, took its stand upon the doctrines of the Vedas more than the previous systems did, and made an attempt to harmonize the preceding philosophies, such as the Sāṁkhya and the Nyāya, with the doctrines of the Vedānta. So it is especially called the Vedānta. Philosophy; and the Sūtras or Aphorisms of Vyāsa are in modern India, the basis of the Vedānta Philosophy. Again, these Sūtras of

1. The Upaniṣads are said to be one hundred and eight in number. Their dates cannot be fixed with certainty,—only it is certain that they are older than the Buddhistic movement. Though some of the minor Upaniṣads contain allusions indicating a later date, yet that does not prove the later date of the treatise, as, in very many cases in Sanskrit literature, the substance of a book though of very ancient date, receives a coating, as it were, of later events in the hands of the sectarians, to exalt their particular sect.

Vyāsa have been variously explained by different commentators. In general, there are three sorts of commentators[1] in India now; and from their interpretations have arisen three systems of philosophy and sects. One is the dualistic or Dvaita : a second is the qualified non-dualistic or Viśiṣṭādvaita; and a third is the non-dualistic or Advaita. Of these, the dualistic and qualified non-dualistic include the largest number of the Indian people. The non-dualistic are comparatively few in number. Now I will try to lay before you the ideas that are contained in all these three sects; but before going on, I will make one remark,—that these different Vedānta systems have one common psychology, and that is, the psychology of the Sāṁkhya system. The Sāṁkhya psychology is very much like the psychologies of the Nyāya and Vaiśeṣika systems, differing only in minor particulars.

---

1. The commentaries are of various sorts, such as the Bhāṣya, Ṭīkā, Tippani; Churni, etc.,—of which all except the Bhāṣya are explanations of the text or difficult words in the text. The Bhāṣyas is not properly a commentary, but the elucidation of a system of philosophy out of texts, the objects being not to explain the words, but to bring out a philosophy. So the writer of a Bhāṣya expands his own system, taking texts as authorities for his system.

   There have been various commentaries on the Vedānta. Its doctrines found their final expression in the philosophical Aphorisms of Vyāsa. This treatise, called the Uttara Mīmāṁsā, is the standard authority of Vedāntism,—nay, is the most authoritative exposition of the Hindu scriptures. The most antagonistic sects have been compelled, as it were, to take up the texts of Vyāsa, end harmonize them with their own philosophy. Even in very ancient times, the commentators on the Vedānta philosophy formed themselves into the three celebrated Hindu sects of dualists, qualified non-dualists, and non-dualists. The ancient commentaries are perhaps lost; but they have been revived in modern times by the post-Buddhistic commentators, Śaṅkara, Rāmānuja, and Mādhva. Śaṅkara revived the non-dualistic form, Rāmānuja, the qualified non-dualistic form of the ancient commentator Bodhāyana, and Mādhva, the dualistic form. In India, the sects differ mainly in their philosophy; the difference in rituals is slight, the basis of their philosophy and religion being the same.

All the Vedantists agree on three points. They believe in God, in the Vedas as revealed, and in cycles. We have already considered the Vedas. The belief about cycles is as follows :—All matter throughout the universe is the outcome of one primal matter called Ākāśa; and all force whether gravitation, attraction or repulsion, or life, is the outcome of one primal force called *prāṇa*. *Prāṇa* acting on Ākāśa is creating or projecting[1] the universe. At the beginning of a cycle, Ākāśa is motionless, unmanifested. The Prāṇa begins to act, more and more, creating grosser and grosser forms out of Ākāśa,—plants, animals, men, stars, and so on. After an incalculable time, this evolution ceases and involution begins, everything being resolved back through finer and finer forms into the original Ākāśa and Prāṇa, when a new cycle follows. Now there is something beyond Ākāśa and Prāṇa. Both can be resolved into a third thing called Mahat,—the Cosmic Mind. This Comic Mind does not creat Ākāśa and Prana, but changes itself into them.

We will now take up the beliefs about mind, soul and God. According to the universally accepted Sāṁkhya psychology, in perception, in the case of vision, for instance,—there are, first of all, the instruments or *Karaṇas* of vision,—the eyes. Behind the instruments—the eyes—is the organ of vision or *Indriya,*—the optic nerve and its centres,—which is not the external instrument, but without which the eyes will not see. More still is needed for perception. The mind or *Manas* must come and attach itself to the organ. And besides this, the sensation must be carried to the intellect or *Buddhi,*—the determinative, reactive state of the mind. When the reaction comes from *Buddhi,* along with it flashes the external world and egoism. Here then is the will; but everything is not complete. Just as every picture,

1. The word which is "creation" in your language is, in Sanskrit, exactly "projection," because there is no sect in India which believes in creation as it is regarded in the West—a something coming out of nothing. What we mean by creation is projection of that which already existed.

being composed of successive impulses of light, must be united on something stationary to form a whole, so all the ideas in the mind must be gathered and projected on something that is stationary—relatively to the body and mind,—that is, on what is called the Soul or Puruṣa or Ātman.

According to the Sāṁkhya philosophy, the reactive state of the mind called *Buddhi* or intellect, is the outcome, the change, or a certain manifestation of the *Mahat* or Cosmic Mind. The *Mahat* becomes changed into vibrating thought; and that becomes in one part changed into the organs and in the other part into the fine particles of matter. Out of the combination of all these, the whole of this universe is produced. Behind even *Mahat*, the Sāṁkhya conceives of a certain state which is called *Avyaktam* or unmanifested, where even the manifestation of mind is not present, but only the causes exist. It is also called Prakṛti. Beyond this Prakṛti, and eternally separate from it, is the Purusha, the Soul of the Sāṁkhya, which is without attributes and omnipresent. The Puruṣa is not the doer but the witness. The illustration of the crystal is used to explain the Puruṣa. The latter is said to be like a crystal without any colour, before which different colours are placed, and then it seems to be coloured by the colours before it, but in reality it is not. The Vedantists reject the Sāṁkhya ideas of the soul and nature. They claim that between them there is a huge gulf to be bridged over. On the one hand, the Sāṁkhya system comes to nature, and then at once it has to jump over to the other side and come to the soul, which is entirely separate from nature. How can these different colours, as the Sāṁkhya calls them, be able to act on that soul which, by its nature, is colourless? So the Vedantists, from the very first, affirm that this soul and this nature are one.[1] Even the dualistic

1. The Vedānta and the Sāṁkhya philosophy are very little opposed to each other. The Vedānta God developed out of the Sāṁkhya's Puruṣa. All the systems take up the psychology of the Sāṁkhya. Both the

Vedāntists admit that the Ātman or God is not only the efficient cause of this universe, but also the material cause. But they only say so in so many words. They do not really mean it, for they try to escape from their conclusions, in this way. They say there are three existences in this universe,—God, soul, and nature. Nature and soul are, as it were, the body of God, and in this sense it may be said that God and the whole universe are one. But this nature and all these various souls remain the beginning of a cycle do they become manifest; and when the cycle ends, they become fine, and remain in a fine state.

The Advaita Vedantists—the non-dualists—reject this theory of the soul, and having nearly the whole range of the Upaniṣads in their favour, build their philosophy entirely upon them. All the books contained in the Upaniṣads have one subject, one task before them,—to prove different from each other through all eternity. Only at the following theme : "Just as by the knowledge of one lump of clay we have the knowledge of all the clay in this universe so what is that, knowing which we know everything in the universe?" The idea of the Advaitists is to generalize the whole universe into one,—that something which is really the whole of this universe. And they claim that this whole universe is one, that is one Being manifesting itself in all these various forms. They admit that what Sāṁkhya calls nature, exists, but say that nature is God. It is the Being, the *Sat*, which has become converted into all this,—the universe, man, soul, and everything that exists. Mind and *Mahat* are but the manifestations of that one *Sat*. But then the difficulty arises that this would be pantheism. How came that *Sat* which is

---

Vedānta and the Sāṁkhya believe in the infinite Soul, only the Sāṁkhya believes there are many souls. According to the Sāṁkhya, this universe does not require any explanation from outside. The Vedānta believes there is the one Soul. which appears as many : and we build on the Sāṁkhya's analysis.

unchangeable, as they admit (for that which is absolute is unchangeable), is to be changed into that which is changeable and perishable? The advaitists here have a theory which they call *Vīvarta Vāda* or apparent manifestation. According to the dualists and the Sāṁkhyas, the whole of this universe is the evolution of primal nature, according to some of the Dualists, the whole of this universe is evolved from God. And according to the Advaitists proper, the followers of Śaṅkarācārya, the whole universe is the *apparent* evolution of God. God is the material cause of this universe, but not really, only apparently. The celebrated illustration used, is that of the rope and the snake, where the rope appeared to be the snake, but was not really so. The rope did not really change into the snake. Even so this whole universe as it exists, is that Being. It is unchanged, and all the changes we see in it are only apparent. The changes are caused by Deśa, Kāla, and *Nimitta* (space, time, and causation), or, according to a higher psychological generalisation, by *Nāma* and *Rūpa* (name and form). It is by name and form that one thing is differentiated from another. The name and form alone cause the difference. In reality, they are one and the same. Again, it is not, the Vedāntists say, that there is something as phenomenon and something as noumenon. The rope is changed into the snake apparently only; and when the delusion ceases, the snake vanishes. When one is in ignorance, he sees the phenomenon and does not see God. When he sees God, this universe vanishes entirely for him. Ignorance or *Māyā*, as it is called, is the cause of all this phenomenon,—the Absolute, the Unchangeable, being taken as this manifested universe. This *Māyā* is not absolute zero not non-existence. It is defined as neither existence nor non-existence. It is not existence, because that can be said only, of the Absolute, the Unchangeable, and in this sense-*Māyā* is non-existence. Again it cannot be said it is non-existence; for if it were, it could never produce the phenomenon. So it is something which is neither; and in the Vedānta philosophy, it is called Anirvachaniya or inexpressible. *Māyā* then is the real cause of this universe, *Māyā* gives the name and form to what Brahman or God gives the material; and the latter seems to have been transformed into all this. The Advaitists, then, have no place for the individual soul. They say individual souls are created by *Māyā*. In reality, they cannot exist. If there were only one existence throughout, how could it be that I am one, and you are one, and so forth? We are all one, and the cause of evil is the perception of duality. As soon as I begin to feel that I am separate from this universe, then first comes fear, and then comes misery. "Where one hears another, one sees another, that is small. Where one does not see another, where one does not hear another, that is the greatest, that is God. In that greatest is perfect happiness. In small things there is no happiness."

According to the Advaita philosophy, then this differentiation of matter, these phenomena, are, as it were for a time, hiding the real nature of man; but the latter really has not been changed at all. In the lowest worm, as well as in the highest human being, the same divine nature is present. The worm form is the lower form in which the divinity has been more overshadowed by *Māyā*; that is the highest form in which it has been least overshadowed. Behind everything the same divinity is existing, and out of this comes the basis of morality. Do not injure another. Love every one as your own self, because the whole universe is one. In injuring another, I am injuring myself; in loving another, I am loving myself. From this also springs that principle of Advaita morality which has been summed up in, one word,—self-abnegation. The Advaitist says this little personalized self is the cause of all my misery. This individualized self, which makes me different from all other beings, brings hatred and jealousy and misery, struggles and all other evils. And when this idea has been got rid of, all struggle will cease, all misery vanish. So this is to be given up. We must always hold ourselves ready, even to give up our lives for the lowest beings. When a man has become ready even to give up his life for a little insect, he has reached the perfection which the Advaitist wants to attain; and at the moment when he has become thus ready, the evil of ignorance falls away from him, and he will feel his own nature. Even in this life, he will feel that he is one with the universe. For a time, as it were, the whole of this phenomenal world will disappear for him, and he will realize what he is. But so long as the *Karma* of his body remains, he will have to live. This state, when the veil has vanished and yet the body remains for some time, is what the Vedāntists call the *Jīvan Mukti*, the living freedom. If a man is deluded by a mirage for some time, and one day the mirage disappears,—if it comes back again the next day or at some future time, he will not be deluded. Before the mirage first broke, the man could not distinguish between the reality and the deception. But when it has once broken, as long as he has organs and eyes to work with, he will see the image, but will no more be deluded. That fine distinction between the actual world and the mirage, he has caught, and the latter cannot delude him any more. So when the Vedāntist has realised his own nature, the whole world has vanished for him. It will come back again, but no more the same world of misery. The prison of misery has become changed into *Sat*, *Cit*, *Ānanda*,—Existence Absolute, Knowledge Absolute, Bliss Absolute,—and the attainment of this is the goal of the Advaita Philosophy.

The Vedāntic Doctrine of the Future Life[1]

Pandit Sitanath Tattvabhushan

1. Refutation of Materialism

In Hindu Philosophy, one misses the elaborate and long-drawn arguments for the immortality of the soul which form a prominent feature of the philosophical Theology of Europe. The explanation of this is no doubt to be found in the general unanimity of Hindu philosophers as regards the doctrine in question. All the six orthodox schools of Hindu Philosophy agree in thinking of the soul as not only immortal, but also as eternal. The heterodox school of Buddhist Philosophy, too, accepts the doctrine in a modified form. It is only out-and-out Materialists ike the Cārvākas that questioned it. There was therefore little occasion for our philosophers spending time and energy in proving that the soul does not perish with the body. But that the Materialist's arguments were not left quite unheeded, appears from controversial passages here and there in Hindu philosophical works,—passages which are apparently directed against the heretics just mentioned. For instance, in his commentary on the fifty-third and fifty-fourth aphorisms of the third *pada*, third chapter, of the *Brahmasūtras*, Śaṅkara first states and then argues against the views of the Lokayatikas or Cārvākas. The aphorisms commented upon occur in a place where no one would expect them, which shows perhaps that they were the result of an after-thought on the part of the author and

1. Reprint from, "the Indian Review".

the little interest he felt in the superficial speculations of the Materialists. I shall however, give the substance of both the arguments of these philosophers as stated by Śaṅkara and his refutation of those arguments. The reasonings of the Materials amount to this :

> "Though consciousness is hidden in external objects, it becomes manifest in these objects when they form an organism just as the intoxicating power hidden in certain objects is manifested when they are made into wine. There is, therefore, no soul apart from the body, which is capable of either going to heaven or attaining liberation. The properties of an object are those that exist and cease to exist in its absence. Heat and light are, in this sense, properties of fire. Now, the vital functions, sensibility, memory and the like, which are believed to be properties of the soul, are found in the body, and not found without the body. They are, therefore, not the properties of an extra-organic object, but really properties of the body."

Śaṅkara's reply, which is an amplification of the aphorisms referred to, is, in substance, this :

> "If the properties of the soul are to be set down as properties of the body because they exist, while the body exists, why should not they be concluded as *not* properties of the body for their not existing while the body exists. Form and such other qualities, which are really properties of the body, exist so long as the body exists; but the vital functions and the rest do not exist in the body after death. Besides, form and other properties like it are perceived even by others, but the properties of the soul, sensibility, memory, etc., are not perceived by anyone else than the soul to which they belong. Then again, one knows the existence of these properties in the body while it lives; how can one be sure that, at the destruction of one body, they are not

transmitted to another? Even the possibility of this refutes Materialism. Then, as to the true character of consciousness, the Materialist will perhaps admit that consciousness is the knowledge of matter and material objects. If so, he must also admit that inasmuch as matter and material objects are objects of consciousness, it cannot be their property. For matter to perceive matter is as impossible as it is for fire to burn itself, and for a dancer to climb upon his own shoulders. Form and other properties of matter cannot, we see, make themselves or other properties their objects. Inasmuch, therefore, as consciousness makes both internal and external things, its object, it is not a material property. If its distinction from material objects be admitted, its independence of them must also be admitted. Moreover, its identity in the midst of changing circumstances proves its externality. Remembrance and such states of the mind become possible only because the knowing self is recognised as the same in two successive states. Thus, in the consciousness, 'I saw this before', the seeing and the recognising self is known as the same. The argument that because preception takes place while the body exists, therefore it is a property of the body, has already been refuted. It is as valid an argument as that, because perception takes place while such materials as lamps, etc., are present, therefore it is a property of lamps etc. The body is only an instrument of perception like lamps, etc. Nor is the body absolutely necessary even as an insrument of perception inasmuch as a variety of perception takes place in the state of dreaming, when the body is inactive. Thus the existence of the soul, as something different from the body, is an irresistible fact."

II. The Law of *Karma*

The other pivot on which the Vedāntic doctrine of

immortality turns, is the doctrine of *Karma*,—the doctrine that every action must be followed by its proper effect. This doctrine is sometimes stated in such an abstract shape as to appear like a law of mechanical causality; but really, in its application to rational beings, it has an ethical aspect also. As an ethical law, it lays down, when stated in its broadest form, that every moral action must have a moral effect. In its popular form it prescribes happiness as the result of every virtuous act, and suffering, of every vicious act. But thus started, it looks very much like the Christian doctrine of justice,—the doctrine that every virtuous act deserves happiness as its reward and every vicious act necesistates suffering as its punishment. Reward and punishment are personal acts,—the awards of a personal judge, and the Christian doctrine of justice is necessarily connected with that of such a judge. Hindu thinkers, on the other hand, distinctly deny the personal character of the law of *Karma*. In the thirty-fourth aphorism of the first *pada*, second chapter of the *Brahmasūtras*, as well as in the commentary thereon, the results of the moral actions of rational beings are described as irrespective of Divine activity and as dependent on the free activity of indiviual agents. The *Bhagavad Gītā* also says, in the fourteenth verse of its fifth chapter : "The Lord creates neither people's actions nor their agency nor the fruits of their actions; in this matter, nature takes its course." Nevertheless, the impersonality of the moral law is not always consistently kept in view by Vedāntists, and the same *Gītā* which speaks rather mysteriously in some places, of nature as a cause other than God, describes the Supreme Being, in other places, as the Dispenser of Heaven and Hell as a reward of virtue and punishment of vice. Even though we may set down such descriptions as only occasional lapses into popular modes of thought, it must be admitted, on the other hand, that the Vedāntic conception of the moral order of the world is not, and could not be purely impersonal. The Universe being the manifestation of a conscious Being, a

Being embodying in himself the highest perfections, and the lives of individual rational beings being so many reproductions of the Divine life, ever tending to perfection, the moral order, with all the vicissitudes of rise and fall, suffering and enjoyment, must be held as teleological at the bottom, as having a grand purpose which it is fulfilling, though gradually, at every step. Though not personal, therefore, in the popular sense, the moral order, or in other words, the law of *Karma*, may be called personal in a higher sense,—in the sense of its fulfilling a Divine purpose. As such, it is a strong proof of the soul's immortality,—its continued moral activity in another sphere of life when one is closed to it. Every moral action, as the law lays down, must have a moral effect. If the effect is pleasant, the pleasantness in only incidental; it must lead to a certain elevation or degradation of the soul, as the case may be, but ultimately to the former,—to moral progress. If the effect is painful, the pain is only an instrument, like pleasure, for bringing about a certain moral effect. Moral actions, again, have a certain moral effect. Moral actions, again, have a certain collective effect. They all tend to build a moral character,—a character with fixed tendencies to thoughts, feelings and actions of a definite nature. Every rational being—and a rational being must be moral by virtue of his possessing reason—has such a character at the time of death, and the law of *Karma* demands that this character must be perpetuated,—must continue to have the effects which exist potentially in the moral forces embodied in it. To suppose a cessation of life and activity at the destruction of the body is, first of all, to suppose a violation of the law of universal causation understood in its broadest sense. The law of causation requires not only that every cause should have an effect, but that the effect should be adequate to the cause. Now, human character is an aggregate of moral cause, moral forces; its effects also should therefore be moral, and there can be no moral effects in the true sense without a conscious personal centre of activity,—without the perpetuation, that is, of the lives of moral agents. Secondly, to suppose an extinction of the soul at the death of the body, is to pronounce rational and moral life as purposeless,—to deny the moral order of the universe and to conceive it as the play of blind forces. If, therefore, there is a moral order in the universe, if rational life has a purpose that purpose cannot be anything higher than moral progress,—the attainment of perfection by rational beings; and such a purpose requires the perpetuation of the conscious life of individuals. The gradual elevation of the mere race, to which the moral efforts of individuals contribute,—an idea which seems to satisfy some thinkers,—does not fully meet the requirements of the case. There is no meaning in the elevation of a race unless the individuals composing it are conceived as elevated, and to say that one set of individuals exists in order to contribute to the elevation of another set or generation, is to deny the most essential characteristic of a rational being,—that of its being not an instrument or means to any other being or thing, but an end unto itself. Individuals do indeed contribute to the elevation of other individuals; but to say that an individual lives only for other individuals, is to make everything hopelessly relative to deny the existence of an absolute end and to eviscerate moral worth of its very essence,—its personal character. We thus see that the law of *Karma*, understood as just explained, guarantees the perpetuation of the moral life of every rational being and its gradual progress and final attainment of perfect union with the All-good, the ultimate end of existence.

III. The Law of Evolution Proves Pre-Existence

The next question that concerns us is the form of immortality conceived by the Vedānta. Does the soul remain disembodied in its future life or undergo a process of re-birth? With this question is connected that of the soul's pre-existence, its existence before a particular incarnation. The

Vedānta is decidedly of opinion that every individual soul passes through a practically infinite number of incarnations, —incarnations determined by its own moral activity and determining it in turn. The formation of a soul, *i.e.*, of a complex intellectual and moral organism, in the course of a few months or years, it apparently conceives as an impossibility. It will appear so also to the modern intellect if we take a number of most important facts into serious consideration. It is undeniable that we are born with definite intellectual and moral characters. Circumstances indeed affect and contribute to the formation of character; they, however, do not act upon empty minds and souls equal and identical in their blankness, but upon clearly defined moral powers and tendencies of infinite variety both in quality and quantity. If, in mature life, all formations, whether intellectual or moral, demand a history, an explanation in the form of a series of previous actions, and all differences a difference of history, does not the complexity and variety of endowments with which our present life begins, demand a similar explanation,—a similar history protected into the unknown past? A striking confirmation of the Vedāntic doctrine of the soul's pre-existence is supplied by the theory of evolution now so widely accepted. This theory seems distinctly to militate against the current supposition that the human soul is the work of about nine months' time. The human body has an almost incalculably longer history behind it. Its present form, with its nice adaptations and its wonderful capacity for multiplying itself, is the result of a series of evolutions extending through millions of years, during which it has passed through innumerable lower and tentative forms. It is a law of Nature that the time required for the evolution of an organism is long in proportion to its richness, niceness and complexity. The human mind, then—the richest, nicest and most complex of organisms,—far from requiring only nine months for its formation, would seem to demand a much longer period than any physical or physiological structure whatever. The theory of the transmission of acquired powers from father to son, cannot, it seems, go farther than explaining the superior richness and adaptability of the organisms with which succeeding generations are favoured compared with those possessed by their ancestors. The net result of experience, the acquired niceness of the organism, its fitness for longer action and thought may be, as it is said to be, transmitted to its reproductions. But unless the favoured organisms are occupied by superior minds, unless the laws that govern physiological evolution are acknowledged as obtaining in the spiritual world also, the current theory of transmitted experience does not seem sufficient to explain the variety and complexity of the human soul at its birth. The direct transmission of powers from one soul to another, and the origin of the soul of the child from that of the father,—suppositions that underlie current thinking on the subject,—are theories without any rational grounds whatever, and are hardly even conceivable. On the other hand, the analogy of physiological evolution points to a parallel process of spiritual evolution,—the gradual development of souls by experience gathered in each life, and their re-birth in fresh lives, the extent of their development determining the quality of the organisms occupied by them. In these re-incarnations, the souls may be conceived as carrying with them the result of their previous experiences, with the details dropped from memory, but the substantial progress in intellectual and moral power uninterrupted and ready to determine, and be increased by fresh experience.

IV. What Sleep and Re-waking Proves

Now, if these considerations help to solve the problem of pre-existence, they also help to solve the allied problem of re-incarnation. But I shall discuss the latter problem a little further. I have, in some of my writings, reffered to the phenomena of sleep and re-waking and forgetting and recollecting as having very important bearing on the philosophy of mind, and as facts from which our old Vedāntists drew the legitimate conclusions. I shall now show how these phenomena help in solving the problem of re-incarnation. It seems to me that, in relation to this problem, they have a double bearing, (1) they prove the continuance of the contents of the individual consciousness, with all their variety and limitations intact, even without the instrumentality of the body, and (2) they show the necessity of the body for the re-manifestation of these contents after their suspense in death. In profound dreamless sleep, our individuality, or rather the manifestation of individual life, suffers a partial suspense. The wave that constitutes it seems to return to the ocean. But this temporary suspense of individuality is not a merging, not a total sublation, of difference. The contents of every individual life are maintained intact,—in all their fulness and distinction. There is no loss and no mingling. When the time comes each individual starts up from the bosom of the Eternal, the ever-waking, with its wealth of conscious life undiminished, with its identity undimmed. Every one gets back what was his own and nothing but his own. There seems to be separate chambers in the Eternal Bosom for each individual to rest soundly and unmolested. Now, this fact seems to prove that the contents of our conscious individual life can exist in the Eternal Consciousness, with their totality and difference intact, even in the absence of the body, and its organs. However, instrumental our brain-cells and other organs may be in the re-production of the contents of consciousness in the state of re-waking, they cannot explain their persistence in the hours of sleep; far less can they be identified with those contents. It is not the body—not the brain, nor the nerves—that can be said to sustain thought. The contents of consciousness can be retained only in a conscious being. To say that they can exist in an unconscious form,—in a so-called 'sub-conscious region'—is to be actually guilty of a contradiction. Thoughts can persist, can retain their essence and identity, only in a thinking being remaining conscious and self-identical in the midst of change. The reproduction of such contents in us as 'I am the same being now that I was before,' 'this object is the same that I saw yesterday,' 'this idea is the same that occurred to me before I slept, and so on, implies that, during the temporary lapse of individual life, these ideas are retained as ideas and not as anything else in the very Being who is the basis of our lives, a Being who is thus seen to have an eternal, un-changing, ever-conscious aspect of his nature besides his intermittent manifestation as 'our' consciousness. As Śaṅkara says in his commentary on the *Brahmasūtras* II. 2, 31, 'Unless there exists one relating principle in the past, present and future, one, which is unchangeable and sees all things, the facts of remembrance, recognition, etc., which depend upon mental impressions requiring space, time and occasional cause, cannot be explained."

V. Individuality Requires Organism

But if the phenomena of sleep and awaking prove the continuance of the individual consciousness in the Universal, and its independence of physical conditions for this continuance, they also prove the independent of that life on such conditions for its actual manifestation. Sleep indicates the temporary exhaustion of nervous power. When, by continual activity, the nervous sysem has lost its strength, and requires refreshment from rest, it ceases to work, and the cessation of its activity is accompanied by a temporary suspense of consciousness in its individual manifestation. It is only when the strength of the organs has bean restored by sufficient rest, that the flow of thoughts and feelings that constitutes individual life re-commences, and the identity and continuity of individual, consciousness is re-established. In the waking state also, the health and vigour of mental life are found determined by the soundness and strength of the organism, and injuries to the organs specially connected with the manifestation of consciousness, are seen to materially affect the order and vividness of this manifestation. A valid induction from these patent facts is that the re-appearance of individual consciousness after the dissolution of the present body will require a fresh organism with essentially the same properties. We cannot indeed be absolutely sure that there are no other conditions of the re-manifestation of consciousness than those with which we are acquainted. But in the absence of any proof of the existence of such conditions, we cannot say that there are probably such conditions; nay we can hardly assert even their possibility. It seems barely possible that, as is asserted, at a certain stage of development, individuals acquire the power of disembodying themselves,—extricating themselves from their gross bodies and continuing their conscious lives in a subtle body imperceptible to the senses. That come such environment is required for the individual soul, seems to be axiomatic from its nature as a finite being. The *Sūkṣma Śarīra* spoken of in our theological books, the body that consists of the five vital airs, the five organs of knowledge in their subtle forms as powers, the five organs of action conceived in the same fashion, and egoity or reflected self-consciousness,—the body which is described as the vehicle of the soul's migration to the *Pitṛloka* and the *Brahmaloka*,—the regions of the *manas* and the Divine regions,—seems to be too fine for the purpose, which it is conceived as fulfilling. For locomotion and activity in space, a material body having extension and parts is necessary, and such a body must be supposed to belong to even the most and richly endowed of souls in the other world. But the evolution of such a fine ethereal body must be conceived to follow the same slowly acting laws that obtain in the region of gross-matter, and also to be dependent upon a corresponding growth of spiritual power. Admitting, therefore, the evolution of such a body in extraordinary cases, it may be safely laid down that so far as ordinary individual self is concerned, there is not the slightest probability of its reproduction and actual continuance except in connection with an organism similar to that which we possess in our present life.

VI. Ethical Life Implies Society, and Society Embodied Beings

From another point of view, re-incarnation seems to be the most probable form of immortality. The conditions of ethical progress would apparently be absent in a disembodied existence. The ethical life must be social. There is neither morality nor spirituality for an isolated being. Virtue is indeed personal, individual. There is no meaning in the purity of a society in which the individuals are not pure. But the purity of individuals and their continued growth in righteousness imply their inclusion in a society of which the members owe duties to one another, and in which a free exchange of thoughts and sentiments and as active co-operation in good work are possible. These things are inconceivable in a state of existence in which souls are disembodies; for it is through our bodies that we are able to communicate with one another. The very conditions of that spiritual life, then, which makes immortality necessary and desirable, require that souls should be re-born either in this very world or in others more or less similar to this.

VII. Objection from Forgetfulness Answered

An ever-recurring objection to the doctrine of pre-existence and re-incarnation is that we have no memory of a previous existence and cannot possibly remember the events of this life if we should be re-born, and that the enjoyment or suffering of the fruits of actions which have passed out of memory, involves an apparent injustice. The phenomena of sleep and re-waking and those of forgetting and recollecting, to which I have already referred, supply an answer to this objection. They prove an important truth which is often overlooked, and the overlooking of which lies at the basis of the objection just mentioned. That truth is that by passing out of our memory a fact does not cease to have connection with our mental life, and even to determine it materially. In an independent, self-sustained mind like the divine, the presence or absence of an idea can mean nothing less than its presence or absence in consciousness. If anything could possibly pass out of its cognisance, it would cease to have any existence for it. But this is not true of our finite minds, which are contained in and perpetually sustained by the Infinite. Facts are constantly going out of our individual consciousness and returning to it from the Divine mind, which form its eternal basis, and in which they are perpetually held. At the present moment, for instance, when I am intent upon writing this paper, how few of the manifold facts of my life are actually present with me! But they are nevertheless determining my present action from the background of my consciousness, in which they lie hidden. How many events have preceded and made it possible ! Most of them cannot, by any efforts I may make, be recalled, and will not perhaps revisit my mind any more. Some can be recalled, but are absent now. Others are starting into consciousness from the dark chambers of the mind in which they lay concealed only a few moments back. My present action is, it is clear, due to a certain permanent form which the mind has taken as the combined effects of these various classes of facts, and to the recurrence of a certain number of them. In the same manner, the moral character which I now possess, and which determines the ethical quality of my present actions is the combined result of a long series of thoughts, feelings and actions, many of which have passed entirely out of my consciousness, and many more which may be recalled only with great difficulty. But all these facts, are, in a sense, present with me in their effect, *i.e.*, my character, and if I now suffer in consequence of sins committed before, but now forgotten or enjoy the fruits of righteous conduct equally forgotten, I do not feel myself wronged in the one case or specially favoured in the other. In sound dreamless sleep, again, the facts of life, as we have already seen, beat a complete retreat from the field of consciousness and leave it utterly empty so far as its individual manifestation is concerned. But they are, by no means, lost in consequence of this temporary disappearance, and do not cease to determine waking life. Now, considered in the light of these facts, the objections to pre-existence, and re-incarnation reffered to are seen to be groundless. That we have at present no recollection of any previous state of existence, does not, in the first place, prove that it will never come back to our memory. For aught we know, its re-appearance may be waiting for conditions to be hereafter fulfilled. In the second place, even if it should so happen that such facts will never recur to us under any circumstances, it would not follow that they never occurred and are not determining our present life. As we have already seen, the richness and complexity of our minds even at the moment of birth, and their speedy development in definite lines under the varying circumstances of this life, point to a long mental history through which we have passed is the un-remembered past. In the third place, if, in our present life, we have to lose and gain constantly in consequence of actions which we have utterly forgotten, but which have, nevertheless, left lasting effects on our character, there can be no injustice in our enjoying or suffering the fruits of actions done in previous states of existence, and which though forgotten now, have yet made us what we are. And finally, it may also be that the few years during which we live in forgetfulness of our past lives, are, in proportion to the actual span of our existence, a much shorter period than are our hours of dreamless sleep in proportion to then total extent of our present life. The alleged recollection of previous states of existence by many persons characterised by uncommon purity of heart, is a subject which I simply mention and pass by; its discussion would be beyond the limited scope of this paper.

VIII. From Animal to Man

I shall refer to one more aspect of Vedāntic doctrine of the future life before I close. The law of evolution in the physical and physiological world points, as we have seen, to a similar law in the spiritual world. Does not the same law, we may now ask, testify to the reasonableness of the Vedāntic view that the animating principles of all creatures are substantially of the same nature and the transmigration of these principles from one species to another is quite possible? If man's body is linked to, and is the development of, the bodies of the lower animals where is the unreasonableness of thinking that his soul also has passed through a similar process of gradual development, having animated lower organism in the more remote periods of its pre-existence, gaining in intelligence and moral strength as it migrated into higher and higher organism and at last attaining humanity both physically and spiritually? Current European thought draws a hard and fast line between man and the lower animals and practically sets down the latter as soulless beings. Apart from the progress of philosophical speculation, the recent discoveries of natural historians as regards the highly developed social feelings of some of the lower animals and the existence in them of sentiments akin to the ethical, have been showing more and more clearly, day by day, the hastiness of such, a view, and it now seems impossible to imagine a gap between human consciousness in its lowest forms and the consciousness of the higher brutes. It seems quite probable therefore that psychological science will, in not a very distant future, confirm the anticipating of the Vedānta Philosophy and link together all conscious existence by a law similar to the law of physiological evolution. We shall then see with the eyes of science, as we already see with the eye of intellectual intuition, that the humanity of which we are so proud is an acquisition which has come to us as the result of a long struggle carried on through millions of years, leading us, under the slow but beneficial law of *karma*, through organic and spiritual conditions of an infinitely diverse nature, to that which seems to be the nearest to God. But the reverse process—from humanity to animality—which the old Vedāntists seem to have thought as likely as the other, seems to be quite improbable in the light of both natural and moral science Progress—from seed to tree, from child to man, from the jelly-fish to the highest mammalia, from barbarism to the highest civilisation—is the order of Nature, and so, while the teachings of the Vedānta, interpreted scientifically, inspire the hope that we shall one day be gods and partake of the divine blessedness, they leave no room for the fear that we may one day descend to that brute condition from which we have risen.

The Vedānta—Its Theory and Practice[1]

Swami Saradananda

Our subject this evening is the philosophy of the *Vedānta* and its application to the life of man. This high system of philosophy was evolved in India, thousands of years ago, but it is difficult to determine the precise date it was first evolved. We find its existence long before Buddhism and long before the age of the *Ramāyāṇa* and the *Mahābhārata,* the two great pre-Buddhistic epics of India. By examining all the different religions and sects that exist in India, we find the principles of the *Vedānta* underlie each one of them. Nay more, the *Ṛṣis* or seers of thoughts, the fathers of the *Vedānta,* claim that its principles underlie all the different religions that exist on the face of the earth and all that will come in future even. The goal which the *Vedānta* points at is the goal to which all religions, all society, all humanity, are rushing either consciously or unconsciously, through the process of evolution.

One great peculiarity of this philosophy is that it is not built around one person or prophet. It is founded on the "latter portion or the knowledge portion of the Vedas," as the term *Vedānta* shows. The term *Veda* is derived from the Sanskrit root *Vid,* to know, means, according to the oldest Hindu commentator, all the super-sensuous knowledge that has been revealed to man up to the present and that which will be is future. And to the books which kept the record of

1. A lecture delivered in America.

this knowledge, the term *Vedas* became applied later. Then the Vedic commentator goes on saying that this super-sensuous knowledge might be revealed not only to Hindus but to other people, and their experience should be regarded as *Vedas* also. The *Vedas* were divided into two great divisions, 'the work portion' which teaches man how, by the performance of duty, the observance of morality and other acts, he might go to heaven, a better of enjoyment, and "the knowledge portion" which teaches him that not even the enjoyments of heaven should be his aim inasmuch as they too are fleeting and transitory, but to go beyond all relativity and find in himself the Divine, the Centre of all Knowledge and power. Of course it took ages for the Hindu mind to evolve this system of philosophy.

Speaking of philosophy, we must always keep in mind that it never went against religion in India. They always went hand-in-hand. And religion, in order to appeal to man has a whole, should not only appeal to his heart but to his intellect also and therefore must have a sound basis of metaphysics. For is not man a compound being, a combination nation of reason and emotion and will? Can any religion satisfy him which does not fulfil all his highest aspirations on these fields?

The rapid march of Science and the wonderful discoveries it is making every day by the study of the external and the material world, is striking terror at the hearts of many. They seem to think that the foundation of religion is being undermined day by day and that the whole social fabric on this foundation is in imminent danger. But the seers of old who, by their study of the internal world, found the basis of religion, of morality, of duty, and, in short, of everything in that Unity which forms the background of this universe, that ocean of Knowledge, Bliss, Absolute from which the Universe has come out, if they were here to-day, would have rejoiced to find that, instead of undermining, Science is making the basis of religion stronger than ever inasmuch as it is rapidly approaching towards the same goal, the same Unity. And it must be so; for is not the Universe one connected whole? Is not the division of it into external and internal an arbitrary one? Can we ever know the external *per se?* Then again we speak of the natural laws which govern the external; but are laws anything else than the method or manner in which our mind connects into a link a series of phenomena? This Universe according to the *Vedānta* is one connected mass. Start from the external and you come to the internal and *vice versa.* It has come out of the Infinite ocean of Knowledge and Bliss and will go back to it again. It is evolving and involving from all eternity. View it as one unit and it can have no change, no motion. It is perfect and all change is within it. For change and motion is only possible when there is comparison, and comparison can only be made between two or more things. Again this chain of evolution and involution, of manifestation and returning to the unmanifested or seed form of nature, can have no beginning in time. To admit a beginning of it would be to admit the beginning of the Creator and not only that, but that he must be a cruel and partial Creator, who has produced all these diversities at the outset. Then again there would arise another difficulty, the Creator, the first cause, must either have been perfected or imperfected by the ere creation. So, according to the *Vedānta,* the creation is as much eternal as the Creator himself, only it sometimes remains in a manifested state and sometimes in an unmanifested. What then is the purpose, the motive of this creation, this eternal flow of evolution and involution ? The answer which the *Vedānta* gives is that it is a play of the Infinite. You cannot ascribe any motive to the perfect, the Absolute, without making Him imperfect. The infinite, the perfect, must have no motive to compel It to create. The Infinite must be absolutely free and independent, and the very conception of the finite, the relative, implies the existence of the Absolute. The Absolute is the only real existence and the Universe is but a speck in that infinite ocean of Knowledge and Bliss. He is playing with Himself and projecting this world of phenomena. He is appearing through all these masks of imperfection and at the same time He is remaining One and perfect in all splendour and glory. "He vibrates, and He does not vibrate. He is far and He is near; Ha is within all and He is without all this world of phenomena." "As the web-wombed spider projects and takes back the thread, as hair grows in the head of a man (without any effort), so this universe comes out of that infinite ocean of Knowledge and Bliss and goes back to It again.

Science by tracing the evolution to its cause has arrived at the laws of the survival of the fittest and sexual selection, for the change of one species into another. The *Vedānta* is one with it as regards the truth of the evolution, but differs from it inasmuch as it says that the cause of the change of one species into another is the struggle of the Divine within every form, to manifest Itself better and better. As one of our great philosophers has said, in the case of the irrigation of a field, where the tank is placed in a higher level, the water is always trying to rush into the field but is barred by a gate. Upon the gate, the water will rush in by its own nature. This struggle of the Divine has produced or evolved higher and higher forms up to the man form. It is going on still, and it will be completed only when the Divine will manifests Itself perfectly, without any bars or bolts to hinder Its expression. This highest point of evolution transcends even the conscious existence and so we shall call it the super-conscious existence. This stage of development has been reached by individuals long ago. Christ and Buddha and all the other great teachers which the world has produced, attained to that state. The whole of humanity is approaching towards that unconsciously. But is such a stage possible where the evolution will attain its completion? The *Vedānta* says it is. Every solution presupposes an involution. To admit an unending chain of will, will be to conceive motion in a straight line, which modern science has proved to be impossible. But what would take society ages and ages to attain, individuals can attain even in this life and have attained it as proved by the religious history of the world. For what are all the bibles but the records of experience of men who attained to that stags? Examine them and read between the lines and you will find that the same stage which the *Vedānta* expresses in the famous aphorism as "Thou art that Infinite Ocean of Knowledge and Bliss," (*Tat tvam asi*), is that which was expressed by Buddha as attaining to *Nirvāṇa* [perfected state] and by Christ as becoming as perfect as the Father in Heaven, and by the Muhammadan Sufis as becoming one with the Truth. The *Vedānta* claims that this idea of the oneness of *man* with the Divine, that the real nature of Him is infinite and perfect, is to be found in every religion in India or outside of it; only in some, the idea is expressed through mythology and symbology. It claims that what one man or a few men attained long before is the natural inheritance of all men and every one will attain to it sooner or later. Man, therefore, according to the *Vedānta*, is Divine, and everything that is strong, good and powerful in human nature is the expression of Divinity within him.

In this super-conscious existence lies the basis of all ethics. Attempts have been made in the present time to find a permanent basis of morality within the relative to no effect. Every one of us feels within himself that morality and unselfishness and doing good to others are good, and without these, neither the individual nor the nation can develop. Even men standing outside the pale of any religion are advancing them on utilitarian grounds, that we must do that which brings the greatest amount of good to the greatest number. But if we question why should we do that, why should I look upon my brother as myself and not try to secure the greatest amount of good to myself alone, even at the sacrifice of all else, no plausible answer is given. The answer which the *Vedānta* gives to this question is that you and I are not separate from this Universe. It is by mistake we think ourselves to be distinct and unconnected entities, independent of one another. All history, all science show that it is just the opposite, that this Universe is one connected whole, look at it from the external ocean of matter, in which our bodies but represent so many different points. Behind the external there is that one vast ocean of mind, in which our minds but represent so many different whirlpools and behind that is the Soul, the Self, the Absolute and Perfect. Everything in human life points towards this oneness. Our love, our sympathy, kindness, and doing good to others all are but expressions conscious or unconscious of this oneness of man with the universe. Consciously or unconsciously, every man feels it; consciously or unconsciously he tries to express it, that he is one with the universal Being and as such every soul his soul, and every body his body, that by injuring others he injures himself and by loving others he loves himself.

This gives rise to a subtle but unfounded question. Shall we lose our individuality when we attain the super-conscious stage, the highest point of evolution? The *Vedānta* questions in its turn, are we individuals as yet in the proper sense of the term? Does individuality mean the changing element in man or does it apply to the un-changeable essence in him? Do you apply the term individuality to the body and mind of man which is changing every minute? If so, there is no occasion for the former question inasmuch as we are losing or changing our individuality every minute of our existence. Think what great change have we, each one of us, undergone since we were born, think what a change for the wicked when he becomes a good member of society, or the primitive man when he becomes civilized, or think what great change of a barbarous individuality when through the process of evolution, the ape form changes into the man form? Do we lament the change of individuality in these cases? The *Vedānta* says, by developing your individuality, you rise to a point where you became a perfect individual. You change your apparent individuality, for a better and real one. The process of evolution is from lawlessness, through law, beyond law; from the unconscious, through the conscious, beyond the conscious. Our conscious existence, where every action is accompanied with a feeling of egoity, does not cover the whole of our existence. During sleep or in performing actions which are known as the automatic actions, there is no feeling of egoity present and yet we do exist though we enter a stage which is below, the conscious and inferior to it. In the higher stage of development also there is no feeling of egoity, but it is infinitely superior to the conscious. Apparently in a superficial view, the highest and the lowest stages of development seem to be one and the same but there is as much difference between the two as between darkness produced by the want of light and darkness produced by the excess of light and known in science as the polarisation of light. There is an illiterate and ignorant man, he enters, and comes out a sage, a prophet, a great seer of thought. He discovers in himself the eternal fountain-head of all knowledge and power; he finds the kingdom of heaven within. "For him," say the Vedas, "all doubts [and hankerings] vanish for ever and all selfish knots of the heart are cut asunder, the endless chain of cause and effect fades and dies for him who attains the Highest."

This attaining the super-conscious existence has been described in many religions as seeing and realising and feeling God. The rapid march of reason has proved beyond a doubt, that all our ideas of God are perfectly anthropomorphic, that we are creating our own mental representation. What is the necessity then for worshipping God? Why shall I worship my own mental creation? The history of evolution shows how the idea of God grows and develops with the growth of the man. Low from fetichism and animism, he comes to polytheism and thence to monotheism. Suggested by his own dreams or the love of his dead ancestors, or the stupendous forces in nature, the idea of a future existence dawns in his infant mind and he tries to peep behind the screen of the senses. How, in his search after the super-sensuous, he comes up gradually through the stages of ancestor-worship and nature-worship, to the recognition of many spirits or gods behind all the different mighty forces of nature and lastly how he comes to the conception of one supreme ruler at the head of these different gods and pays his homage to Him. Reason will say that, although this worship of the super-sensuous was a great motive power in bringing out his powers and developing his mind, yet all this time he has been worshipping his own mental creations, and now that his eyes have been opened, he ought to discard all these mistakes ideas of God. The *Vedānta* does not deny that all these different ideas of God are anthropomorphic but it asks in its turn, are not all our ideas of the external the same? Can we ever know the world but as our mind represents it to us, and has not science proved already that the senses are deceptive and can never know thing as they are? Therefore, if it is reasonable to reject all our ideas of God because they are anthropomorphic, it is reasonable also to throw away every other idea from the mind, but how many of us are willing to do so and have the power of doing so? Then again, though all that we know of anything are what our minds represent them to be, yet they help us in developing ourselves, and bringing us higher and higher. Then lastly what the *Vedānta* has to say in this point is that man is not wrong or mistaken in his worshipping all these different ideas of God, only he has been travelling from lower to higher truths. His progress in his world is not from error to truth but from lower and lower truths to higher and higher ones. Everything in this world, even truth itself is relative. What is truth for one state of things or one plane of existence is not truth for another state or another plane and the different ideas of God are nothing less than the different views of the Absolute, the Infinite from different planes of the relative. Supposing, for instance, we make a journey to the Sun, our view of the Sun changes every minute we proceed. With every step in advance we see newer and newer vision of the same Sun. The Sun which appeared to be a bright little disc grows larger and larger till at last when we reach the Sun itself, we see the Sun in its entirety. We know the Sun as it is. The Sun has not changed all the time, but our views of it have changed till at last we got the full view of the luminary. This is the progress of man towards the Infinite. His View of the Infinite has never become perfectly *nil*, but through the limitations of his senses, his intellect and all, he sees only a little bit of the infinite and worships it as God. The fault is not with the Infinite but with his own limited faculties. As he grows, these limitations become less and less and he sees the Infinite better and better till at last all his limitations fade away as mists before the rising Sun, and he grasps the Infinite in its entirety : he discovers in himself the Infinite ocean of Knowledge and Bliss. This has been beautifully expressed in the Vedas. "Two birds of bright golden plumage, inseparable companions of each other, are sitting on the same tree, the one on the higher and the other on the lower branches of it." The upper bird not caring to taste the sweet and bitter fruits of the tree, sits majestic in his own glory and sees the lower one tasting the fruits. As the lower bird gets the taste of the bitter fruit of the tree, he grows disgusted and looks up to the splendid vision above him of the upper bird and draws himself nearer to him. He forgets again the glorious vision in his love for the fruits of the tree and goes on tasting them as before till he tastes another bitter fruit. He grows disgusted again and advances a little more towards the bright vision before him. So on he alvances till at last when he reaches the upper bird, the whole vision changes and he finds himself to be the upper bird who was sitting in all splendour and majesty all the time.

The goal being thus the same in all religions, the *Vedānta* has no quarrel with any. It looks upon all the different religions as so many different ways for attaining that one indivisible ocean of Knowledge and Bliss. "As the different rivers, having their sources in different mountains, roll down through crooked or straight paths and at last come into the ocean—so all these various creeds and religions taking their start from different stand-points and running through crooked or straight courses, at last come unto Thee, Oh, Lord." The *Vedānta* condemns nobody, for it looks upon man not as he is at the present moment, but what he really is. It reaches that sooner, or later every man will discover his real nature and will know himself as the source of all knowledge, power and bliss. Will or *nil*, every man is advancing towards that through every act that he is doing here. The worker by doing good to others, the philosopher by developing his reason, the lover of God by developing and directing his emotions all, all will attain the super-conscious plane, the highest stage of development. What if a man be an atheist or agnostic? The question is, is he sincere and is he ready to sacrifice himself for the good of others and for the truth that he has known? The *Vedānta* says there is no fear for him. He will come to higher and higher truths and ultimately attain the highest. Allow infinite variation in religious thoughts. Follow your own but do not try to bring everybody to the same opinion. It can never be, for is not unity, in diversity the law of nature? And is not the goal the same though the roads are different? Do not make yourself the standard for the universe but know that Unity forms the background of this universe and whatever way man might travel, at last he will arrive at that.

The Vedānta for the World[1]

Swami Vivekananda

Religion—Our Life Principle

"A very small amount of religious work performed brings a very large amount of result"—are the eternal words of the author of the *Gītā*, and if that statement wanted an illustration, in my humble life I am finding every day the truth of that great saying. My work, gentlemen of Kumbakonam, has been very insignificant indeed, but the kindness and the cordiality of welcome that have met me at every step of my journey from Colombo to this city are simply beyond all expectations. Yet, at the same time, it is worthy of our traditions as Hindus, it is worthy of our race; for here we are the Hindu, race, whose vitality, whose life-principle, whose very soul, as it were, is in religion. I have seen a little of the world, travelling among the races of the West and the East; and everywhere I find among nations one great ideal which forms the backbone, so to speak, of that race. With some it is politics, with others it is social culture; others again have intellectual culture and so on for their national background. But this, our mother-land, has religion and religion alone for its basis, for its backbone, for the bed-rock upon which the whole building of its life has been based. Some of you may remember that, in my reply to the kind address which the people of Madras sent over to me in America, I pointed out the fact that a peasant in India has, in

1. Speech by Swami Vivekananda, at Kumbakonam, Madras, on his return in 1897 from the Chicago Parliament of Religions.

many respects, a better religions education than many a gentleman in the West, and to-day beyond all doubt, I myself am verifying my own words. There was a time when I would feel rather discontented at the want of information among the masses of India and the lack of thirst among them for information, but now I understand it. Where their interest lies, they are more eager for information than the masses of any other race that I have seen or have travelled among. Ask our peasants about the momentous political changes in Europe, the upheavals that are going on in European society. They do not know anything of these, nor do they care to know; but those very peasants,—even in Ceylon, detached from India in many ways, cut off from a living interest in India—I found the very peasants working in the fields there had already known that there was a Parliament of Religions in America, and that one of their men had gone over there, and that he had some success. Where, therefore, their interest is and there they are as eager for information as any other race; religion is the one and the sole interest of the people in India. I am not just now discussing whether it is good to have the vitality of the race in religious ideals or in political ideas, but so far it is clear to us, that for good or for evil, our vitality is concentrated in our religion. You cannot change it. You cannot destroy one thing and put in its place another. You cannot transplant a large growing tree from one soil to another and make it immediately take root there. For good or for evil the religious ideal has been flowing into India for thousands of years, for good or evil the Indian atmosphere has been filled with ideals of religion for shining scores of centuries, for good or evil we have been born and brought up in the very midst of these ideals of religion, till it has entered into our very blood, and tingles with every drop of it in our veins, and has become one with our constitution, become the very vitality of our lives. Can you give such a religion up without the rousing of the same energy in reaction, without filling the channel which that mighty river has cut out for itself in the course of thousands of years? Do you want that the Ganges should go back to its icy bed and begin a new course? Even if that were possible, it would be impossible for this country to give up her characteristic course of religious life and take up a new career of politics or something else for herself. You can only work under the law of least resistance, and this religious line is the line of least resistance in India. This is the line of life, this is the line of growth, and this is the line of well-being in India—to follow the track of religion.

This World—The Goal of Others

Aye, in other countries, religion is only one of the many necessities in life. To use a common illustration which I am in the habit of using, my lady has many things in her parlour, and it is the fashion now-a-days to have a Japanese vase, and she must procure it; it does not look well without it. So my lady, or my gentleman, has many other occupations in life; a little bit of religion also must come in to complete it. Consequently she has a little religion. Politics, social improvement, in one word, this word, is the goal of the rest of mankind, and God and religion come in quietly as the helpers out of the world; their God is, so to speak, the being who helps to cleanse and to furnish this world of ours;—that is, apparently, all the value of God for them. Do you not know how, for the last hundred or two hundred years, you have been hearing again and again out of the lips of men who ought to have known better, from the mouths of those who pretend, at least, to know better, that all the arguments they produce against this Indian religion of ours is this,—that our religion does not conduce to well-being in this world, that it does not bring to us handfuls of gold, that it does not make robbers of nations, that it does not make the strong stand upon the bodies of the weak, and feed themselves with the life's blood of the weak. Certainly our religion does not do that. It cannot march cohorts, under whose feet the earth trembles, for the purpose of destruction and pillage and the ruination of races. Therefore, they say—what is there in this religion? It does not bring any grist to the grinding mill, any strength to the muscles. What is there in such a religion?

Ours the only True Religion, because it goes beyond the World and Teaches Renunciation

They little dream that that is the very argument with which we prove our religion to be good and true. Ours is the true religion because it does not make for this world. Ours is the only true religion because this little sense-world of three days' duration is not to be, according to it, the end and aim of all, is not to be our great goal. This little earthly horizon of a few feet is not that which bounds the view of our religion. Ours is away beyond, and still beyond; beyond the senses, beyond space, and beyond time, away, away beyond, till nothing of this world is left there and the universe itself becomes like one drop in the transcendent ocean of the glory of the soul. Ours is the true religion because it teaches that God alone is true, and that this world is false and fleeting, and that all your gold is dust, and that all your power is finite, and that life itself is often-times an evil; therefore it is that ours is the true religion. Ours is the true religion, because above all, it teaches renunciation, and stands up with the wisdom of ages to tell and to declare to the nations who are mere children of yesterday in comparison with the hoary antiquity of the wisdom that our ancestors have discovered for us here in India—to tell them in plain words, "Children, you are slaves of the senses; there is only finiteness in the senses; there is only ruination in the senses; the three short days of luxury here bring only ruin at last. Give it all up, renounce the love of the senses and of the world; that is the way of religion." Through renunciation is the way to the goal and not through enjoyment. Therefore, ours is the only true religion. Aye, it is a curious fact that, while nations after nations have come upon the stage of the world, played their parts vigorously for a few moments and died almost without leaving a mark or a ripple on the ocean of time, here we are, living, as it were, an eternal life. They talk a great deal of the new theories about the survival of the fittest, and they think that it is the strength of the muscle which is the fittest to survive. If that were true, any one of the aggressively known old-world nations would have lived in glory to-day, and we, the weak Hindus—a young English lady once told me, what have the Hindus done; they never even conquered one single race!—even this race, which never conquered even one other race or nation, lives here three hundred million strong. And it is not all true all its energies are spent, that atavism has seized upon every bit of its body;—that it is not true. There is vitality, enough, and it comes out in torrents and deluges when the time is ripe and requires it. We have, as it were, thrown a challenge to the whole world from the most ancient times. In the West they are trying to solve the problem how much a man can, possess, we are trying here to solve the problem on how little a man can live. This struggle and this thick, difference has to go on still for some centuries. But if history has any truth is it, and if prognostications ever prove true, it must be that those who train themselves to live on the least supply of things and to control themselves well, will, in the end, gain the battle, and that all those who run after enjoyment and luxury, however vigorous they may seem for the moment, will have to die and become annihilated.

The Vedānta alone can Cure the Evils of the West

There are times in the history of a man's life, nay the history of the lives of nations, when a sort of world-weariness becomes painfully predominant. It seems that such a tide of world-weariness has come upon the Western World. There too they have their thinkers, great men; and they are already finding out that it is all vanity of vanities, this race after gold and power; many, nay most, cultured men and women there are already weary of this competition, this struggle, this brutality of their commercial civilisation, and they are looking forward towards something better. There is a class which still clings on to political and social changes as the only panacea for the evils in Europe, but among the great thinkers there other ideals are growing. They have found out that no amount of political or social manipulation of human conditions can cure the evils of life. It is a change of the soul itself for the better that alone will cure the evils of life. No amount of force, or government, or legislative cruelty will change the conditions of a race, but it is spiritual culture and ethical culture alone that can change wrong racial tendencies for the better. Thus, these races of the West are eager for some new thought, for some near philosophy; the religion they have had, Christianity, although imperfectly understood and good and glorious in many respects, is, as understood hitherto, found to be insufficient. The thoughtful men of the West find in our ancient philosophy, especially in the *Vedānta*, the new impulse of thought they are seeking, the very spiritual food and drink they are hungering and thirsting for. And it is no wonder.

The Vedānta alone is the Universal Religion for Mankind

I have become used to hear all sorts of wonderful claims put forward in favour of every religion under the sun. You have also heard, quite within recent times, claims put forward in favour of Christianity by a great friend of mine, Dr. Barrows, that Christianity is the only universal religion. Let me consider this question a while, and lay before you my reasons why I think that it is the *Vedānta*, and the *Vedānta* alone that can become the universal religion of man, and that none else is fitted for that role.

For it is not built Round the life of any Personal Founder

Excepting our own, almost all the other great religions in the world are inevitably connected with the life or lives of one or more founders. All their theories, their teachings, their doctrines and their ethics are built round the life of a personal founder from whom they get their sanction their authority, and their power; and strangely enough upon the historicality of the founder's life is built, as it were, all the fabric of such religions. If there is one blow dealt to the historicality of that life as has been the case in modern times with the lives of almost all the so-called founders of religion—we know that half of the details of such lives is not now seriously believed in and that the other half is seriously doubted—if this becomes the case, if that rock of historicality, as they pretend to call it, is shaken and shivered, the whole building tumbles down, broken absolutely; never to regain its lost status. Everyone of the great religions in the world excepting our own, is built upon such historical characters; but ours rests upon principles. There is no man or woman who can claim to have created the *Vedas.* They are the embodiment of eternal principles; sages discovered them; and now and then the names of these sages are mentioned, just their names; we do not even know who or what they were. In many cases we do not know who their fathers were, and almost in every case we do not know when and where they were born. But what cared they, these sages, for their names? They were the preachers of principles, and they themselves, as far as they went, tried to become illustrations of the principles they preached. At the same time, just as our God an impersonal and yet a personal God so in our religion, a most intensely impersonal one, a religion based upon principles, and yet it has an infinite scope for the play of persons; for what religion gives you more incarnations, more prophets and seers and still waits for infinitely more? Says the *Bhagavad Gītā* that Incarnations are infinite, leaving ample scope for as many as you like to come. Therefore if any one or more of these persons in India's religious history, any one or more of these Incarnations, and any one or more of our prophets, are proved not to have been historical, it does not injure our religion a bit; even then it remains there firm as ever, because it is based upon principles, and not on persons. It is vain to try to gather all the peoples of the world around a single personality. It is difficult to make them gather together even around eternal and universal principles. If it ever becomes possible to bring the largest portion of humanity to one way of thinking in regard to religion, mark you, it must be always through principles and not through persons. Yet, as I have said, our religion has ample scope for the authority and influence of persons. There is that most wonderful theory of *Iṣṭa*, which gives you the fullest and the freest choice possible among these great religious personalities. You may take up any one of the prophets or teachers as your guide and the object of your special adoration; you are even allowed to think that he whom you have chosen is the greatest of the prophets, the greatest of all the *Avatāras;* there is no harm in that, but you must keep on a firm background of eternally true principles. The strange fact is here, that the power of Incarnations has been holding good with us only so far as they are illustrations of the principles in the *Vedas*. The glory of Śri Krishna is that he has been the best preacher of our eternal religion of principles and the best commentator on the *Vedānta* that ever lived in India.

It is in Harmony with Science

The second claim of the *Vedānta* upon the attention of the world is that, of all the scriptures in the world, it is the one scripture the teaching of which is in entire harmony with the result that have been attained by the modern scientific investigations of external nature. Two minds in the dim past of history, cognate to each other in form and kinship and sympathy, started, being placed in different circumstances, for the same goal through different routes. The one was the ancient Hindu mind, the other the ancient Greek mind. The latter started in search of that goal beyond by analysing the external world. The former started by analysing the internal world. And even through the various vicissitudes of their history, it is easy to make out these two vibrations of thought tending to produce similar echoes from the goal beyond. It seems clear that the conclusions of modern materialistic science can be acceptable, harmoniously with their religion, only to the *Vedāntins*, or Hindus as they call them. It seems clear that modern materialism can hold its own; and at the same time approach spirituality by taking up the conclusions of the *Vedānta*. It seems to us, and to all who care to know, that the conclusions of modern science are the very conclusions the *Vedānta* reached ages ago; only in modern science, they are written in the language of matter. This, then, is another claim of the *Vedānta* upon modern Western minds, its rationality, the wonderful rationalism of the *Vedānta*. I have myself been told by some of the best scientific minds of the day in the West how wonderfully rational the conclusions of the Vedānta are. I know one of them personally who scarcely has time to eat his meals, or go out of his laboratory, and who yet would stand by the hour to attend my lectures on the *Vedānta;* for, as he expresses it, they are so scientific, they so exactly harmonise with the aspirations of the age and with the conclusions which modern science is coming to at the present time. Two such scientific conclusions drawn from *Comparative Religion,* I would specially like to draw your attention to; the one bears upon the idea of the oneness of things.

Universalities of Religions and Toleration Recognised by the Vedānta alone

We observe in the histories of Babylon and among the Jews an interesting religious phenomenon happening. We find that each of those Babylonian and Jewish peoples were divided into so many tribes, each tribe having a god of its own, and that these little tribal gods had often a generic name. The gods among the Babylonians were all called Baals, and among them, Baal Merodac was the chief. In course of time, one of these many tribes conquer and assimilate the other racially allied tribes, and the natural result would be that the god of the conquering tribe would be placed at the head of all the gods of the other tribes. Thus the so-called boasted monotheism of the Semites was created. Among the Jews, the gods went by the name of Moloch. Of these, there was one Moloch which belonged to the tribe called Israel, and he was called the Moloch Yahva, or Moloch Yava. Then this tribe of Israel slowly conquered some of the other tribes of the same race, destroyed their Molocha, and declared its own Moloch to be the Supreme Moloch of all the Molochs. And I am sure most of you know the amount of bloodshed, of tyranny, and of brutal savagery, that this religions conquest entailed. Later on, the Babylonians tried to destroy this supremacy of Moloch Yahva, bat could not succeed. It seems to me that such an attempt at tribal self-assertion in religious matters might have taken place on the frontiers of India also. Here too all the various tribes of the Aryans might have come into conflict with one another for declaring the supremacy of their several tribal gods; but India's history was to be otherwise, was to be different from that of the Jews. India was to be alone the land— of all lands—of toleration and of spirituality, and therefore the fight between tribes and their gods did not take place long here; for one of the greatest sages that was ever born anywhere found out here in India even at that distant time—which history cannot reach—tradition itself dares not to peep the gloom of that past when the sage arose—and declared, "He who exists is one, the sages call him veriously"—*Ekaṃ sat viprā bahudhā vadanti*—one of the most memorable sentences that was ever uttered, one of the grandest of truths that was ever discovered; and for us Hindus, this truth has been the verb backbone of our national existence. For throughout the vista of the centuries of our national life, this one idea, *Ekaṃ sat viprā bahudhā vadanti,* comes down, gaining strength and vigour as it rolls along, gaining in volume and in fulness, till it has permeated the whole of our national existence, till it is mingled in our blood, and has become one with us in every grain. We love that grand truth in every grain, and our country has become the glorious land of religious toleration. It is here and here alone that they build temples and churches for the religions which have come in with the object of condemning our own religion. This is one very great principle that the world is waiting to learn from us. Aye, you little know how much of intolerance is yet abroad. It struck me more than once that I would have to leave my bones on foreign shores owing to the prevalence of religious intolerance. Killing a man is nothing for religion's sake; to-morrow they may do it in the very heart of the boasted civilisation of the West, if to-day they are not really doing so. Outcasting in its most horrible forms would often come down upon the head of a man in the West, if he dared to say a word against his country's accepted religion. They talk glibly and smoothly here in criticism of our caste laws. If you go to the West and live there as I have done, you will know that even the biggest professors you hear of are arrant cowards and dare not tell, for fear of public opinion, a hundredth part of what they hold to be really true in religions matters.

Therefore the world is waiting for this grand idea of universal toleration. It will be a great acquisition to civilisation. Nay, no civilisation can exist long unless this idea enters it. No civilisation can go on growing before fanaticism stops sad bloodshed stops and brutality stops. No civilisation can begin to lift up its head until we look charitably upon each other, and the first step towards that much-needed charity is to look charitably and kindly upon the religious convictions of each other. Nay more, to understand that not only should we be charitable towards each other, but positively helpful to each other, however different our religious ideas and convictions may be. And that is exactly what we in India do, as I have just related to you. It is here in India that Hindus have built and are still building churches for Christians, and mosques for Mahomedans. That is the thing to do. In spite of their hatred, in spite of their brutality, in spite of their cruelty, in spite of their tyranny, and in spite of the filthy language they are always given to uttering, we will and we must go on building churches for the Christians and mosques for the Mahomedans till we conquer through love—till we have demonstrated to the world that love alone is the fittest thing to survive and not hatred, that it is gentleness that has the strength to live on and to fructify, but not mere brutality and physical force.

The Spiritual Oneness of the Whole Universe

The other great idea that the world wants from us today, the thinking *part* of Europe and the whole world— more, perhaps, the lower classes than the higher, more the masses than the cultured, more the ignorant than the educated, more the weak than the strong—is that eternal grand idea of the spiritual oneness the whole universe. I need not tell you today, men from this Madras University, how the modern researches of Europe have demonstrated through physical means the oneness and the solidarity at the whole universe, how, physically speaking, you and I, the sun and the moon and the stars, are all but little waves or wavelets in the midst of an infinite ocean of matter, and how Indian psychology had demonstrated ages ago that, similarly, both body and mind are but mere names of little, wavelets is the ocean of matter,—the *samaṣṭi*, and how, going one step further, it is shown in the *Vedānta* that, behind that idea of the unity of the whole show, the real soul in also one. There is but one Soul throughout the universe, all is but one existence. This great idea of the real and basic solidarity of the whole universe has frightened many, even in this country; it even now finds sometimes more opponents than adherents; I tell you, nevertheless, that it is the one great life-giving idea which the world wants from us to-day and which the mute masses of India want for their uplifting, for none can regenerate this land of ours without the practical application and effective operation of this ideal of the oneness of things. The rational West is earnestly bent upon seeking out the rationality, the *raison d'etre* of all its philosophy and its, ethics; and you all know well that ethics cannot be derived from the mere sanction of any personage, however great and divine he may have been,—of one who having been born but yesterday has had to die a few minutes after. Such an explanation of the authority of ethics no more appeals to the highest of the world's thinkers; they want something more than human sanction for ethical and moral codes to be binding, they want some eternal principle of truth as the sanction of ethics. And where is that eternal sanction to be found except in the only infinite reality that exists, in you and in me and in all, in the self, in the Soul? The infinite oneness of the soul is the eternal sanction of all morality, that you and I are not only brothers—even literature voicing man's struggle towards freedom; children have preached that you—but that you and I are really one. This is the dictate of Indian philosophy. This oneness is the rationale of all ethics and all spirituality. Europe wants it to-day just as much as our down-trodden masses do, and this great principle is even now unconsciously forming the basis of all the latest political and social aspirations that are coming up in England, in Germany, in France, and in America. And mark it, my friends, that in and through all the literature voicing man's struggle towards freedom, towards universal freedom, again and again you find the Indian *Vedāntic* ideals coming out prominently. In some cases, the writers do not know the source of their inspiration, in some cases; they try to appear very original, and a few there are bold and grateful enough to mention the source and acknowledge their indebtedness to it.

Faith in Ourselves—The Secret of all Greatness

My friends, when I was in America, I heard it once complained that I was preaching too much of *Advaita*, and too little of Dualism. Aye ! know what grandeur, what ocean of love, what infinite, ecstatic blessings and joy there are in the dualistic love-theories of worship and religion. I knew it all. But this is not the time with us to weep even in joy, we have had weeping enough; no more, is this the time for us to become soft. This softness has been on us till we are dead; we have became like masses of cotton. What our country now wants are muscles of iron and nerves of steel, gigantic wills which nothing can resist, which can penetrate into the mysteries and the secrets of the universe, and will accomplish their purpose even if it meant going down to the bottom of the ocean and meeting death face to face in every fashion. That is what we want, and that can only be created, established and strengthened by understanding and realising the ideal of the *Advaita*, the ideal of the oneness of all. Faith, faith, faith in ourselves, faith, faith in God, this is the secret of greatness. If you have faith in all the 330 millions of your mythological gods and in all the gods which foreigners have now and again sent into your midst, and still have no-faith in yourselves, there is no salvation for you. Have faith in yourselves, and stand upon that faith and be strong; that is what we need. Why is it that we 300 millions of people have been ruled for the last one thousand years by any and every handful of foreigners who chose to walk over our prostrate bodies? Because they had faith in themselves and we had not. What did I learn in the West, and what did I see behind those talks of frothy nonsense of the Christian religious sects saying that man was a fallen and hopelessly fallen sinner? There, inside the national hearts of both Europe and America resides the tremendous power of the men's faith in themselves. An English boy will tell you—"I am an Englishman, and I will do anything." The American boy will tell you the same, and so will every European boy. Can our boys say the same thing here? No, not even the boys' fathers. We have lost faith in ourselves. Therefore to preach the *Advaita* aspect of the *Vedānta* is necessary to rouse up hearts of men, to show them the glory of their souls. It is therefore that I preach this *Advaita*, and I do so not as a sectarian but upon universal and widely acceptable grounds.

There is Divinity Residing in Every Thing

It is easy to find out the way of reconciliation that will not hurt the dualist or the qualified monist. There is not one system in India which does not hold the doctrine that God is within, that divinity resides with all things. Every one of our *Vedāntic* systems admits that all purity and perfection and strength are in the soul already. According to some, this perfection sometimes becomes, as it were contracted, and at other times it becomes expanded again. Yet it is there. According to the *Advaita*, it neither contracts nor expands, but becomes hidden and uncovered now and again. Pretty much the same thing in effect. The one may be a more logical statement than the other, but as to the result, the practical conclusions, both are about the same; and this is the one central idea which the world stands in need of, and nowhere is the want more felt than is this, our own motherland.

Ourselves Responsible for all Our Miseries

Aye, my friends! I must tell you a few harsh words. I read in the newspapers, when one of our poor fellows is murdered or ill-treated by an Englishman, how the howls go all over the country : I read and weep, and the next moment comes to my mind the question who is responsible for it all. As a *Vedāntist* I cannot but put that question to myself. The Hindu is a man of introspection, he wants to see things in and through himself through the subjective vision.

I, therefore, ask myself who is responsible, and the answer comes every time, "Not the English, No! they are not responsible. It is we who are responsible for all our misery and all our degradation, and we alone are responsible. It is we who are responsible for all our misery and all our degradation, and we alone are responsible." Our aristocratic ancestors went on treading the common masses of our country under foot, till they became helpless, till, under this torment, the poor, poor people nearly forget that they were human beings. They have been compelled to be merely hewers of wood and drawers of water for centuries, so much so that they are made to believe that they are born at slaves, born as hewers of wood and drawers of water. And if anybody says a kind word for them, with all our boasted education of modern times, I often find our men shrink at once from the duty of lifting up the down-trodden.

Heredity no Argument to Prove Our Weakness

Not only so, but I also find that all sorts of most demoniacal and brutal arguments, called from the curse ideas of hereditary transmission and other such gibberish from the Western world, are brought forward in order to brutalise and tyrannise over the poor all the more. In the Parliament of Religions in America, there came among others a young man, a Negro-born, a real African Negro, and he made a beautiful speech. I became interested in the young man, and now and then talked to him, but could learn nothing about him. But one day in England, I met some Americans, and this is what they told me—that this boy was the son of a Negro chief in the heart of Africa, and that one day another chief became angry with the father of this boy and murdered him and murdered the mother also to be cooked and eaten; but that the boy fled. And after passing through great hardships, travelling through a distance of several hundreds of miles, he reached the sea-shore and that there, he was taken in to American vessel and brought over to America.

And this boy made that speech! After that, what was I to think of your doctrine of heredity !

Proclaim the God in you and be Great

Aye, Brahmins!—If the Brahmin has more aptitude for learning on the ground of heredity than the Pariah, spend no more money on the Brahmin's education, but spend all on the Pariah. Give to the weak, for there all the gift is needed. If the Brahmin is born clever, he can educate himself without help. If the others are not born clever, let them have all the teaching and the teachers they want. This is justice and reason as I understand. These our people, therefore, require to hear and to know what they really are, these down-trodden masses of India, Yea, let every man and woman and child without respect of caste or birth or weakness or strength, hear and know that behind the strong and the weak, behind the high and the low, behind every one, there is that Infinite Soul assuring the infinite possibility and the infinite capacity of all to become great and good. Let us proclaim to every soul— *Uttiṣṭhata Jāgrata, prāpya vāran nibodhata*—"Arise, awake and stop not till the goal is reached." Arise, awake; awake from this hypnotism of weakness. *None* is really weak; the soul is infinite, omnipotent, and omniscient. Stand up, assert yourself, proclaim the God within you, do not deny. Too much of inactivity, too much of weakness, too much of hypnotism, has been and is upon our race. O ye modern Hindus, de-hypnotise yourselves. The way to do that is found in your sacred books. Teach yourselves, teach every one his real nature, call upon the sleeping soul to see how it rises. Power will come, glory will come, goodness will come, purity will come, and every thing that is excellent will come, when this sleeping Soul is roused to self-conscious activity. Aye, if there is any thing in the *Gītā* that I like, it is these two verses, coming out strong, as the very gist, the very essence of Krishna's teaching—"He who sees the Supreme Lord dwelling alike in all beings; the Imperishable in things that perish, sees indeed. For seeing the Lord as the same, everywhere present, he does not destroy the Self by the Self, and then he goes to the highest goal."

Growth, Expansion and Development on National Lines

Thus there is a great opening for the *Vedānta* to do beneficent work both here and elsewhere. The wonderful idea of the samenss and omnipresence of the Supreme Soul has to be preached for the amelioration and elevation of the human race, here as elsewhere,—wherever there is evil and wherever there is ignorance and want of knowledge, I have found out in my experience that, as our scriptures say, all evil comes by relying upon differences, and that all good comes from faith in equality, in the underlying sameness and real oneness of things. This is the great *Vedāntic* ideal. To have the ideal is one thing, and to apply it practically to the details of daily life is quite another thing in every case. It is very good to point out an ideal, but where is the practical way to reach it? Here naturally comes the difficult question which has been uppermost for centuries in the minds of our people, the vexed question of caste and social reformation. I must frankly let his audience know that I am neither a caste-breaker nor a mere social reformer. I have nothing to do directly with your castes or with social reformation. Live in any caste you like; but that is no reason why you should hate another caste, or another man. It is love and love alone that I preach, and I base my teaching on the great *Vedāntic* truth of the sameness and omnipresence of the Soul of the Universe. For the last one hundred years nearly, our country has been flooded with social reformers and various social reform proposals. Personally, I have no fault to find these reformers. Most of them are good well-meaning men, and their aims too are very laudable on certain points; but it is quite a patent fact that these one hundred years of social reform has produced no permanent and valuable result appreciable throughout the country. Platform speeches have been sent out by the thousand, denunciations have been hurled upon the devoted head of the Hindu race and its civilisation in volumes after volumes and yet no good practical result has been achieved; and where is the reason for that? The reason is not hard to find. It is in the denunciation itself. In the first place, as I told you before, we must try to keep our historically acquired character as a people; I grant that we have to take great many things from other nations, that we have to learn many lessons from outside; but I am sorry to say that most of our modern reform-movements have been inconsiderate imitations of Western means and methods of work, and that surely will not do for India; therefore it is that all our recent reform movements have had no result. In the second place, denunciation is not at all the way to do good. That there are evils in our society even the child can see, and what society is there where there are no evils. And let me take this opportunity, my countrymen, of telling you that in comparing the different races and nations of the world I have been among, I have come to the conclusion that our people are, on the whole, the most moral and the most highly godly, and our institutions are, *in their plan and purposes*, best situated to make mankind happy. I do not therefore want any reformation. My ideal is growth, expansion, development an national lines. As I look back upon the history of my country, I do not find, in the whole world, another country which has done quite so much for the improvement of the human mind. Therefore, I have no words of condemnation for my nation. I tell them "You have done well : only try better." Great things have been one in the past in this land; there is both time and room for greater things to be done. I am sure you know that we cannot stop. If we stop, we die. We have either to get forward or to go backward. We have either to progress or to degenerate. Our ancestors did great things in the past, but we have to grow into fuller life and march on even beyond their great achievements. How can we now go back and degenerate ourselves? That cannot be; that must not be; going back will lead us to national decay and death. Therefore, let us go forward and do yet greater things : that is what I have to tell you, I am no preacher of any momentary social reform. I am not trying to remedy evils. I only ask you to go forward and to complete the practical realisation of the scheme of human progress that has been laid out in the most perfect order by our ancestors. I only ask you to work to realise more and more the *Vedāntic* ideal of the solidarity of man and his inborn divine nature. Had I the time, I would gladly show you how every bit of what we have now to do was laid out years ago by our ancient law-givers, and how they actually anticipated all the different changes that have taken place and are still to take place in our national institutions. They also were breakers of caste, but they were not like our modern men. They did not mean by the breaking of caste that all the people in the city should sit down together to a dinner of beefsteak and champagne, nor that all fools and lunatics in the country should marry when, where, and whom they chose, and reduce the country to a lunatic asylum, nor did they believe that the prosperity of a nation is to by gauged by the number of husbands its widows get. I am yet to see such a prosperous nation.

The Ideal Man is the Brahmin

The ideal man of our ancestors was the Brahmin. In all our books stands out prominently this ideal of the Brahmin. In Europe, there is My Lord the Cardinal who is struggling hard and spending thousands of pounds to prove the nobility of his ancestor, and he will not be satisfied until he has traced his ancestry to some dreadful tyrant, who lived on a hill, and watched the people passing through the streets, and, whenever had the opportunity, sprang out on them and robbed them. That was the business of these nobility-bestowing ancestors, and My Lord Cardinal is not satisfied until he can trace his ancestry to one of these. In India, on the other hand, the greatest princes seek to trace their descent to some ancient sage, dressed in a bit of loin-cloth, living in a forest, eating roots, and studying the *Vedas*. It is there that the Indian prince goes to taste his ancestry. You are high caste when you can trace your ancestry to a Ṛṣi, and not before that. Our ideal of high birth, therefore, is different from that of others. Our ideal is the Brahmin of spiritual culture and renunciation.

What is True Brahmin-ness?

By the Brahmin ideal what do I mean ? The ideal Brahminness is that in which worldliness is altogether absent and true wisdom is abundantly present. This is the ideal of the Hiṇdu race. Have you not heard how it is declared that he, the Brahmin, is not amenable to law, that he has no law, that he is not governed by kings, and that his body cannot be hurt? That is perfectly true. Do not understand it in the light which has been thrown upon it by interested and ignorant fools, but understand it in the light of the true and original *Vedāntic* conception. If the Brahmin is he who has killed all selfishness and who lives and works to acquire and to propagate wisdom and the power of love, a country that is inhabited by such Brahmins altogether, by men and women who are spiritual and moral and good, is it strange to think of that country as being above and beyond all law ? What police, what military are necessary to govern them? Why should any one govern them at all? Why should they live under a government? They are good and noble; they are the men of God; they are our ideal Brahmins.

The Ideal of Caste

We read that in the *Satya-yuga*, there was only one caste to start with, and that was that of the Brahmin. We read in the *Mahābhārata* that the whole world was in the beginning peopled with Brahmins, and that, as they began to degenerate, they became divided into different castes, and that, when the cycle turns round, they will all go back to that Brahminical origin. This cycle is now turning round, and I draw your attention to this fact. Therefore our solution of the caste question is not degrading those who are already high up, is not running amuck through food and drink, is not jumping out of our own limits in order to have more enjoyment; but it comes by every one of us fulfilling the dictates of our *Vedāntic* religion, by our attaining spirituality, and by our becoming the ideal Brahmin. There is a law laid on each one of you here in this land by our ancestors, whether you are Aryans, or non-Aryans, Ṛṣis or Brahmins, or the very lowest out-castes. The command is the same to you all, and that command is that you must not stop at all without making progress and that, from the highest man to the lowest *Pariah*, every one in this country has to try and become the ideal Brahmin. This *Vedāntic* idea is applicable only here but over the whole world. Such is our ideal of caste, meant for raising all humanity slowly and gently towards the realisation of the great ideal of the spiritual man who is non-resisting, calm, steady, worshipful, pure, and meditative. In that ideal there is God.

What shall your Work be Now?

How are these things to be brought about? I must again draw your attention to the fact that cursing and vilifying and abusing do not and cannot produce anything good. They have been tried for years and years, and no valuable result has bees obtained. Good results can be produced only through love, through sympathy. It is a great subject, and it requires several lectures to elucidate all the plans that I have in view, and all the ideas that are, in this connection, coming to my mind day after day. I must therefore conclude, only reminding you of this, fact, that this ship of our nation, O Hindus, has been usefully plying here for ages. To-day, perhaps, it has sprung a few leaks; to-day perhaps, it has become a little worn; and if such is the case, it behoves you and I, children of the soil, to try our best to stop these leaks and holes. Let us tell our countrymen of the danger, let them awake, let them mend it. I will cry at the top of my voice from one part to the other of this country to awaken the people to know their situation and their duty therein.

Suppose they do not hear me, still I shall not have one word of abuse for them, not one word of curse. Great has been our nation's work in the past, and if we cannot do greater things in the future, let us have this consolation, let us all die and sink together in peace. Be patriots, love the race which has done such great things for us in the past. Aye, the more I compare notes the more I love you, my fellow-countrymen; you are good and pure and gentle; and you have been always tyrannised over; such is the irony of this material world of *Māyā*. Never mind that; the spirit will triumph in the long run. In the meanwhile, let us work and let us not abuse our country, let us not curse and abuse the weather beaten and work-worn institutions of our thrice-hold motherland. Have not one word of condemnation, even for the most, superstitious and the most irrational of its institutions, for they also must have served to do us good in the past. Remember always that there is not in the world one other country whose institutions are really better in their aims and objects than the institutions of this land. I have seen castes in almost every country in the world; but nowhere is their plan and purpose so glorious as here. If caste is thus unavoidable, I would rather have a caste of purity and culture and self-sacrifice than a caste of dollar. Therefore, utter no words of condemnation. Close your lips and let your hearts open. Work but the salvation of this land and of the whole world, each of you thinking that the entire burden is on your shoulders. Carry the light and the life of the *Vedānta* to every door and rouse up the divinity that is hidden within every soul. Then, whatever may be the measure of your success, you shall have this satisfaction, that you have lived, worked, and died for a great cause. In the success of this cause, howsoever brought about, is centred the salvation of humanity here and hereafter.

Vedānta in Daily Life[1]

Swami Abhedananda

It has been asked again and again whether the teachings of Vedānta, sublime though they are, can be applied to our practical every-day life. Some people have an idea that, being a philosophy, Vedānta must by speculative, like any other philosophy of Europe and America, that it gives a few grand theories which can never be carried into practice. Such statements would be true if Vedānta were simply a philosophy and not a religion.

In order to become a religion, the teachings of Vedānta must be intensely practical, because where theory ends, there is the beginning of true religion. Vedānta gives not only the principles of the highest philosophy, but it also teaches the practical methods which are necessary to make it a religion. If the ideals of Vedānta do not cover the whole field of life, if they do not enter into every plane of our thoughts, nay of our very existence in home life, in social and business life, in moral and spiritual life, than we must reject them as mere theories of a speculative philosophy, and must not call Vedānta a religion. The ideals of Vedānta, however, are so broad and so universal in their scope that for the last four thousand years, men and women, living in retirement, in caves and forests, as well as those holding the most responsible positions in society and in the state, have successfully harmonized their lives with those ideals, and have proved them to be intensely practical.

1. A lecture delivered in America.

There is an impression among some people that the teachings of Vedānta are fit for those only who live like ascetics, is caves and forests, but not for those who lead a busy American's life. Such people are entirely mistaken, because they do not know that the truths of Vedānta were first discovered and practised, not by ascetics who dwelt in caves or forests, but by kings and monarchs, ministers and statesmen who lived the busiest and most luxurious lives that we can imagine. If we read the Upaniṣads, the Epics—Mahābhārata, and Rāmāyaṇa—and other historical works, we find that there were not only Hindu minister and statesmen, but kings sitting on their thrones, discharging their royal duties of governing the states and of looking after the welfare of their many subjects; and living a busier and much more responsible life than that of an ordinary businessman of the present day, found ample time and opportunity to study Vedānta and to carry out its sublime tenets in their practical lives. When such persons could live the ideal life as given by Vedānta, what can we say of ourselves? We are not half as busy as they were. I can quote from the Upaniṣads many names of the ancient Hindu monarchs who faithfully followed the teachings of Vedānta while fulfilling the duties of their royal position. They not only lived up to the ideals of Vedānta, but taught others, and were considered by the people as the living example of this practical philosophy. Those who have read the *Bhagavad Gītā*, or "The Song Celestial" as Sir Edwin Arnold calls it, will remember that the great commander of a huge army, standing in the battle-field, in the midst of the din of battle at Kurukshetra, found time to discuss the ideals of Vedānta and succeeded in applying them in practice.

Many of you have seen and heard the late Swami Viekananda. He was a living example of the practical side of Vedānta. Up to the last moment of his life he worked like giant under all conditions, favourable or unfavourable, bearing all kinds of hardship, discomfort and tribulation, and never moving an inch from the highest ideal of this great philosophy and religion of Vedānta. He lived a pure and chaste life always, working for others, trying to help humanity without seeking any return for his labour. He showed to the world what a true *Karma Yogī* was like. In other words, he proved by his example that, even in this age of materialism and commercialism, one can be a sincere worker who always works for others, and lives for the good of humanity, without being guided by selfish motives or selfish desires.

The most practical side of Vedānta which will appeal to American minds, is the *Karma Yoga*. *Karma Yoga* is that branch of Vedānta which teaches that we, should always work and fulfil all the duties of life, house-hold, social or official but, at the same time, we must not consider that the performance of these duties is the highest aim and ideal of our life. On the contrary, we must regard these duties and the work of our daily life as a means to a higher end. We should also remember that every one of these works brings us new experience, makes us realize the transitoriness of earthly objects, purifies our inner nature and uplifts our souls, if it be not guided by any selfish motive. Vedānta teaches that any work which proceeds from extreme selfishness is wrong and wicked, and we should avoid it. Moreover, it tells us that every action, must bring a similar reaction; that all good or unselfish works produce evil results such as sorrow, suffering, misery, disease and death. Holding this ideal before his mind, and applying it to his practical life, a student of Vedānta can go anywhere and live under any conditions, without device from the path of righteousness and virtue; under all circumstances, he will live a pure, unselfish life and remain contented. This is the simplest and easiest thing to practise.

First of all, we should form an ideal, and few people have their ideals. We think that we possess the highest ideal, but that may be only for a short time; next moment perhaps, the ideal has vanished, and we do not know the purpose of life, or why we are here. Therefore, our mode of expression is very poor and it proceeds entirely from selfishness. Selfishness is the result of ignorance. We do not know the laws, nor do we understand how we ought to live. We look after ourselves and take care of ourselves because that is the nearest thing to us. But we must not forget that any person in any country, possessing a fair amount of earnestness and sincerity, will get from this practice of *Karma Yoga* wonderful results, most beneficial in this life and hereafter, if he knows the ideal, and if he follows it at every moment of his life. On the contrary, if we consider that the work which we are performing is the highest aim of life, that there is no further ideal, then our life will not be worth living. But whose ever holds the highest ideal and walks in the path of unselfishness is virtuous, is unselfish, is righteous and is spiritual.

Every householder should study *Karma Yoga* and understand the philosophy of work, and, applying those teachings to the daily life, he will eventually attain to the highest ideal of all religions. If he believe in a personal God or in an impersonal God, or in any divine incarnation like Christ or Buddha or Krishna or Ramakrishna, what should he do? He should every night, before retiring, offer the results of his daily works, both good and bad, to Him; and, by this method, he will become free from the law of *Karma*, the law of action and reaction, and reach the highest goal of salvation in the end. The works of our daily lives will be transformed into acts of worship when we have learnt to offer their results to the Supreme Lord of the universe, and this can be accomplished by any man or woman, engaged in any kind of profession or business. It is the easiest method by which we can make the religion of Vedānta enter into every plane of our daily life, and herein lies the secret of great success, of freedom, of unselfishness,—that is, either offer the results of your works to God, or work as an act of worship. He who has learned to offer the results of his daily works to the

Almighty has learned the secret of work and is always peaceful and contented. This will be beneficial to all those who live the busiest lives, engaged in any kind of work. Works are neither low nor high; every work is great, and every work will be a means to the attainment of divinity.

This *Karma Yoga* is a method by which we can get greater results by less output of our energy. The majority of people in every country waste their energy in unnecessary rush and worry for the results; they have no patience to wait for the results, and what is the effect? They shatter their nerves and suffer from nervous prostration. The lack of self-control and this nervousness they will overcome if they understand the secret of work and the laws of action and reaction, of cause and sequence, that every action must bring its result, whether we worry over it or not. It must; and what a great saving it would be, if, instead of wasting that energy in worry, we could devote it to doing a other works and let the results take care of themselves! We must do our best and stop there. After performing your best, you cannot do any better, and what is the use of worry? If we lived this way, then we should be great workers.

Vedānta teaches that the less passion for work there is, the greater and more we work. If we read the lives of all the great workers of the world, we find that they were wonderfully calm men. Men and women of impulsive nature cannot do great work, cannot be steady workers : they will lose their heads. Persons who are easily disturbed by passions like anger, jealousy, hatred, ambition and selfishness cannot accomplish much. They will shatter their nerves and eventually become useless. As we find in this country, persons who are impulsive can do great work for the moment, but in the reaction, they break themselves to pieces. They suffer from nervous prostration. Therefore, self-control is the secret of great work, success in business, health and longevity. This we learn from Vedānta. What can be more practical or beneficial than to gain self-control and exercise it in everyday life ?

Vedānta teaches how to be strong, physically, mentally and spiritually. Physical strength proceeds from mental strength, and mental strength in its turn is the outcome of spiritual strength. Spiritual strength must be at the back of mental and physical strength, and that spiritual strength will come to those who live the right kind of life, who understand the laws which govern lives. The knowledge of these laws will make us free from committing mistakes, and this knowledge comes through the study of Vedānta. The practice of *Rāja Yoga* will help us in acquiring that knowledge. That branch of Vedānta which is called *Rāja Yoga* is the most practical of all applied sciences. Every step of this science depends entirely upon practice. It must enter into the daily life of every individual. Take, for instance, one of the teachings of *Rāja Yoga,*—concentration. How absolutely helpful and necessary this power of concentration is! Nothing can be achieved without it; no one can accomplish anything without possessing some amount of this power : no one can become a great artist, astronomer or physician; no one can have success, even on the Stock Exchange, without this power of concentration. It is absolutely necessary for success in business, and this power we acquire through the practice of *Rāja Yoga*.

The same power of concentration can be applied for material prosperity as for spiritual advancement. If we want material prosperity, we can use our power of concentration in that direction and get wonderful results. If we are spiritually-minded, we can gain spiritual results by it. Concentration, when practised for spiritual results, will gradually lead us to meditation, and meditation will eventually direct the soul into the state of God-consciousness, and then we shall be able to realize the true nature of the soul and its relation to God. Thus you can understand how in Vedānta the highest ideals of true religion are made into a practical science which is intensely useful and beneficial in every possible way.

Another practical side of Vedānta is the science of breath. Anyone who understands this science of breath and possesses physical, mental and spiritual strength, can stand the sudden changes of weather, can go through any hardship without being broken to pieces. Those who have practised regularly the lessons as given in the Yoga classes held under, he auspices of the Vedānta Society of New York will know how wonderful the teachings of this science of breath are and what wonderful powers can be attained. The students of Vedānta will eventually gain perfect health. By gaining control over your breath, you will make your system do anything you like. You will bring every inch of your muscle and nerve-centres under your control. As breathing exercises bring physical results, so mental powers are developed by the regulation of breath. The power of self-control is bound to come to one who has learnt the control of breath or one who has faithfully practised the breathing exercises as given by the Swamis from India. The utility of this wonderful science is proved by medical practitioners, mental scientists, and by those who teach physical culture or voice culture. Again, when this breath is brought under control, it brings peace of mind. When the mind is directed towards the Supreme Ideal, you will obtain spiritual enlightenment, in which you will discover the past and future of your soul-life. Thus *Rāja Yoga* when properly applied to our daily lives will make us strong physically, mentally and spiritually.

A student of Vedānta does not require any special or separate training in ethics or religion, because the highest ideals and the practical side of ethics are includes in the teachings of Vedānta, and, if we try to live according to the ideals of Vedānta, we cannot but be ethical. For instance, one of the injunctions of practical ethics is to be truthful. Now, why should we be truthful if, by telling lies, we can gain more and enrich ourselves? The question has never been answered by any system of ethics so rationally as by Vedānta. Vedānta tells us that truthfulness is not a mere virtue, but it is the means of attaining the absolute Truth. The absolute Truth is revealed to those only who are absolutely truthful in thought, word and deed. Moral weakness and selfishness lie at the bottom of falsehood, therefore we should abandon it. We should shun the company of those who are untruthful; and although we may go through all kinds of suffering, sorrow, misery, and changes of fortune, still we must not give up the ideal of truthfulness, we must hold on to it until the last breath has passed out of our body, because truthfulness will lead to absolute Truth. The eternal Truth is never gained by falsehood but by truth.

Another ethical law which is considered to be the highest law in all religions is : "Love thy neighbour as thyself." Now, here we can ask the same question : Why should I love my neighbour as myself? Like Christianity, Vedānta teaches this ideal. Christianity teaches it as, a dogma based upon the authority of the Scriptures, and does not give any reason why and what for, but Vedānta gives the rational explanation and tells us why we should love our neighbours as ourselves : Because the true Self of our neighbour is one with our true Self. And that recognition of this spiritual oneness, when understood, is the meaning of love. Love means spiritual oneness, oneness of two souls,—that is true love. Where there is true love; there is divinity, there is the manifestation of God, and that divine love reigns in the heart and soul of a student of Vedānta and therefore he loves all humanity. When the same love which we call human love is not backed by selfishness, it becomes divine love, and that divine love is the means by which we can realize God. God can be realized through divine love; therefore we should practise in our daily lives that unselfish love which is the highest, and never encourage or practise that which is called love but which means something different, which is based upon selfishness, which produces attachment and brings bondage in the end. We should not practise or encourage it, otherwise, we shall be the sufferers, and the ideal of love, which is divine, will not be attained by us.

The highest aspiration of the individual soul is fulfilled when it realizes spiritual oneness with the Divine Being, and that spiritual oneness or divine love is the central ideal of Vedānta. Vedānta teaches that there is one existence, one reality, one Truth, one God, one life, one Spirit. All these differentiations and distinctions, which we perceive with our senses, are fictitious and unreal, they are, all on the surface; but go below the surface and there you will see the undercurrent of one spirit; and when that oneness is properly realized, when we have understood that we are parts of that one stupendous whole, the Universal spirit, how can we help loving that whole? We must love, we cannot help loving and through that divine love we realize the highest ideal of our lives. A student of Vedānta, who recognizes that spiritual oneness, sees that one Universal Spirit is manifesting through all living creatures, and all human beings, and therefore he loves all human beings; through all animals, and therefor he loves all animals. The most practical result of this love this recognition of oneness, is that a student of Vedānta never injures or kills any living creature, because he knows that there is one life, that the difference between an animalcule and a human being is only in degree but not in kind. The same life-force is expressed in so many ways and wherever the humanitarian ideas of Vedānta are preached, there prevails compassion for everybody : there is compassion for poor animals, there hospitals are built, not only for men, women and children, but for lower animals, and there is to be found the desire to take care of the poor, suffering animals just as you would take care of the poor, suffering brother. Therefore a student of Vedānta does not kill any animal for food, because he says : "When I cannot give life to any living creature, what right have I to take it? Let it stay on and live; it has its purpose to fulfil; I must not interfere." And having this ideal in his mind he does good to all, and he world rather give his own life than take the life of another. Such a soul is a great blessing to humanity, as also to all living creatures. The practice of this ideal will bring the most wonderful results which are morally and spiritually perfect. We should teach our children that lower animals possess life and feelings. From our childhood, we have been taught that lower animals have been created for our food. Now we must change that idea and teach children that they are fulfilling certain principles of life, that they are on certain grades of evolution, and, in course of time, they will become human beings; we must be kind to them, and so in practical life we should learn compassion, and that compassion, when properly carried out, will lead to divine love and realization of the Supreme.

The teachings of Vedānta drive away the fear of death, because they say that death cannot attack our souls; we are immortal; by our birthright we are children of that Universal Spirit, and therefore we are immortal. Fear of death will never trouble the mind of a student of Vedānta. "As we throw away our old worn-out garment, so the soul throws away the garment of the old body at the time of death and manufactures a new one, according, to its thoughts and deeds." What a great consolation is this! That we are no longer dependent upon the whim of an anthropomorphic God; that we have not been created out of nothing by the sudden whim of a Creator, but that our souls existed in the past and shall exist after death, that our pleasures and sufferings are the results of our own actions, that we are responsible for our future happiness and misery. We are not going to eternal perdition, nor are we born in sin and iniquity. Thus the teachings of Vedānta take away all fear of death and make us happy and contented in our earthly career. What can be more beneficial to us in our practical life?

Another great help in practical life which we get from Vedānta is the knowledge of the Divine Being. The Divine Being is not far from us; He is the soul or our souls; He is dwelling within us! He is both personal and impersonal, and beyond both; He can be worshipped under any name, in any form, by anyone, under any sect, creed or denomination; He is one and eternal and when we understand this, all religious animosities, quarrels, fights cease for ever. Then we consider all sectarians as our brothers and sisters; we embrace them as children of God. What could be more practical than this! Can a sectarian do so? Can an orthodox Christian embrace a Mahomedan or a Buddhist? Very few possess so broad and liberal a mind as to embrace another belonging to another religion, but Christ Himself would have embraced a Mahomedan or Buddhist or any heathen as the child of divinity, of his Heavenly Father, and we should follow that example. We should try to live up to it, and then in our daily lives, we shall be able to understand that secret by which we shall attain to the highest wisdom, of spiritual oneness, that will make us free. This is the meaning of salvation, emancipation from bondage, from ignorance and selfishness. According to Vedānta, that salvation does not begin in the grave; but it should begin right here and now; and Vedānta shows us the way to attain to that salvation and perfection in this life. And when that knowledge and divine wisdom, come, all darkness is dispelled and the divine powers begin to flow through our souls and produce their results; then we rise above the animal and material plane and slime with the spiritual light of the eternal sun.

Now we can see how all these teachings of the different branches of Vedānta fit into the different departments of our lives and how practical Vedānta is. Not only this, there is another thing, which we should not forget, that Vedānta includes the truths that have been discovered by different branches of science and shows us how those truths can be applied to our daily lives according to lives; how we can mould our daily lives according to these ideals and direct our efforts towards the highest goal, which is one. No other religion has done that; no other religion has ever been able to harmonize with the different branches of science or with the different philosophies of the world; but Vedānta includes all sciences, all philosophies and all religions, and therefore it is universal. A student of Vedānta can be a Christian; Mahomedan, Buddhist or a heathen, or an agnostic. Distinctions of caste, creed, nationality, are never recognized in the light of Vedānta. Wherever the truths of Vedānta are preached, there prevail peace, tranquillity, self-control and spiritual enlightenment. If we understand the teachings of Vedānta and live up to the ideals, then we shall be able to say with the old philosopher Schopenhauer : "Vedānta has been the solace of my life, and it will be the solace of my death."

Glossary

Āditya : Lit. means: Sun or *sūrya*. In the *śāstras* it is mentioned that Ādityas are twelve in number, viz. 1. Dhātṛ, 2. Mitra, 3. Aryaman, 4.Rudra, 5. Varuṇa, 6. Sūrya, 7.Bhaga, 8. Vivasvat, 9. Pūṣan, 10. Savitṛ, 11. Tvaṣṭṛ and 12. Viṣṇu.

Ānanda: Lit. means: happiness, joy, delight, pleasure, etc. *Ānanda* or Bliss is the nature of *Śakti* and it is also the essential nature of Paramaśiva along with *cit*. It is the state of *mukti* or *mokṣa* or *nirvāṇa* in which the self becomes free from all fetters. In Indian Philosophical contexts, *ānanda* or Bliss is a characteristic of the Brahman, others being *sat* and *cit* are too known its characteristics.

Aṇu* or *paramāṇu : Both the terms are synonymous and denote an atom, i.e. an indivisible particle of matter.

Bhairava: Lit. means: terrible, frightful, horrible, formidable, etc. The letter *'bha'* of this word indicates *bharaṇa* or maintenance of the world, and *'va'* indicates *vamana* or projection of the world. Thus, Bhairava is one who brings about the *sṛṣṭi, sthiti* and *saṁhāra* of the universe. He is Lord Śiva who is known as Bhairava. A Tāntric *sādhaka* may consider himself as a Bhairava.

Bhūta : Lit. means: being, existing, gross physical element, etc. *Bhūta is* primarily the concept of creature with both idea of being or originated and becoming or in process. It is an entity which 'was produced' a creature, living or insentient. The term refers to the whole process of evolution and to particular stages at the same time. There are five *bhūtas* (elements), viz. earth, water, fire, air and space. These are also known as *mahābhūtas*.

Caitanya: Absolute Consciousness characterized by *svātantrya*, absolute autonomy and knowledge *(jñāna)* and activity *(kriyā)*.

Citi: It means the Absolute Consciousness, i.e. consciousness in its Initial and unconditioned state. The consciousness-power of the Absolute brings about the world process. It is also known as *cit*.

Citta: 'The empirical mind'. The limited individual consciousness, the psychological status of the individual is known as *Citta*.

Dīkṣā : Lit. means consecration for a religious ceremony, initiation in general. *Dīkṣā* is of two kinds, viz. Vedic and Tāntric. In order to lead a religious life as prescribed by the Vedas and texts of Vedic tradition, a formal initiation is required, but it is not as important as in the case of Tāntric *sādhanā*, in which it is an essential precondition. Abhinavagupta defines *dīkṣā* as 'a process of imparting real knowledge *(jñāna)* and a preceptorial instruction which removes the bondage of *pāśa*. Such kind of benediction and benevolent act is known as *dīkṣā* :

dīyate jñāna sadbhāvaḥ kṣīyate paśuvāsanā/
dāna kṣapaṇasaṁyuktā dīkṣā teneha kīrtitā.// (Tantrāloka).

According to the Śāradā Tilaka, 'that which gives spiritual knowledge *(divya jñāna)* and brings the annihilation of baset propensities *(pāpa)* are verily the initiation *(dīkṣā)*. The Kulārṇava Tantra presents a detailed analysis of different categories of initiation. It speaks about seven kinds of *dīkṣā*, *viz. kriyā, varṇa, kalā, sparśa, vāk, dṛk,* and *mānasa*. According to the Rudrayāmala, *dīkṣā* is of three types, viz. *āṇavī, śaktī, śāmbhavī.*

Hence, *dīkṣā* is a spiritual enrolment to carry on scientific research with the self. It is not a religious anointment but an esoteric discipline. It is not a faith but an inner conviction. It is not ritualistic ostentation but a mystic necessity. However, in Tāntric *sādhanā* the evil deeds are purified through *dīkṣā*.

Guru: A teacher or a preceptor who teaches the essential truth is known as *guru*. Guru may be said to be the power of Divine Grace. That power of Grace affording a favourable opportunity to the aspirant is the means to unraveling of the secret of the *mantra*. The word *guru is* often used in the sense of any elderly person, male or female, who is entitled to get respect. The parents and *ācāryas* are often regarded as the three highest *gurus*. According to the Manusmṛti (2.141-42), *guru* is one who performs the *saṁskāras* and imparts Vedic education. *Guru* is the pivot of Tāntric *sādhanā*, the one who dispels darkness. The Śiva-sūtra (2.6) says: *'gurupāyaḥ."* It means, the *guru* who has attained self-realization can alone help the aspirant for acquiring it. The Mālinīvijaya Tantra (II.10) also says: *'sa gurumatsamaḥ prokto mantravīryaprakāśakaḥ.'* Here, Lord Śiva is addressing Pārvatī as: "One who knows all the principles in their essentials, being able to throw light on the virility or efficiency of *mantras*, is a real *guru* like me." Hence, it is said that *'gṛṇāti upadiśati tāttvikamarthamiti guruḥ.'*

Īśvara: Lit. means :God. The word *īśvara* is derived from the root *is-* 'to rule, be master of', with the suffix *varac* according to the Aṣṭādhyāyī (3.2.175). The Nirukta (3.12) says: *'īśvaraḥ sarveṣāmindriyāṇāṁ gopāyitātmā', i.e. īśvara* is treated here as the soul. The Vedas believe in *Īśvara*. The Cārvāka, Buddha, Jaina, Sāṁkhya and Mīmāṁsā darśanas do not believe in God. But, on the other hand Nyāya, Vaiśeṣika, Yoga, Vedānta, *darśanas* believe in *īśvara* (God).

Jīva: Lit. means : a bonded being, *paśu, aṇu, puruṣa, etc.* The term is also used to denote' individual self or soul'. The Buddhists reduce it to a stream of thought or a series of cognitions. The Nyāya-vaiśeṣikas hold it as a unique substance, to which all cognitions, feelings and conations belong as attributes. The Mīmāṁsaka says that it is a substance which has the capability of consciousness. *Jīva* remains under the control of *māyā* and seeks for liberation through the performance of various auspicious deeds, sacrifices, *vratas*, serious meditation and regular practice of *yogic sādhanās*.

Kālī: Lit. means: 'the Black one'. Goddess Kālī is one of the most popular deities, worshipped mainly by the Hindus. In the Devīmāhātmya section of Mārkaṇḍeya Purāṇa (VII.5ff.) it is stated that She merged from the forehead of the Divine Mother who became black with anger as the demons headed by Caṇḍa and Muṇḍa came to attack her. Kālī came out with a big hideous face and a dreadful appearance. More or less fearful forms of the deity with the name Mahākālī or Bhadrakālī are described in the works like the Kāraṇāgama, Bhaviṣya Purāṇa, Devī Purāṇa, etc. Kālī is generally considered in twelve aspects or forms. The twelve Kālīs as presented by Abhinavagupta, a great scholar of Kashmir Śaivism, are: (1) Sṛṣṭi Kālī, (2) Rakta Kālī, (3) Sthitināśa Kālī, (4) Yama Kālī, (5) Saṁhāra Kālī, (6) Mṛtyu Kālī, (7) Bhadra Kālī, (8) Mārtaṇḍa Kālī, (9) Paramārka Kālī, (10) Kālāgnirudra Kālī, (11) Mahākāla Kālī, (12) Mahābhairavaghora-Chaḍḍakālī. Kālī or Parāśakti or Parāsaṁvid or Universal Consciousness, always manifests powers of *sṛṣṭi*, *sthiti* and *saṁhāra*.

Linga: Lit. means: a mark, sign, token, an emblem, a badge, symbol, a distinguishing mark, characteristic, etc. From etymological sense *liṅga* is that by which mark, one being or word is cognized whether one is male, female, eunuch or masculine, feminine, neuter. The commentator of Amarakośa, Rāmāśramī comments on the term as *'liṅgayate anena, ligi gatau halaśca iti ghañ.'* The Ajitāgama (Kriyāpāda, Ill. 17cd-18ab) defines liṅga as: *'layaṁ gacchanti bhūtāni saṁhāre nikhilāni ca nirgacchanti yataścāpiliṅgokistena hetunā.'* The Tantrāloka (V.113-114) also says: *'atra viśvamidaṁ līnam atrāntaḥsthaṁ ca gamyate'*—it is from the liṅga the universe comes into being and dissolves in it. Generally, *liṅga* has been a popular object of worship in India started from prehistoric to modern period. The Āgamic tradition uses the term *liṅga* mostly in the sense of arch-symbol and a formal representative of Lord Śiva. The Kūrma Purāṇa describes about the origin of *liṅga* and its worship. The Liṅga Purāṇa also speaks about the Śivaliṅga and its symbolical components. It also praises the style of worshipping *liṅga* along with its pedestal. The Vāmana Purāṇa lauds several holy places where ancient *liṅgas* are established. There are twelve *(dvādaśa) jyotirliṅgas* of Lord Śiva being worshipped in India since ancient times.

Mala: Lit. means: dross, dirt, impurity, dust, any impure Matter, etc According to Kashmir Śaivism, *mala* is that which covers and conceals the real nature of the Divine Consciousness. It is a limiting condition which hampers the free expression of the spirit. It is of three types, viz. *āṇava mala, māyīya mala* and *kārma mala*. Āṇava mala is the primary limiting condition which reduces the universal consciousness to an aṇu or the empirical individual. Māyīya mala is the limiting condition brought about by *Māyā* that gives to the soul its gross and subtle body. *Kārma mala* is the limiting condition brought about by the *vāsanās* under the influence of desire. It is the force of those *vāsaṇās* that carries the *jīva* from one life to another.

Maṇḍala: Lit. means: round, circular. The Amarakośa defines the term *Maṇḍala:* as: *'cakravalaṁ to maṇḍalam* (1.3.6), *bimbo'strī manḍḍalaṁ triṣu* (1.3.15) and *pariveṣastu paridhirūpasūryaka, maṇḍale* (1.3.32).' It means, a sensible horizon, a circle or ring, disc of the sun or moon and halo. In the Taittirīya Saṁhitā (V.3. 9.2) *'maṇḍaleṣṭakā'* is used to denote circular bricks. The Bṛhadāraṇyaka Upaniṣad (V.5.2) refers to the person in the orb *Maṇḍala:* of the, sun *(etasmin maṇḍale puruṣa)*. In the later Vedic and Sanskrit Literature *Maṇḍala* is used to mean a circular diagram or figure drawn on any altar and *pūjā* ritual. In Śulbasūtras also it specifically refers the squaring of a circle *(caturaśraṁ maṇḍalaṁ*–Āpastamba Śulbasūtra, 3.2-3). *Maṇḍala* worship is very popular and even important in Tāntric rituals. In Śaivite tradition various *maṇḍalas* are worshipped in different months. Several *maṇḍalas* are described in the Śāradā Tilaka, Pauṣkara Saṁhitā and other Tāntric texts. The Buddhist Tantras also describe *maṇḍalas e.g. Sarvatobhadra* etc. Now a days *Maṇḍala* worship is a common feature in any *pūjā* rituals.

Mantra: It is a sacred or mystic formula for recitation. The word *mantra is* composed of two letters *'man'* and *'tra'*. *Man* implies *mananāt* (by pondering), and *'tra'* implies *'trāyate* (protects). Hence, *mantra* means that which protect or save by pondering. Yāska says: *mantra mananāt* (Nirukta, VII.12) which means Vedic verses are derived from the root *man-*, 'to think'.The Kulārṇava Tantra says *'mantra'* is so called since it saves from all dangers, as the aspirant thereby is led to ponder over God of immeasurable refulgence that is the only principle in the world. The Śāradā Tilaka (6.3) divides *mantras* into three categories, viz. the male *mantra*, female *mantra* and neuter *mantra*. The masculine *mantras* end in *'hum'* and *'phaṭ'*, female with *'svāhā'* and neuter *mantra* with *'namaḥ'*. Purāṇas and some Smṛtis prescribe short *mantras* of five, six, eight, twelve, thirteen. and more syllables as very efficacious for securing all objects. The best Vedic *mantra* is the Gāyatrī (Ṛgveda, 111.62. 10). The Atharvaveda (XIX.71.1) calls it Vedamātā. The Tāntric works (rituals) have their own sacred *mantras*, but they also employ Vedic *mantras*, e.g. *'tryambakaṁ yajāmahe sugandhim'...* (RV.7.59.12) is addressed to Rudra, but is known as *mahā-mṛtyuñjaya mantra* or *mṛtasañjīvanī mantra* in Tāntric works and is prescribed for purifying the mind in the Mahānirvāṇa Tantra (8.243). Similarly, the Gāyatrī *mantra* is employed by the Tāntrikas (vide Śāradā Tilaka, XXI.108 and Prapañcasāra Tantra, which devotes two chapters, i.e. 19 & 30 for explaining *pranava mantra* or *oṁkāra)*. The Mahānirvāṇa Tantra (III.14-37) recommends that *'om sac-cid-ekaṁ brahma' is* the best of *mantras*, that those who perform the *pūjā & upāsanā* of the Highest *Brahma* or Supreme Lord, are in need of no other *sādhanā* and that by the mere perfection of that sacred *mantra* the individual self merges in Brahma. The Buddhist Tantras also claimed ti show the way to the attainment of various worldly objects and even Nirvāṇa through the *mantras*.

Māyā: Generally it means deceit, jugglery, witchcraft, fraud, trick, etc. The Amarakośa (2.10.11) records the term in the sense of magic *(indrajāla)* and Kṣīrasvāmin comments on this as: *'mātyasyāṁ viśvaṁ māyā.'* According to the Abhidharmakośa Bhāṣya (V.49), *māyā is* used in the sense of magic which deceives others *(parvañcanā māyā)*. The term is very frequently used in the Ṛgveda in the sense of magic *(māyābhiraśvinā yuvam-* ṚV V.78.6; *indromāyābhiḥ pururūpa īyate--ṚV* 6.47.18). According to Śaṅkara the world is called *māyā,* because of its unreality. *So, māyā* is the root of every creation. But different philosophical schools develop different thoughts on this concept of *māyā*. According to Kashmir Śaivism Parama Śiva have two forms of Śakti--Cit Śakti and Māyā Śakti. They may be called Vidyā-māyā and Avidyā-māyā. The nature of Vidyā-māyā is to help in the attainment of Parama Śiva with her power of *hlādinī* and *saṁvita*. It accelerates the process of evolution. Whereas *avidyā-māyā* brings about the crudification of self. It creates the phenomenal world. With the power of her *āvaraṇa* and *vikṣepa* it obscures, limits and blinds the Self. But these two powers or functions of Śiva are not independent and separable. *Māyā* creates five principles or powers known as *kañcukas*, which limit the knowledge and power of the Universal Self. These five *kañcukas* are: *kalā, (aśuddha) vidyā, rāga, niyati & kāla*. It is with these sheaths that *māyā* enwraps *puruṣa*. The microcosm goes into deep slumber and forgets his Divine nature and origin.

Mokṣa: Lit. means: salvation, liberation, emancipation, release, *nirvāṇa, mukti, apavarga,* etc. It is the last of the four goals of a human being *(puruṣārtha)*, the remaining three being righteousness *(dharma)*, material well-being *(artha)*, and sexual pleasure *(kāma)*. The Amarakośa (1.5.6) records the term *mokṣa* as a synonym of *mukti* along with other terms like: *kaivalya, nirvāṇa, śreyas, niḥśreyas, amṛta* and *apavarga*. Kṣīrasvāmin comments on the same as: *mokṣaḥ pāśebhyaḥ ātmanaḥ pṛthakbhāvaḥ*--free from the bindings of one's self. The Laghu Yoga-Vāsiṣṭha (6.1.9) defines the term as: *aśeṣeṇa parityāgo vāsanānāṁ ya uttamaḥ, mokṣa ityucyate*, i.e. abandonment of all sorts of desires *(vāsanās)* is the best means of liberation. Hence, to be freed from all sorts of sufferings is known as *mokṣa*. It is rightly defined by Śabdakalpadruma as: *'mokṣyate duḥkhamanena.'* This is the main subject of discussion in all the Indian philosophical systems. The Vedānta, Sāṁkhya Yoga, Nyāya-vaiśeṣika, Mīmāṁsā, Buddha, Jaina, Kashmir Śaiva Darśana, etc.have treated it according to their own philosophical thought.

Mudrā: Lit. means: a seal, an instrument for sealing or stamping; a stamp, print, mark, impression; an image, a sign; name of certain positions of fingers practiced in devotion or religious worship. Generally it is known as posture of the body, especially of hands needed for *yogic* exercise and spiritual attainment. It is called *mudrā* (root *mud-* 'to rejoice', 'to please', with the suffix *rak* and *tāp)*, because it gives the bliss of spiritual consciousness. The derivative meaning of the term *mudrā* is: *'mudaṁ harṣaṁ rāti dadāti iti mudrā'*--it gives delight in the heart. *Mudrās* like Abhaya, Varada, Dharmacakra, Bhūmisparsa, Namaskāra, etc. are commonly found in iconic representation symbolizing the quality associated with the deity. The Haṭhayoga Pradīpikā devotes a complete chapter on *mudrās*. Some of which are: Mahāmudrā, Mahāvedha, Khecarī, Mahābandha, Uḍḍīyyānabandha, Mūlabandha, Jālandharabandha, etc. However, the scholars explain *mudrā* in different ways denoting mystic pose of the hand', manual signs indicative of various ideas', finger signs', hand poses adopted during meditation or exposition.

Nāda: Lit. means: loud roar, shout, cry and sounding in general. The Amarakośa (1.6.22) refers it as a synonym of *śabda*. The Nighaṇṭu (III.16.9) records it as a synonym of *stoṭa*, i.e. 'one who praises'. However, most of the related words of *nāda* bear the etymological sense of the verbal root nad- 'to sound' or 'to praise'. In the Tāntric literature *nāda* is related with creation. When the Supreme Being or Para Śiva begins to manifest itself in creation, its first vibration or the primordial sound is known as *nāda*, which is actually the manifestation of the consciousness of the Supreme Being revealed as sound. The Divine pleasure of this union, i.e. Śiva and Śakti is called *nāda*, As the supreme seed, the primeval sound nāda abides in all living beings.

Nirguṇa: The term *guṇa* means quality, virtue, cord, etc., while *nirguṇa* which is opposite to *saguṇa*, means having no cord or string or without good qualities or virtues, bad, worthless, vicious, etc. The term *nirguṇa* appears several times in the Upaniṣads in the sense of devoid of all qualities or properties. Basically the terms *saguṇa* and *nirguṇa* are associated with Brahman, viz. *Saguṇa* Brahman & *Nirguṇa* Brahman. *Nirguṇa* Brahman is unqualified Absolute. The best method of describing it, therefore, is by negative terms (*neti-neti*). The concept of *Nirguṇa* is found in the Upaniṣads, Epics, Purāṇas and other texts of Indian tradition. In the Śvetāśvatara Upaniṣad (VI. 11), Brahman or God is described as omnipotent, omniscient, omnipresent, an observer and devoid of all qualities. Hence, *Nirguṇa* devoid of (*guṇas*) qualities is an attribute of Brahman, and without which Brahman cannot be defined in the Upaniṣadic texts.

Parama Śiva : He is known as the Supreme or the Absolute of Tāntric Philosophy. Parama Śiva is the *purṇa-ahantā*, self-luminous and pure-consciousness. The *purṇa-ahantā* is the essence of ParamaŚiva. He is also known as the Supreme Reality. Besides, He is of the nature of Bliss and complete in Himself. He holds in Himself the un-manifested universe as an idea. That reality out of which thirty-six *tattvas* evolve and into which all of them get absorbed. At the same time, He transcends the Universe. He is the transcendental Reality, Pure Intelligence as well as the one all-including Supreme Experience. Hence, Parama Śiva is both transcendent and immanent. He is Truth, Consciousness and Bliss.

Paśu: The empirical individual bound by ignorance (*avidyā*) or spiritual nescience is known as *paśu*. Abhinavagupta explains it in his Paramārthasāra (verse 16) as: '*māyāparigrahavaśād bodho malinaḥ pumān paśurbhavati.*' *Puruṣa* is the finite subject who takes a finite individual I-consciousness, having limited power to know and to do, as his self. Having lost his finiteness, he is known as '*aṇu*', a finite being. He sees that everything and everyone as different from him. Such viewpoint of diversity and such finitude are the main impurities of such individual I consciousness, which being fastened by the chains of ignorance and finitude, is known as *paśu*, a bonded being.

Pīṭha: Lit. means: a seat, a chair, stool or shrine of a deity (usually a goddess). In the Amarakośa (2.6.138) the term is recorded as a synonym of *āsana* to mean 'seat' or more specifically a chair or stool. At present the term is mostly focused on the senses of the seat of a deity, an altar, a pedestal, a religious seat, or throne of the *āśramas*. Various holy *pīthas* of Goddess Śakti are famous in India. Tantracūḍāmaṇi records a list of 51 *pīṭhas*, widely known as holy resorts of Śakti origin of which is associated with Dakṣayajña legend describing the falling of 51 pieces cut-off from the body of Satī. Each *pītha* is supposed to contain a limb of *Devī* Satī, a presiding goddess and her Bhairava. Some of the famous Śakti *pīthas* are: Varanasi, Kañcī, Kāmākhyā, Kurukshetra, Ujjayinī, Hiṅgulā, Jvālāmukhī, etc. There are also some minor *pīṭhas*, known as *upapīṭhas*. The Hevajra Tantra and Kalikāpurāṇa enumerate four *pīṭhas*, viz. Jālandhara, Oḍiyāna, Pūrṇagiri, and Kāmarūpa. The Devī Bhāgavata Purāṇa records 108 *pīṭhas*. A complete list of 108 Śakti *pīṭhas* along with the 108 names of the goddess is formed for the first time in the Matsya Purāṇa (13.25-53). The Tāntric and Purāṇic texts have elaborately discussed various Śakti *pīṭhas* and its religious importance.

Prajñā: It stands for perfect knowledge, which liberates an individual mind from the miseries and torments of life and removes the veil of ignorance.

Prāṇa: Lit. means: breathe. It is derived from the root-*pṛ*- 'to fill, to nourish, to satiate. The term *prāṇa* is traditionally derived from the conjunction of *pra-an + ac* (cf. *ānīdavātaṁ svadhayā tadekam*–Ṛgveda X.129.2), which means 'breathing forth' and *prāṇiti jīvati*, means breathes properly and goes on living. The root *an-*, 'to breathe' , with the suffix kvip means one who breaths. *Prāṇa* is defined in the Chāndogya Upaniṣad (1.3.3) as: *'yad vai prāṇiti sa prāṇaḥ'*--that which breaths, is truly breath. In the narrow sense prang denotes one of the vital airs of which five are usually distinguished, viz. *prāṇa*, apāna, vyāna, udāna, and samāna. *Prāṇa* is brahman. It is an all-conditioning, yet inscrutable agent. This is said in the Kena Upaniṣad (1.9) as: *'yatprāṇena na prāṇiti yena prāṇaḥ pranīyate, tadeva brahma tvaṁ viddhi.'* In accordance with the Upaniṣads, Abhinavagupta in his Tantrāloka states that the vital energy is basically one, but it assumes the five specific modes, viz. *prāṇa, apāna*, etc.

Pratyabhijñā: It is a name of Kashmir Śaivism, i.e. Śaiva system of Kashmir. *Prati+abhi+jñā = Pratyabhijñā*. Prati means *pratipam*, i.e. contrary, in other words though known, now appearing as forgotten through delusion. *Abhi* means facing, i.e. close at hand. Jñā means illumination or knowledge. Hence, *pratyabhijñā* means re-cognition of the real self. Since the term means recognition it refers to the way of realizing the soul's identity with Lord Śiva.

Rāga : means mental desire, such as: greed, passion, *etc.*, which lead one to bondage and *Saṁsāra*.

Śakti : Lit. means: energy, power, especially the creative energy that generates and continues to activate the universe. The term *Śakti* is derived from the root *śak-* 'to be able', 'to be powerful', with the suffix *ktin*. Kṣīrasvāmin, the commentator of the Amarakośa comments on the term as: *śakyate anayā jetuṃ Śakti*. The derivative sense of *Śakti* is 'that through which it is possible to conquer or through which something can be conquered (*śakyate jetum ābhiḥ śaktyaḥ)*. The Aṣṭādhyāyī of Pāṇini (3.2.129), uses the term *Śakti* in sense of capability. The primordial female principle or the power of the Supreme Being is treated *Śakti* through the manifestation of the universe is affected. *Parāśakti* is conceived as female principle. It is the energy of Lord Śiva and regarded as the instrumental cause of creation. Besides, Śakti is symbolically represented as the spouse of Śiva and hence, She is the immanent principle of Śiva. Devoid of Śakti, Śiva would be insentient *(jaḍa)* and consequently, as good as 'dead' *(lava)*. Śiva knows Himself only through His Great Śakti She is also the power of freedom of the Lord. Śakti has been addressed as *janani, mātri* and *ambā*. Generally, Śakti or Devī is identified with Vidyāmāyā. With the help of Vidyāmāyā, *jīva* proceeds towards spiritual sublimity. Śakti or Devī helps *jīya* in moving towards Paramaśiva. Without the help of Śakti it is not possible for the *jīva* to attain the Supreme Oneness with Paramaśiva.

Śaṅkara: This is another name of Śiva *'Sam karoti iti Śaṁkaraḥ'*, i.e. one who brings about happiness and welfare is known as Śaṁkara.

Śānti: Lit. means: peace, tranquility, etc. The term *śānti* (fem.) is a mufti-dimensional concept in the Vedic, Purāṇic, Tāntric & Buddhist Literature. It is a word of current usage in the sense of peace or calmness of mind, absence of passion, averting of pain, quiet, etc. It is derived from the root *Sam-* 'to be appeared', 'to kill', 'to stop', etc. Kṣīrasvāmi, the commentator of Amarakośa (3.2.3) says: *'kāmakrodhādyabhāva śānti'*—absence of lust, anger, etc. is known as *śānti*. The indeclinable particle *śam* means welfare, happiness, prosperity, and it is also used in the sense of peace, quiet, etc. Though the word *śānti*. does not occur in the Ṛgveda, but *'śam'* occurs several times in this text. Similarly, in the Vājasaneyi Saṁhitā also *'śum'* occurs a number of times. The word *śānti'* is occurred many a times in the Taittirīya Saṁhitā (6.1.7.7-8, 6.2.2, 6.3.5, etc.) as well as in the Atharvaveda (XIX.9.14). In the Upaniṣads, the word *śānti* is used in the sense of 'peace'. According to Atharvaveda Pariśiṣṭa (LXX.10.4), *śānti* does not occur / happen on account of the following reasons :

apūjanāttu pūjyasya tathāpūjyasya pūjanāt /
antaḥkaraṇadoṣācca hetoḥ śāntirnajāyate //

It means, persons those who are not honouring one who is honourable, honouring one who is not honourable, and keep blemishes in the mind. So, due to, these reasons the peace desiring people never get peace in their life time. The Gītā uses the words *śānti* and *nirvāṇa* to indicate the Bliss of the person who abides in God *(śāntiṁ nirvāṇa paramām* ...). According to the Viṣṇusahasranāma Bhāyṣa (75), Brahman is known as *śānti* as those who have abandoned all attachments find peace in Him. The Agni Purāṇa (263.7-8) describes eighteen *śāntis*. The Kūrma Purāṇa (I.12.66) describes *śānti* as a goddess, whereas it is known as *parva* as mentioned in the Mahābhārata, i.e. *Śānti parva*. In Buddhism, *nirvāṇa* is known as the best *śānti* (peace). The Dhamapada rightly says: *'natthi śānti paramaṁ sukham'*--there is no Bliss, which surpasses the perfect peace. The Nārada Bhakti Sūtra (VI.1.60) records that love is the nature of peace and it is of the nature of Supreme Bliss.

Sāvitrī : This was one of the most important philosophical doctrines of the Ṛgveda, in which the creative principle is symbolized as Savitā, the impeller of all and his energy as Sāvitrī. Savitā and Sāvitrī are known as an inseparable pair. Sūrya is the great deity, Savitā and his energy is

Sāvitrī which he is radiating through out the space and each one of the living organisms in the plant, animal and human kingdoms is receiving that Sāvitrī or solar light. In the Sāvitrī Upaniṣad nine Savitā -Sāvitrī pairs are enumerated as:

	Savitā	Sāvitrī
1.	Agni	Pṛthvī
2.	Varuṇa	Āpaḥ
3.	Vāyu	Ākāśa
4.	Yajña	Chandāṁsi
5.	Stanayitnu	Vidut
6.	Āditya	Dyauḥ
7.	Manas	Vāk
8.	Puruṣa	Strī

The above (list) is almost similar in the Jaiminīya Upaniṣad Brahmaṇa, Ch.4, Tāṇḍya 28, which shows that the doctrine of Sāvitrī Vidyā was specially featured in the Sāmaveda tradition. The Gopatha Brahmaṇa (1.1.53) is also explains in detail the Sāvitrī doctrine and records twelve pairs of Savitā -Sāvitrī.

Siddhis: Super-natural powers attained through the practice of *yoga*. These *siddhis* are eight in number, viz. *aṇimā, laghimā, mahimā, garimā, prāpti, prākāmya, vaśitva*, and a s *īśitva.*

Śraddhā: Lit. means: trust, faith, belief and confidence. Belief in divine revelation or religious faith is known as *śraddhā.* It is very much extolled in Vedic literature and occurs in the Indian religious tradition as an essential element in the making of the truthful man. *Śrat* is *satyam* and the faculty which accepts truth as its cardinal virtue is called *Śraddhā (śraddhīyate asmat iti śraddhā).*

Śrī: Goddess Lakṣmī, the deity and consort of Lord Viṣṇu, who embodies the qualities of prosperity and beauty. She is worshipped especially by the Vaiṣṇavas as inseparable from Viṣṇu.

Tryambaka: Lit. means Lord Śiva The word *ambaka* is understood as the eye, and Śiva is therefore represented as the deity with three eyes and hence called Virūpākṣa. The three eyes are are taken to be Sūrya, Candra, and Agni corresponding to the triadic conceptions employed in the Vedic cosmogony. Śiva's *Śakti* Māheśvarī is also represented as the Goddess with three eyes both in sculpture and painting. Agni is also called *Tryambaka* because of his three births on the three different levels of manifestation (ṚV X.45.1), each birth requiring one mother.

Vidyā: Lit. means: knowledge (from the root *vid-* 'to know') learning, lore, science, etc. *Vidyā* is stated to be fourteen, i.e. the four Vedas, six *aṅgas* (Vedāṅgas), Dharmaśāstra, Mīmāṃsā, Tarka or Nyāya and the Purāṇas. As knowledge, *vidyā* is of two kinds, viz. *parāvidyā* (spiritual knowledge) and *aparāvidyā* (material knowledge).

Viriñci : Lit. means Brahmā. It is the same as Viriñcā. Both the words denote Brahman, the creator of this whole world/ universe.

Vrata: Lit. means a religious act of devotion or austerity, a vow in general. It is an observance of pious act like fasting on a particular sacred day. In the sense of religious observance the Āpastamba Śrautasūtra *(vratam upaiti-IV.2.6)*, the Kātyāyana Śrautasūtra *(vratopeta-2. 1.11)*, and the Baudhāyana Śrauta-Sūtra (I.1), which includes abstinence from certain things like: *māṣa* (beans), *māṁsa* (flesh) and sexual intercourse. One has to follow certain prescribed rules while observing a particular *vrata. Vrata* also means rituals intended for certain purposes. These are regional and local in character, performed specially by the women folk for averting diseases and calamities, for progeny and prosperity and for other practical purposes of life. The majority of the *vratas* are supposed to produce tangible results. Their performer is endowed with a beautiful form, and he/she gets immense fortune, subdues the enemy, and is rendered free from all earthly calamities including various diseases. In short, all conceivable temporal Bliss can be obtained through *vratas*.

Yantra: Lit. means : restraint, curb, check, bind, fasten, force, etc. The term *yantra is* derived from the root *yam-*, 'to control'. Besides, it also denotes a fetter, band, tie and rain. In the Ṛgveda, (X.149.1) it is used in the sense of bend or fetter. In the Aṣṭāṅgahṛdaya (Sūtrasthāna XXV.3-28), *yantra* is described as instruments of different types of. According to the Sūryasiddhānta (XIII.19-24), various *yantras* were used for measuring time, like: *chāyā-yantra, kapāla-yantra, toya-yantra,* etc. The Mayamata, as an archaeological text, used *yantra* in the sense of a device and machine as: *jala-yantra.* In the Tantric point of view, *yantra* means an amulet, i.e. a mystical or astronomical diagram used as an amulet. This diagram is engraved or drawn on metal, paper, stone, wood or other materials which are worshiped in the same manner as an image. The *yantra* worship is an essential feature of Tantric *sādhanā* and it is also a mystic process of awakening the Divine Power.

Yoni : Lit. means: womb, uterus, vulva, the female organ of generation (cf. *jīvo mṛtasya carati svadhābhiramartyor martyenā sayoniḥ*--Ṛgveda, 1.164.30cd). The term is derived from the root *ya-* 'to unite, to yoke, to push or to worship' towards, etc. Brahman is the *yoni* (main source) of everything. *Yoni* signifies the causal factor that produces a particular class of beings. In the Bhagavad Gītā, Lord Śrī Krisṇa says that His womb is the great sustainer where He places the seed of creation (*mama yonirmahad Brahma tasmin garbhaṁ dadhāmyaham*—XIV.3).